Crafting Cloth Dolls

Crafting Cloth Dolls

A Pageant of Patterns, Techniques, and Ideas from Award-Winning Dollmakers

Miriam Christensen Gourley

The Quilt Digest Press

Chicago New York San Francisco Lisbon London Madrid Mexico City Milan New Delhi San Juan Seoul Singapore Sydney Toronto

Library of Congress Cataloging-in-Publication Data

Gourley, Miriam, 1951–
Crafting cloth dolls : a pageant of patterns, techniques, and ideas from award-winning dollmakers / Miriam Christensen Gourley.
p. cm.
ISBN 0-8442-2084-1
1. Dollmaking 2. Cloth dolls. I. Title.

TT175.G6823 2002
745.592'21—dc21 2001019632

The Quilt Digest Press 
A Division of The **McGraw-Hill** *Companies*

1 2 3 4 5 6 7 8 9 0 SSI/SSI 0 9 8 7 6 5 4 3 2 1

ISBN 0-8442-2084-1

This book was set in Electra by Hespenheide Design
Printed and bound by Star Standard Industries

Cover and interior design by Hespenheide Design
Cover photographs by Sharon Hoogstraten
Cover and interior illustrations by Shauna Mooney Kawasaki

All interior photographs by Sharon Hoogstraten with the following exceptions:
Photograph on page 5 by Scott Zimmerman
Photograph on page 50 by Jan Schou
Photographs on pages 24 (*Mother Moon*), 25 (*Shaker Sister* and *Marcella the Milliner*), 31 (*Peppermint Tea Party*), 54, and 61 by Kevin Dilley of Hazen Photography, Ogden, Utah
Photographs on pages iii, 2, 6, 14, 15, 16, 20, 23, 25 (*Magic*), 26 (*Polly Pinks*), 27 (*Black Aunt Cora*), 30, 31 (*Too Hot for Shoes*), 33, 34, 35 (*Dragon Lady* and *Aurora*), 36, 37, 40 (*Olivia* and *Shadow Dancing*), 46 (*Tribal Woman*), 47, 48, 49, 56, 57, 58, and 59 courtesy of the dollmakers

This book is printed on acid-free paper.

From the moment I met

elinor peace bailey's Victorian Doll,

I knew I wanted to make cloth dolls.

This book is lovingly dedicated to elinor,

my mentor and good friend.

Long live our queen!

Contents

Chapter 4 The Crowning Glory: Hair and Wigs 37

Chapter 5 Costuming the Doll 51

Part Two: A Pageant of Dolls 63

Preface

Welcome to the wonderful world of cloth dolls. I discovered dollmaking more than twenty years ago, and few things give me as much pleasure as creating a new doll to decorate my home or to give as a gift. The immensely talented artists who have contributed dolls or patterns to *Crafting Cloth Dolls* have also experienced this unique joy and are ready to share it with you.

Like every little girl, I played with dolls when I was very tiny. As soon as I was old enough to sew, my sister and I spent hours stitching countless ball gowns and bedding, pinafores and hats for our little playmates. In my midtwenties, at home with my small son, I bought a sewing machine and rediscovered sewing.

Soon after my sewing machine and I became friends, I happened across a doll that had been created by elinor peace bailey. I was completely captivated and began attempting to make my own. I had found my vocation.

If you have never made a doll before, you will find all the help you need to get started in *Crafting Cloth Dolls*. Part One leads you through the process of creating a doll. Part Two offers ten complete doll patterns in an incredible range of styles. Some are primitive folk art; others are detailed sculpted pieces—exotic and magical. The dolls are arranged by skill level, so you will find it easy to choose a pattern that suits your tastes and ability. If you wish to modify a pattern to create a unique doll, all you need to do is refer back to the techniques in Part One to shape the body, craft the hair, or dress the doll as you wish.

Miriam Christensen Gourley

Acknowledgments

My deep appreciation to the dollmakers featured in Part Two who generously shared patterns for their favorite dolls.

My sincere thanks to the sensational doll artists who contributed materials on the following topics:

Armature making, Gloria "Mimi" Winer
Dyeing doll hair, Patti Medaris Culea
Wig making, Antonette Cely
Creative wig making, Bonnie Hoover
Drafting doll clothing patterns, Lynda Larsen
Making shoes, Christine Shively
Making fairy wings, Annie Wahl

Special thanks to Delta® (paints); Americana® (paints) by DecoArt; Hollywood Trims/Prym-Dritz; Loew Cornell (brushes); Bernina of America; Fairfield Processing; All Cooped Up.

Throughout the book, you will find photographs of numerous sensational dolls. Several are award-winning creations, made for Dollmaker's Magic, a special touring exhibit of one-of-a-kind cloth dolls. Dollmaker's Magic has introduced many creative people to this exciting art form. It has also inspired thousands to give dollmaking a try. My thanks to all the artists who made Dollmaker's Magic possible.

Medieval Jester BY MIRIAM CHRISTENSEN GOURLEY, 1999.

Part One
Dollmaking Techniques

Part One explains key techniques that will get you started in creating your own dolls. You will learn how to make a basic doll body that you can then mold to the shape you desire. You'll also discover a variety of options for painting your doll's face, fixing the hair, and creating a costume.

CHAPTER 1

Getting Started

THE ART OF DOLLMAKING, once considered a very specialized craft, has evolved and grown dramatically over the last several years. An important reason for this rise in popularity is the ready availability of new tools and dollmaking supplies.

Even in the smallest crafts shops, there is an incredible variety of fabrics and threads in a wonderful range of textures and color. There is a wide choice of fibers to use for doll hair. There are acrylic paints in every color of the rainbow and permanent-ink, fine-tip marking pens—perfect for drawing fine features on doll faces—are available in several colors. If you prefer clay heads and faces to traditional "rag doll" faces, new materials like Sculpey clay that you can harden in an oven make this option possible and easy. Early dollmakers were limited not only by selection but also by cost. Today, supplies are both easy to find and affordable.

I encourage you to explore the shelves of your local quilting or crafts store and discover the many choices open to you when you decide to make a new doll. If you have previously embroidered your dolls' faces, try using paints or a combination of paints and embroidery instead. If you have used only wool roving in prepackaged colors for hair, try dyeing fibers to new shades. Experiment with fibers you haven't tried before. Dollmaking is a wonderful opportunity for creative freedom. Explore and enjoy!

Feeding the Birds BY MARGERY CANNON, 1994. This 16" (40 cm) doll is built around a wire armature. It was the first cloth doll to appear on the cover of *Contemporary Doll Collector* magazine. The clothing, handmade by Margery, is exquisite. She used soft sculpture to mold the features, mohair for the hair, and glastique for the eyes.

Dollmaking Essentials

Basics

- Embroidery, quilting, blunt craft, and 3½" (9 cm) dollmakers' needles
- Needle threaders
- Pincushion with straight quilting pins
- Safety pins (small)
- No. 2 lead pencils
- Colored pencils, crayons
- Iron-on transfer pencil or pen
- Permanent-ink, fine-tip marking pens

Tracing paper
Paper scissors, pinking shears, fabric shears, small embroidery scissors
Rotary cutter, rotary mat
Strong thread, such as upholstery thread
Sewing thread (cotton/polyester blend, quilting)
Decorative thread for machine (rayon, metallic)
Embroidery floss and hoop
Tweezers
Bamboo skewers, 3½" (9 cm) hemostat, bamboo chopsticks (for stuffing)
Various sizes of dowels (for stuffing)
Glue gun, glue sticks, white tacky glue, white craft glue
Paper-backed fusible webbing
Measuring tape

Painting Supplies

Acrylic paints
Extender medium (to dilute paints)
Brushes of various sizes, from #00 up to ¾" (2 cm) wide
Acrylic clear matte sealer (spray or brush-on)
Round wooden toothpicks
Sponge brush
Paper towels (to dry brushes)
Mixing tray or palette
Blow-dryer (to shorten drying time)
Crackle medium (I like Jo Sonja's brand)
Acrylic gel stain (for antiquing)

Doll Body Materials and Supplies

Unbleached muslin or other suitable flesh-colored fabric
Wool felt
Rit® dye to tint fabric and fiber: cocoa, golden yellow, tan, rose pink, tangerine
Cotton batting, polyester batting
Black tea bags (to tint fabric)
Colander (to drain fiber)
Screen (to dry fiber)
Cotton swabs
Buttonhole twist
Jute, twine

Fiber for Doll Hair

Curly wool crepe
Wool roving
Nubby yarn
Three-ply natural hemp rope
Naturally curled dyed mohair
Various yarns
Natural flax
Camel hair
Embroidery floss

My Studio

Just as the creative process is divided into several steps, my creative space is also sectioned off. When I am in search of ideas for a new doll, the whole world is my workroom. Sometimes, an idea begins to take shape as I gaze in a store window or see a picture in a magazine or storybook; other times, my inspiration comes from reading ancient folktales. Dollmaking is a wonderful way to make sense of life and offers an avenue of creativity that expresses so much of your inner self. Once the seed of an idea is planted, it grows through daily experiences and visual stimuli.

Once I've had enough time to think about an idea, it's time to move to the studio, which consists of two rooms down in my basement. One is the sewing room, complete with a Bernina 1230 and a serger. There are two ironing boards, one that is large and covered with a stained, but favorite elinor peace bailey cover, and the other–smaller–one that's on top of the worktable. The many drawers in the room are filled with thread, needles, ribbons, buttons, zippers, pencils, pens, paper, and myriad other things. The fabric is stacked by color in sectional shelves on one of the walls. Fabric needs to be visible, because it is a source of inspiration to me.

In the sewing room, ideas become reality. Sketches are drawn, patterns are made and altered, fabric is cut, and the doll begins to emerge. The walls of my sewing room are covered with favorite projects from past explorations: a long shelf houses a group of dolls dressed in country fabrics posed next to their little picket fence, baskets of wool, birdhouses, and other items. Underneath the shelf, I have a large worktable with a light over it. As I sit down at this table to cut out a doll body, I always have an idea of the kind of doll I am creating; in fact, there is usually a little pile of fabric, trims, and notions to inspire me, and the pile is added to or subtracted from as the doll evolves. Dollmaking is an evolution. We are never certain of the outcome, because the doll begins to take on a life of its own as the creative process progresses.

My second workroom is for painting, and it is lined with shelves full of acrylic paints and other related products. The old table is covered with paint and blobs of glue-gun drips. The walls are covered with dried flowers, silk flowers, latex flowers, baskets, wreaths, and other items. Cabinets hold the overflow of embroidery floss, and assorted Christmas decorations poke out from baskets and boxes. It's a creator's paradise–and an organized housekeeper's nightmare–and I am a little of both.

Sometimes, when a project is done, it is merely wrapped in plastic, placed in a box, and shipped to a client. Other times, when a book or magazine project is in the works, I move to a third work space. In my family room, against one wall, is my office, complete with a nice desk with cubbyholes, a computer, a fax machine, and files. This is where instructions are written and illustrated, and sent (hopefully) before the deadline looms before me.

All these places are important to me, since I spend so much time in each of them. I have often told people that I am one of the fortunate people who plays for a living. I consider myself very lucky!

CHAPTER 2

Creating the Doll Body

In this chapter you will find help on creating a basic doll body, as shown in *Renaissance Woman* on page 8. This body is easy to make and will get you started in the craft of dollmaking. With just a little practice, you can adapt and redraw the templates quite easily to change the shape or pose of your doll. You can also costume her in any number of ways, as you will see in upcoming chapters.

Summer Fairies by Hedy Katin, 1991.
This beautiful fairy, holding her tiny baby, is made from a silk knit. The face is constructed by stretching and gluing the knit over a Paper Clay mask, such as the one on page 104. Hedy created the fingers by topstitching the hands and stuffing them separately.

Tinting and Dyeing Fabric for the Doll Body

If you wish to add a pink tone to the unbleached white muslin that is usually used for the doll body, use this recipe: Add ⅛ teaspoon (.75 ml) of Rose Pink Rit® Dye and ¼ teaspoon (1.5 ml) of Tangerine Rit® Dye to 3 to 4 quarts (3 to 4 liters) of hot tap water. Mix until the dye dissolves. Place a ½ yard (45 cm) or less of fabric into the dye bath. Stir every few minutes, checking the color until it reaches the desired shade. Squeeze out excess water and rinse the fabric in cool water. Put the fabric in the dryer to heat-set the color, and press.

Tea-dyeing is an easy way to tint fabric to give it an antique look. Fabric may be tea-dyed before cutting out the doll pattern or after the body is sewn (prior to stuffing). Use the following recipe to tea-dye 1½ yards (135 cm) of fabric: Pour 2 quarts (2 liters) of very hot tap water into a large bowl. Add fifteen tea bags and steep for 20 minutes. Remove the tea bags. Add the fabric to the bowl and soak for 30 minutes, stirring occasionally if you wish the color to be even. Squeeze out excess tea. Put the fabric in the dryer to heat-set the color, and press.

If you want to paint the doll's face, neck, and hands, use a very fine muslin with a high thread count. These fabrics are usually more expensive, but the finer the weave, the better the painted surface will look.

Making the Basic Doll Body— Renaissance Woman

There are as many ways of making the doll body as there are dollmakers. The variety of techniques is part of the fun! Here, I have described a technique that is simple but very flexible. Starting out with this basic body form, it is easy to make your doll thinner, fatter, taller, or shorter. You can have her stand, sit, or dance on pointed toes. For this doll, the face is hand-sculpted using a simple needle-sculpting technique described in Chapter 3.

Renaissance Woman Cavils in the Moonlight by Miriam Christensen Gourley, 1999.

SUPPLIES

- 1/2 yard (45 cm) muslin
- Stuffing
- Stuffing and turning tools
- Chenille stems (or pipe cleaners)

Cut all templates on pages 122–125 from muslin. Use a 1/4″ (0.75 cm) seam allowance and set your sewing machine to a smaller stitch length—about 10 to 12 stitches to the inch (4 to 5 stitches to the centimeter).

Constructing the Body

1. Right sides together, stitch template A (left midchest) to template B (center midchest). Trim to scant 1/8″ (0.4 cm) seam allowance and press toward center. Attach template C (right midchest) to other side of template B in same way.
2. Right sides together and matching raw edges, stitch template D (upper chest) to midchest pieces. Trim seam allowance and press toward midchest pieces. This completes top torso front.
3. Right sides together, stitch template E (front abdomen) to top torso. Trim seam allowance and press toward top torso front. This completes body front.
4. Right sides together, stitch template F (left buttock) to template G (midbuttocks). Trim seam allowance to 1/8″ (0.4 cm), and press toward center. Attach template H (right buttock) to other side of template G in same way.
5. Right sides together, stitch template I (upper back) to buttocks. Trim seam allowance to 1/8″ (0.4 cm) and press toward buttocks. This completes body back.
6. With right sides together, align back to front, stitching around entire body but leaving side open as shown. Trim seam allowance to 1/8″ (0.4 cm). Turn right side out. Stuff firmly. Ladder-stitch opening closed.

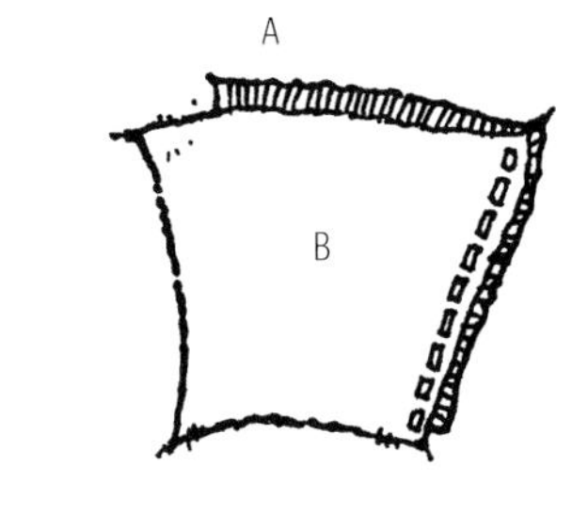

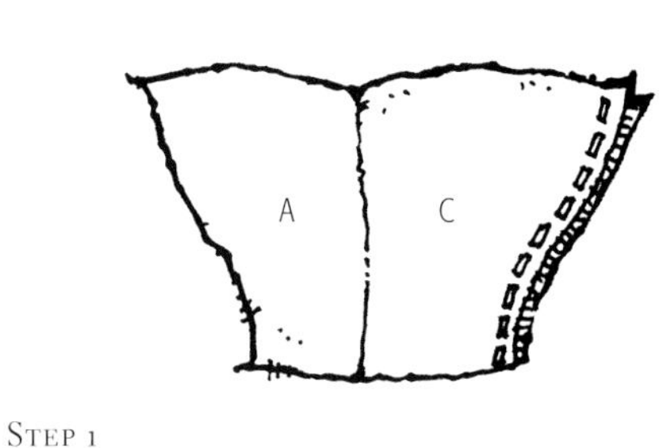

STEP 1

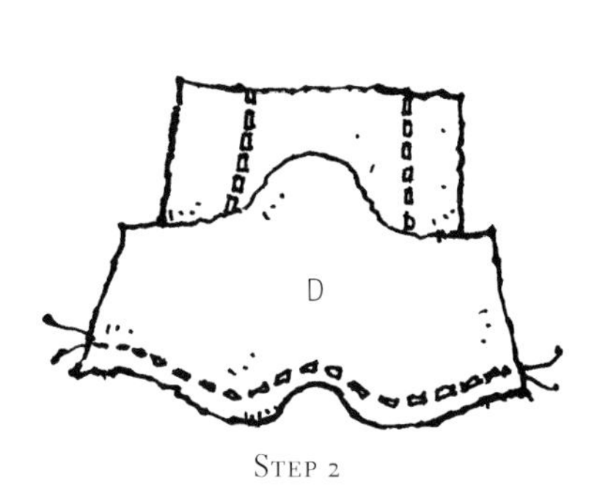

STEP 2

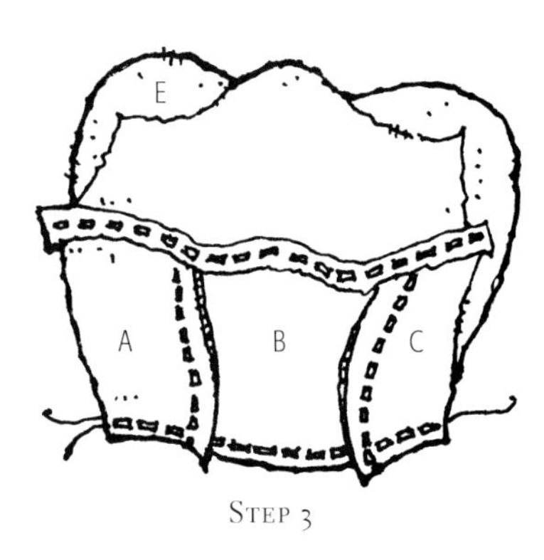

STEP 3

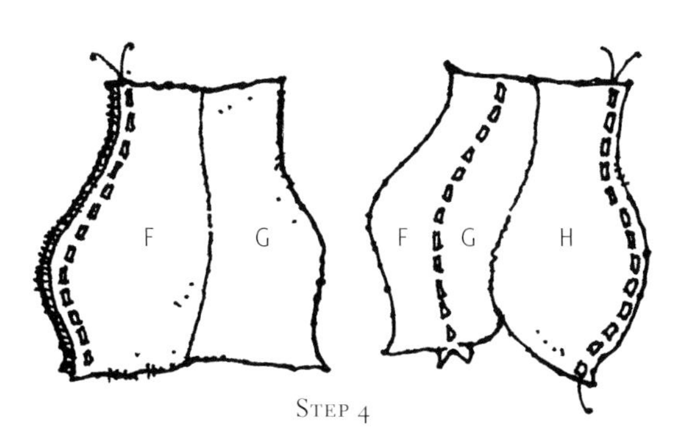

STEP 4

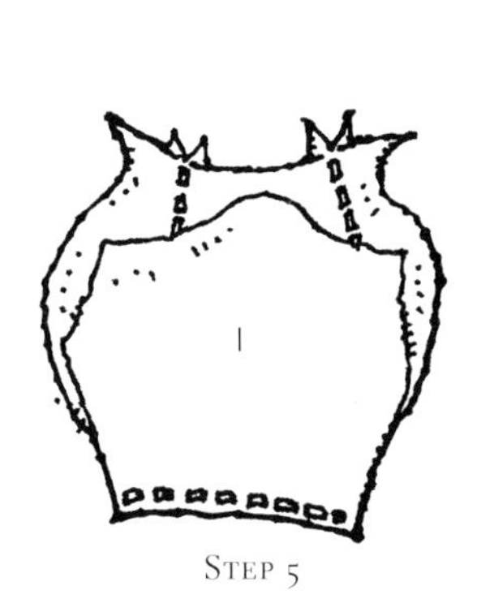

STEP 5

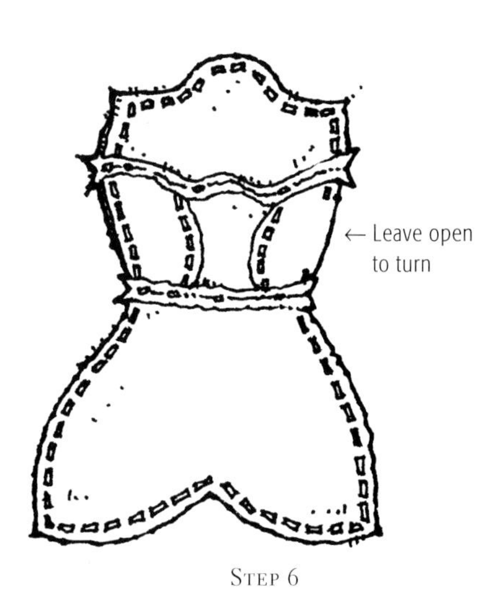

STEP 6

Constructing the Head and Neck

7. Place templates J (head back) and K (head front) with right sides together. Stitch along curve, from top of head to neck edge. Trim seam allowance. Repeat for other side of head.
8. Right sides together, stitch head pieces together, leaving neck open. Trim seam allowance to ⅛″ (0.4 cm).
9. To form curved chin, press upper and lower chin seams on top of each other, lining up seams exactly. Machine stitch a slight curve, about ½″ (1.5 cm) long, to form chin. Trim seam allowance close to stitching and clip under nose. Turn head right side out.
10. Stuff head firmly to neck opening and turn under ⅛″ (0.4 cm) of raw edge. Baste lower neck edge. Sculpt and paint face using face pattern as a guide. The needle-sculpting technique for creating the face is described on page 21 in Chapter 3.
11. Ladder-stitch neck onto upper torso, leaving about ¾″ (2 cm) open at back of neck. Insert more stuffing until neck is very firm. Finish stitching opening closed. Remove basting.

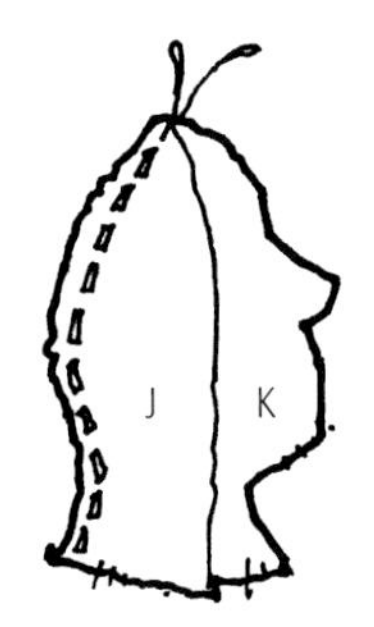

Step 7

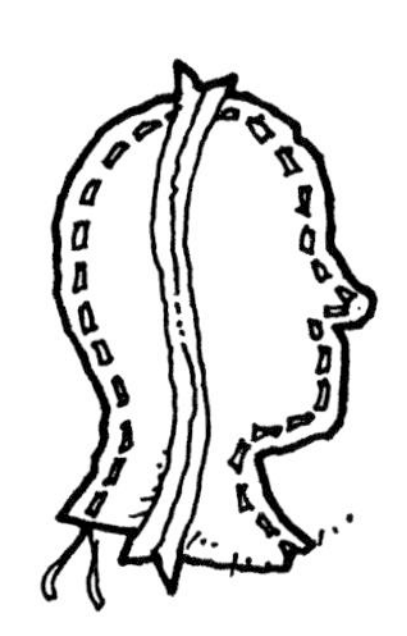

Step 8

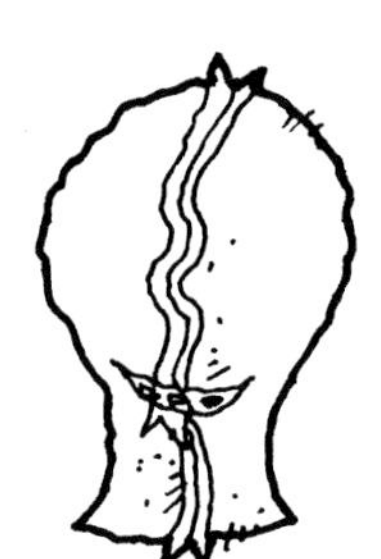

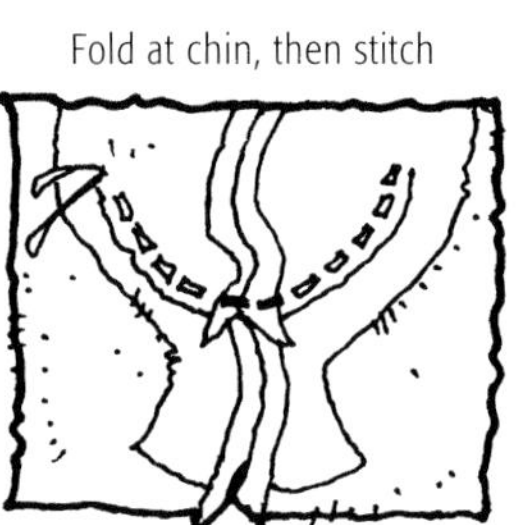

Step 9

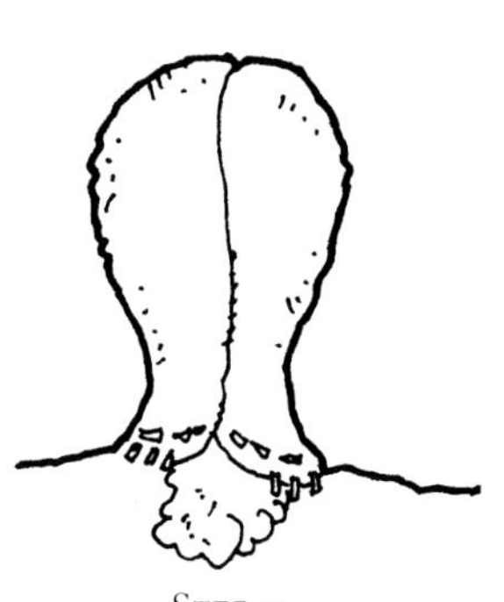

Step 11

Stuffing the Doll

Polyester stuffing is usually used for dollmaking. In most brands, the fibers are combed—they run in one direction and are prone to matting and bunching. I prefer uncombed or random stuffing, since it is easier to mold and works smoothly into corners. Combed fibers are sometimes rolled into a batt; random fibers usually expand when you open the package.

There are several commercial stuffing tools available, such as Dritz for Dolls Stuffing Tool. There are also several items you may have around the house that you can use to help stuff the doll, such as dowels of varying widths. An extra-long chopstick is helpful for stuffing tubular pieces—such as long, thin legs or arms—and bamboo skewers are great for poking stuffing into fingertips and toes. I recommend using a 3½″ (9 cm) hemostat (available from hospital supply stores) to grab small amounts of stuffing to place in hard-to-reach spots. There are commercial stuffing tools available, too, which are very helpful in stuffing small places.

Begin by fluffing small amounts of stuffing, stretching it in all directions, so it doesn't form a ball that may make a lump. Push the stuffing firmly into the doll's body, pushing into outer curves and angles until firm. Add small amounts of stuffing at a time to achieve a smooth, wrinkle-free surface. Gradually work from the outside eges toward the middle of larger body pieces. As you stuff, use your free hand to flatten the stuffed body or limbs. This helps prevent too much roundness.

Molding the Body

There is no single best way to make the doll body. It all depends on the final shape or pose you want to achieve. Lenore Davis used an interesting method that is based on simple dressmaking principles. This technique enabled her to create bodies with a great variety of poses. She divided the body into sections, creating a pattern for each one. She began by sculpting the torso from water-based clay. She then split this up into several sections using imaginary lines—much like the dressmaking torso on page 51—and created a muslin pattern for each section, pinning the muslin pieces to the wet clay with straight pins until all the pieces were in place. She labeled each piece, removed it from the clay, and created a template by drawing around it, adding a seam allowance. She used these very accurate templates to cut the body pieces from muslin. They were then stitched together and stuffed, creating a faithful replica of the original clay torso.

With further inspiration from VaLoy Marchant, I experimented with this method to create *Renaissance Woman Cavils in Moonlight*. Here, I have modified the technique to demonstrate how to make a pattern for a basic decorative doll. If you decide to make *Renaissance Woman*, you will find complete directions for sculpting the face in Chapter 3 (see page 21).

Mustardseed BY LENORE DAVIS, 1996.

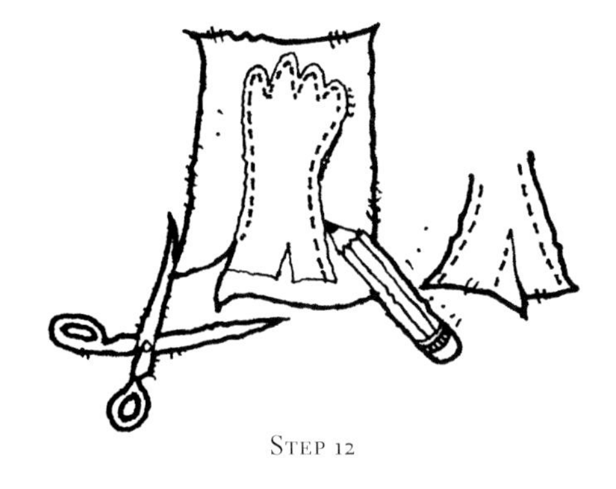

Step 12

Constructing Arms and Fingers

12. Pencil around template L (lower arm and hand) on doubled muslin. Stitch carefully around outer arm and fingers on pencil lines as shown. Trim seam allowance to ⅛″ (0.4 cm) or less and clip to separate fingers. Transfer markings and stitch dart, using scant ⅛″ (0.4 cm) seam allowance. Turn right side out. Repeat for other hand.
13. Right sides together, stitch side seams of templates M (upper arm), leaving top and bottom open. Trim seam allowance to ⅛″ (0.4 cm). Insert L inside M, right sides together, matching raw edges and front and back seams. Stitch together by hand, making very small backstitches. Trim seam allowance to ⅛″ (0.4 cm). Turn right side out. Repeat for second upper arm.
14. Cut four pieces of pipe cleaner, each 2″ (5 cm) long. Bend one end under, and insert bent end into a finger. Repeat until all fingers are filled. Stuff palms of hand with polyester stuffing; fingers are filled with pipe cleaners, allowing ends of pipe cleaners to lie against fabric inside hand (on top of hand; not at palm). Pipe cleaners give the illusion of bones. Continue stuffing arm up to shoulder. Palm should appear padded; top of hand is bony. Repeat for other hand.
15. Pencil around template N (thumb) on doubled muslin. Stitch curved seams, leaving wide end of thumb open. Trim seam allowance to ⅛″ (0.4 cm), including opening. Turn the thumb right side out and stuff. Gather-stitch opening using pencil mark as stitch line. Push raw edges inside as you gather slightly. Knot tightly to hold. Repeat for other thumb.
16. Stitch thumbs to hands, starting at wrist and working around thumb. Stitch arms to shoulders with strong thread.

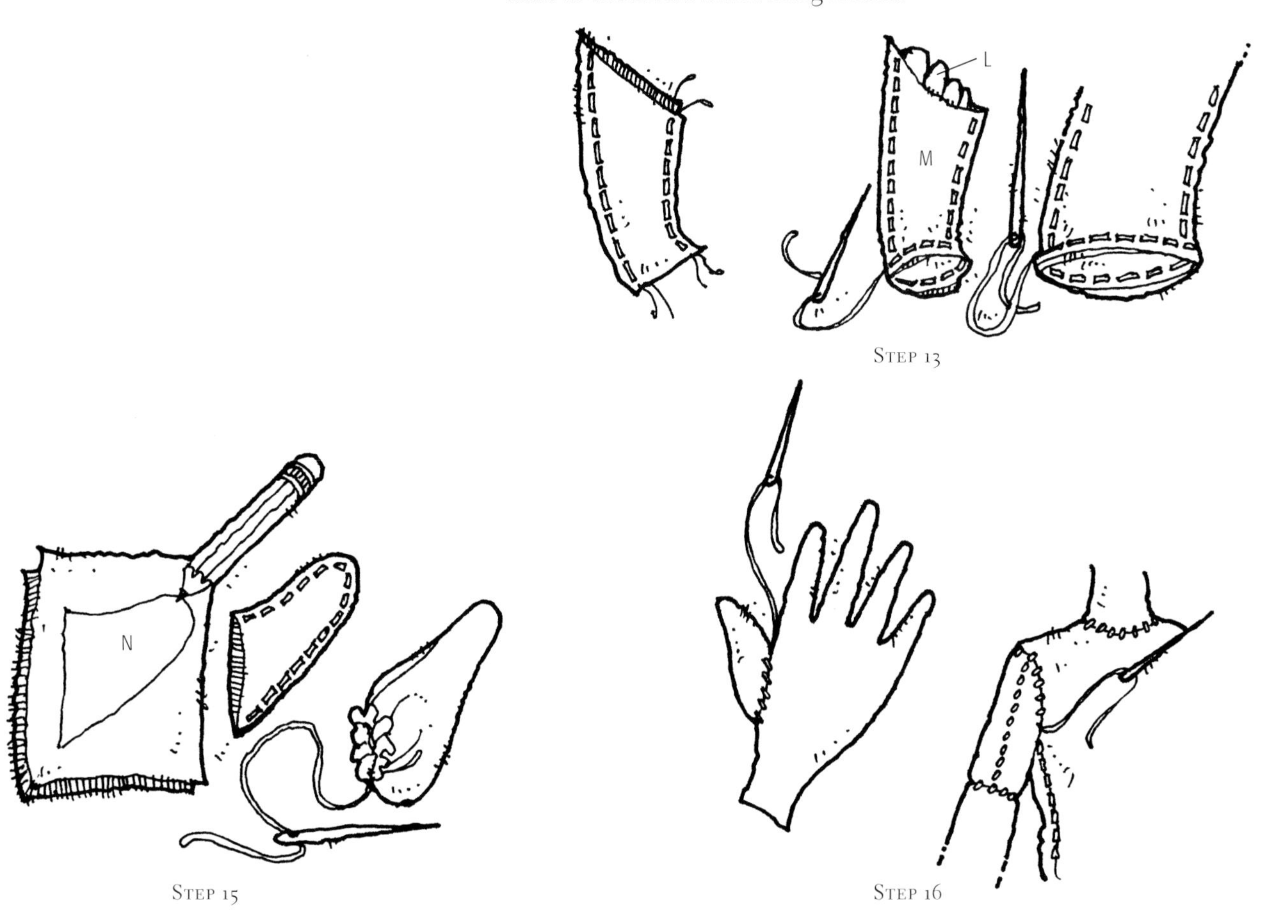

Step 13

Step 15

Step 16

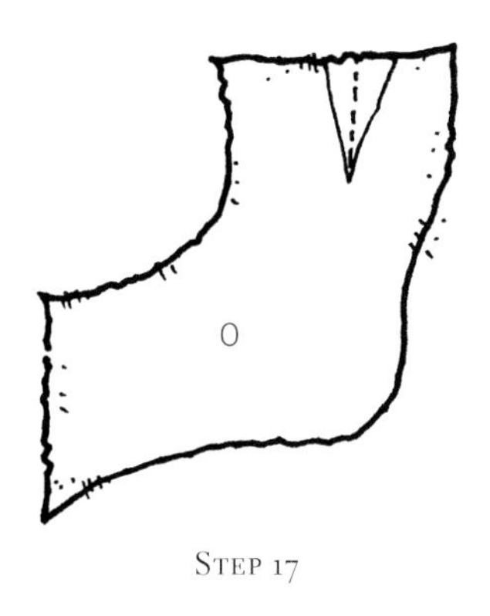

Step 17

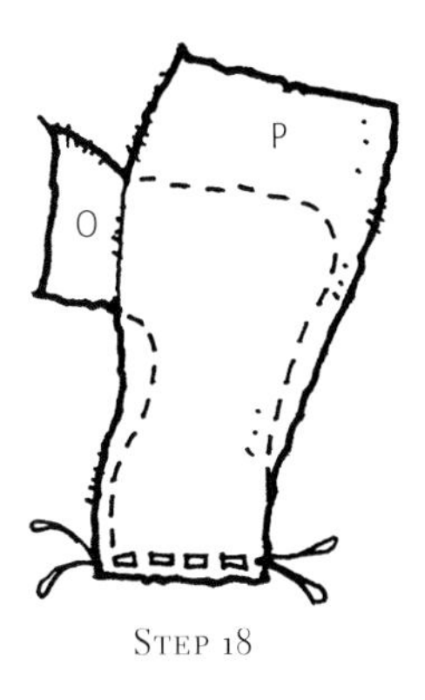

Step 18

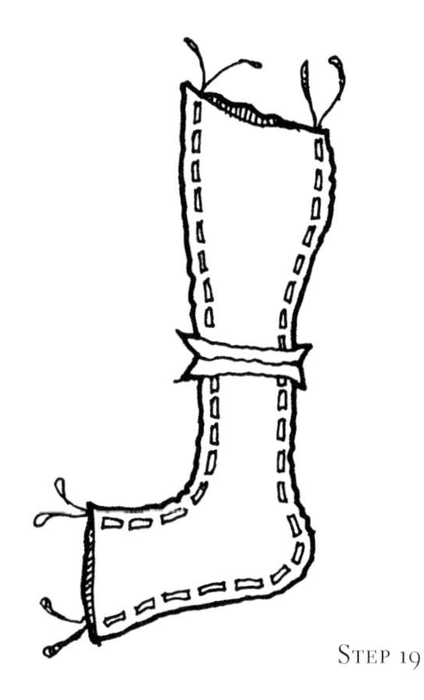

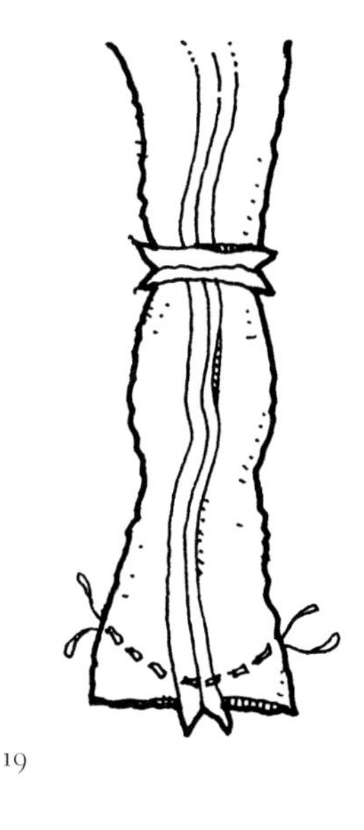

Step 19

Constructing Legs

17. Stitch the darts in each of templates O (left lower leg) and P (right lower leg), starting the dart with a ¼″ (0.75 cm) pucker and tapering to the point.
18. Right sides together, stitch each template O and P to a template Q (upper leg). Trim seam allowance to ⅛″ (0.4 cm).
19. Right sides together and matching raw edges and center seams, stitch leg pieces together, leaving top and bottom open. Align side seams to create flat toe area. Draw a gradual curve across toe area. Machine stitch this curve. Trim seam allowance. Turn leg right side out.
20. Make a small slit in arch of foot as marked on templates O and P. Insert a solid copper electrical wire—length of leg plus 1¼″ (3.2 cm)—into slit, leaving about 1¼″ (3.2 cm) of wire protruding from foot. Seal hole with white craft glue and let dry. Stuff leg firmly around wire using a hemostat, starting at the toes and working upward.
21. Turn under ⅛″ (0.4 cm) seam allowance at top of leg and baste. Stitch legs to body in whatever pose you choose. Remove basting stitches.
22. Needle-sculpt ankle, going back and forth through heel, about 1″ (2.5 cm) or less from the back of heel seam.
23. Lightly draw lines to separate toes. Knot thread and insert needle from below, exiting at first drawn line next to big toe. Tug on thread to pop knot into stuffing. Take a small anchor stitch, then insert needle again at same point. Pull needle through stuffing and exit at other end of first drawn line (tip of foot). Draw thread back along drawn line to first insertion point. Repeat, pulling thread tight to indent dividing line between toes. Make a small knot on underside of foot. Insert needle again at same point and move over to second drawn line. Repeat until all drawn lines are finished.
24. When doll is complete and dressed, insert protruding wire at base of foot to block of wood, which becomes the doll stand.

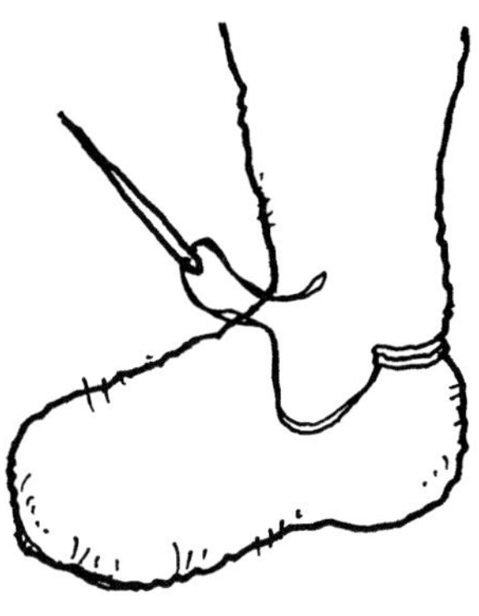

Step 22

You can use this simple technique to have your doll either stand flat on her feet or point her toes. My doll, *Renaissance Woman*, is pointing her toes on one foot. By turning the legs to different angles, it is easy to alter the doll's pose.

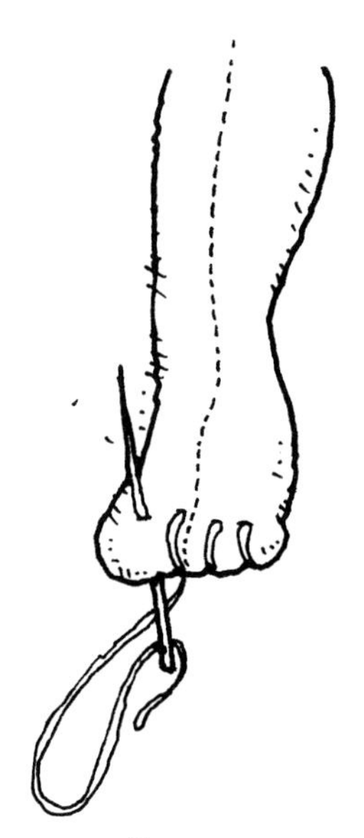

Step 23

Mother's Day BY MARGERY CANNON, 1992.
Margery uses knit fabrics to create her lifelike figures. The armature inside each of her dolls has separate fingers from a sturdy wire, so the doll can hold things without the fingers straightening out. You can see the seam down the front of the face, as well as the front of the legs, and sides of the arms. In a highly detailed creation, using a knit precludes the many different pieces required if you use muslin .

Dolls in All Shapes and Sizes

This basic doll body is extremely versatile. You can finish it by painting it, clothing it, designing hair, or making a wig. All the techniques you need are provided in the chapters that follow. For inspiration, here are several dolls that were created from a similar basic body. Each is unique, and all are quite amazing!

So You Don't Believe in Mermaids BY RUTH LANDIS, 1990.
This rather large creation has wonderful hand and arm construction. The limbs are made by tracing a bent-arm shape (with fingers) on doubled muslin, then stitching on the lines. It is best to use a smaller stitch length when you are making detailed fingers and arm shapes. Double stitch at the elbow for additional strength. Note the exquisite painted face and shadows on the body.

Come Fly With Me BY GLORIA WINER, 1991.
Creating a male doll will involve changing the proportions of the body a great deal. The torso and arms are usually longer than those of a female body, and the legs are a little shorter. To create the torso, think of an inverted triangle, although it's a little exaggerated. Whether it's a fantasy figure, such as this one, or an ordinary human male, remember to observe the differences in hand size, body proportions, and muscular development.

Catbird Woman BY RUTH LANDIS, 1993.
A wooden dowel is used inside the leg and goes into the stand to support this whimsical creature. The face is sculpted to be catlike, and the doll's pose is reminiscent of a dancer. A wire armature inside the body, as well as pipe-cleaner fingers, make it possible to pose the doll in this manner.

Aunt Cora BY VIRGINIA ROBERTSON, 1990.
This wonderful doll is constructed of knit fabric and utilizes extensive face-sculpting and drawing skills. Virginia is considered an expert on creating dolls' faces. She does the needle sculpture first. After sketching the features with a pencil, she uses fine-point ink pens to establish the major lines of the facial features. She then uses colored pencils to shade the areas around the eyes, around the chin line, under the lips and nose, and so on until the face is finished.

Cinderella BY KAREN ABEL, 1990.
Karen created a doll to fit a glass slipper she found at a glassblower's booth at a fair. The body for this doll is graceful and well made. Stuffing is a big part of successful dollmaking, and you will notice the lack of lumpiness. The doll's legs and arms are finely detailed and in good proportion to the doll's body. You can easily adapt my basic body pattern to make this doll by reducing the width of the pattern pieces.

Making an Armature

It is easy to make the basic doll body stand by embedding a simple copper wire through the body or the legs, as described in Step 20 on page 13. The ends of the wire are then pushed into holes in a doll stand.

If you wish to have a freestanding figure, with no stand, making an armature is the best choice. An armature allows you to pose your doll in a variety of ways and offers you a great deal more flexibility than using a doll stand.

Gloria Winer, whose doll *Come Fly With Me* is shown on page 14, shared with me her method of creating an armature. The essential ingredient is vinyl- or plastic-covered wire. Don't use bare steel wire because it will rust; the green, crumbly surface of bare copper wire will oxidize and stain the doll. Aluminum sculptor's wire is too soft to make an armature of this type. It will not hold the doll up. Try to find vinyl- or plastic-covered, single-strand steel or copper wire, available at hardware stores or electrical supply stores.

Prepare the doll pattern in the same way as for the basic doll body. Do not stuff the torso or limbs yet, and do not attach the limbs to the body. This will be done once the armature is in place.

Feeding the Birds BY MARGERY CANNON, 1994.
See caption on page 3.

Supplies

- Vinyl- or plastic-covered wire: heavy (steel) or medium (copper), depending on doll size
- Chenille stems (or pipe cleaners)
- White floral tape
- Wire cutters
- Pliers
- Vise (optional)
- Ruler
- Marking pen
- Scratch awl
- Wooden base, about 1½″ (4 cm) thick
- Paint for base
- Hand or electric drill and set of drill bits

Preparing Armature

1. Measure doll's height. Double that measurement and add 6″ (15 cm). Cut wire to that length.
2. Put two ends of wire together and grasp them with one hand. With other hand, slide up wire, squeezing it together to form a hairpin shape.

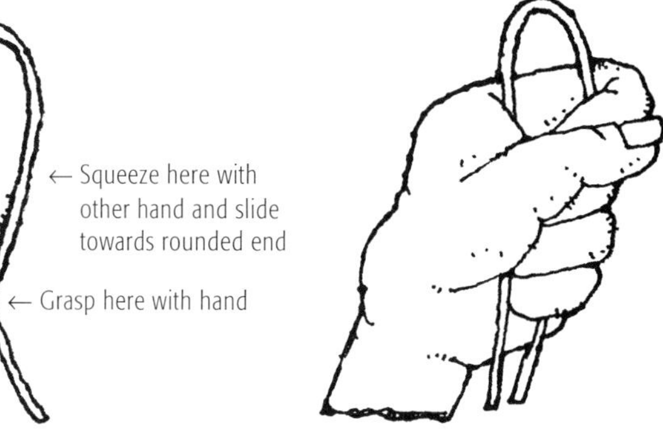

Step 2

3. Squeeze rounded end in pliers until it is quite narrow. Leave it just big enough to get an awl or a screwdriver into loop. Clamp rounded end in vise to hold it, or put awl or screwdriver through rounded end and hold it in one hand.
4. Twist ends of wire until twisted part is 5″ (13 cm) long. If you don't have a vise, hold onto rounded end (using awl or screwdriver) with one hand while you twist with the other.
5. Mark twisted part of armature 2½″ (6.5 cm) from top. This is where arm wire will be inserted.
6. Cut a new 24″ (60 cm) length of wire for arms. Mark center. Push awl through twisted part of armature, 2½″ (6.5 cm) from loop. When you remove awl, it will leave a hole. Push arm wire through hole until center mark is at center of twisted armature.

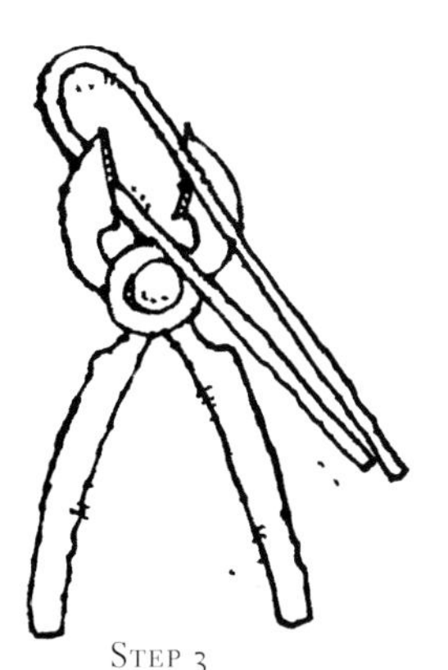
Step 3

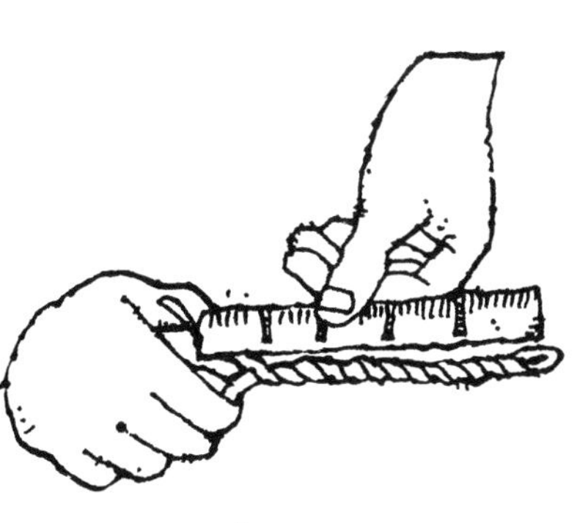

Step 4

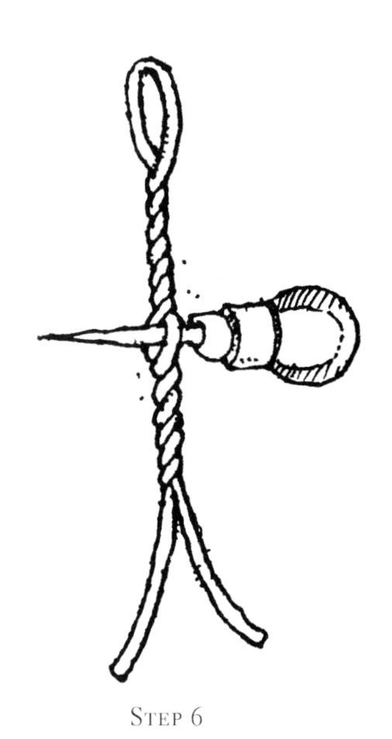
Step 6

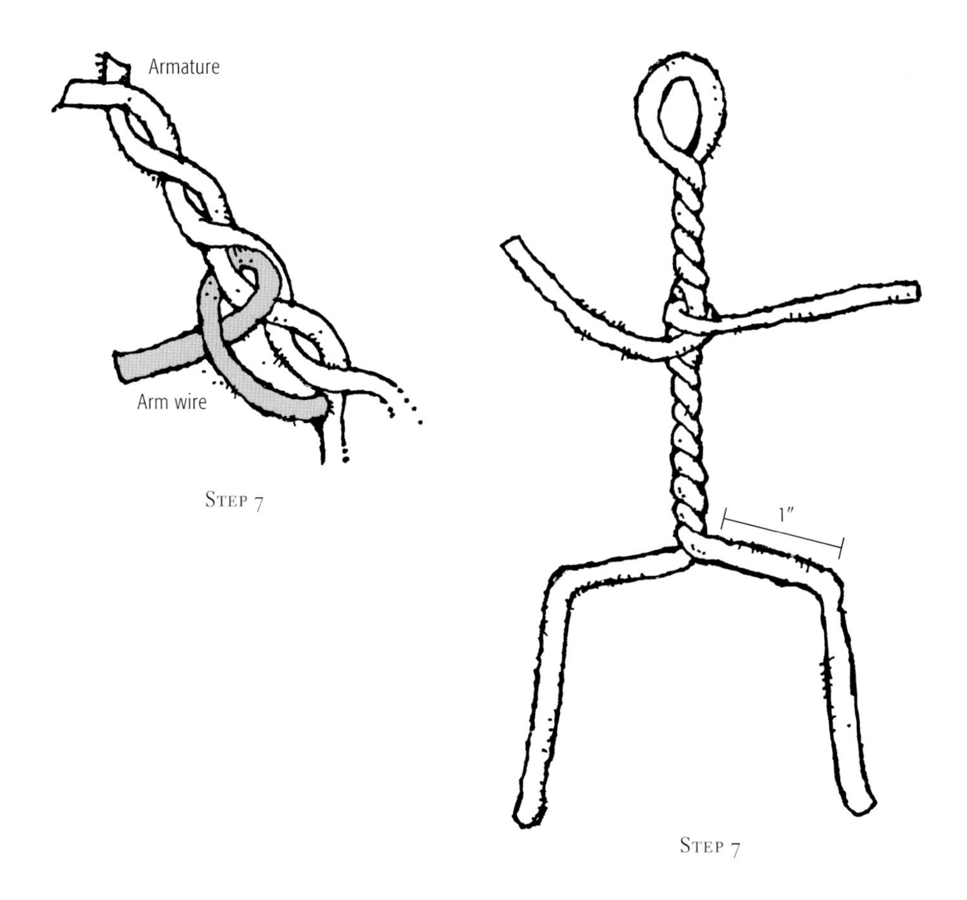

Step 7

Step 7

7. Bend both arms around until arm wire is locked to armature by a loop. Grasp armature with pliers near end of twisted part. Use your fingers to bend legs straight out to either side. Grasp a leg with pliers about 1″ (2.5 cm) from armature and use your fingers to bend leg straight down. Repeat for other leg.

Inserting Armature in Body

8. To insert armature in unstuffed doll body, first pull arm wires straight up. Slip armature inside body. Bend wire back perpendicular to twisted center to form shoulders, then bend arm wires out of your way so you won't poke yourself while stuffing torso. Starting at top, use hemostats to insert stuffing. Keep wire armature in middle of body and stuff north, east, south, and west, revolving around armature. Firmly stuff entire torso.
9. Before stuffing legs, insert a piece of cardboard, cut to fit sole of foot, inside each leg and into foot. Poke wire through cardboard and fabric between ball and heel of foot, right in arch area. (The cardboard facilitates shoemaking, because it gives you a flat surface which is easier to work with.) Bend protruding wire to keep foot from slipping off end. Use a hemostat to stuff toes, working your way up leg, keeping wire in middle. (Protruding wires will be placed into base after legs are stuffed and sewn onto lower torso. You will have to trim some of the excess wire to fit into holes of base.)

Finishing Fingers

10. If you wish to attach wired fingers to ends of arms, with arms down at side, cut off arm wires ½″ (1.5 cm) below crotch. Wrap end of arm wire with white floral tape, stretching tape a little as you wrap to activate wax adhesive. Place wrapped end of arm wire in center of four chenille stems, spaced and sized for inserting into fingers. Wrap them all together with white floral tape. (Note: thumb is sewn on separately and doesn't require a stem.) When stuffing palm and wrist, use a tiny bit of stuffing in palm, but not on top of hand, as chenille stems give the illusion of bones on top side of hand. Use a hemostat and place stuffing in wrist, working your way up arm, surrounding armature. When arms are very firmly stuffed, stitch them to torso.

Mounting Doll on Base

11. Paint base. I prefer to use a wooden base, about 1½″ (4 cm) thick. Position doll with armature wires that protrude through feet touching base. Mark small dot where wires touch base.
12. Select drill bit that makes hole just big enough to hold armature wire. (Pretest bits on scrap wood to find right size.) Drill through base and scrape off any splinters around top or bottom of holes.
13. Put doll on stand so that ends of armature wires stick through bottom of stand. Push down on doll to position securely.
14. Use wire cutters to grip wires on bottom of stand. Squeeze to mark but do not cut through wires. Remove doll and cut wires about ⅛″ (0.4 cm) above marks so wire will not stick out of bottom of stand. Reposition doll, taking care to balance it well. Wire should fit snugly into drilled holes, with no need for glue to hold it in place.

CHAPTER 3

CREATING THE DOLL'S FACE

THE BEAUTY OF A doll is in its face. It is here that the dollmaker gives her work feeling and expression. The slant in the doll's eyes, the color in her cheeks, and the curve of her lip all tell her story. There are several methods you can use to create your doll's face. In this chapter, we shall explore some of the most popular approaches. You will also find photographs of several wonderful dolls whose faces are created using an exciting range of innovative techniques.

The Woman with Too Much on Her Mind BY MIRIAM CHRISTENSEN GOURLEY, 1990. This very busy mother is constructed of muslin. Her face is a flat piece and the back of the head is two almost-half-round shapes. The nose is stuffed and sewn on separately. The texture of the lips and eyes are created by detailed embroidery. The eye shadows are also embroidered. The fingers are constructed separately and tucked into the thumb/hand piece, then stitched in place. The doll's hat is covered with utility bills, children's pictures, and several other reminders of the mother's hectic life.

Sculpting the Face—Renaissance Woman

Needle-sculpting is a technique dollmakers use to mold facial features, such as the nose, the cheeks, and the chin, from stuffed fabric. Quite simply, you use a needle and thread to raise certain areas of the face, manipulating the muslin and stuffing with your fingers until you achieve the shapes you desire. Sculpting the face is sometimes done before the head is attached to the body.

My doll *Renaissance Woman* has a very simple face that is easy to sculpt. To practice the needle-sculpting technique, first prepare the basic stuffed head as described on page 10, then follow the directions here.

Detail of *Medieval Jester* (left). Full doll is shown on page x.
Detail of *Renaissance Woman* (right). Full doll is shown on page 8.

Before You Begin, Practice

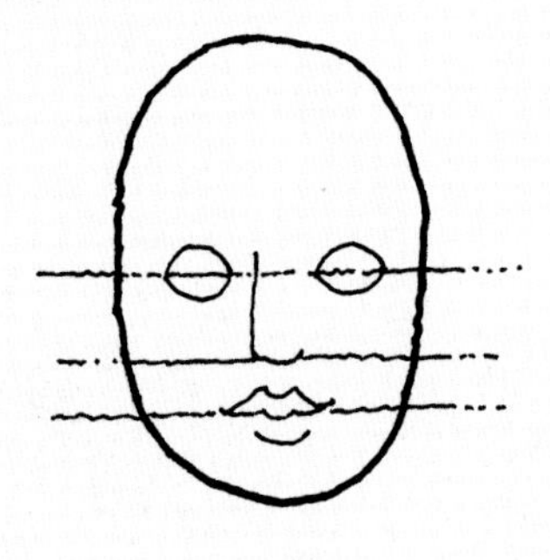

Before you work on your doll's face, practice first by drawing the facial features on a piece of paper. Draw an oval face shape about the size of the finished cloth head. (Remember, the head is stuffed and oval in shape.) To create symmetrical, regularly spaced features on your paper pattern, visually divide the face area in half from top to bottom. Pinch it gently with your fingers to mark the center line. Lightly draw the eyes along the center line, leaving a space the same width as an eye between them. Visually divide the bottom half of the oval and pinch again to create a nose line, marking the bottom of the nose. Use the pattern as a guide to mark the sculpting lines along the side of the nose. (Use template K on page 124 if you are making *Renaissance Woman*.) Pinch the paper again about halfway between the nose line and the base of the oval–this is the lip line. Draw the mouth so that the corners are directly below the center of each eye.

When you have a sketch that pleases you, lightly copy it in pencil onto the completed head (after it is sculpted and painted with a flesh-colored base coat). You can use an art eraser to erase pencil lines if changes need to be made.

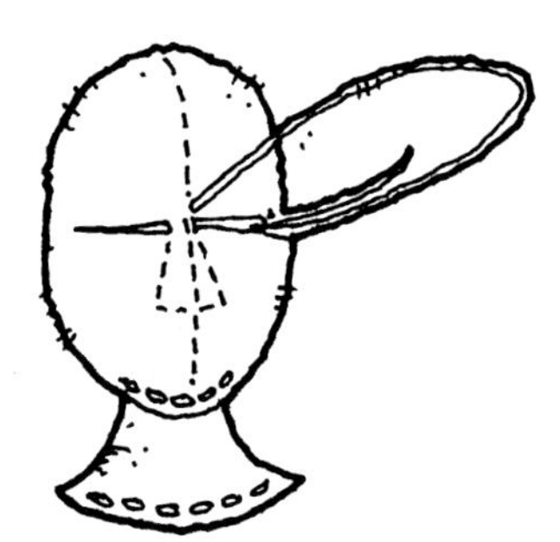

Step 1

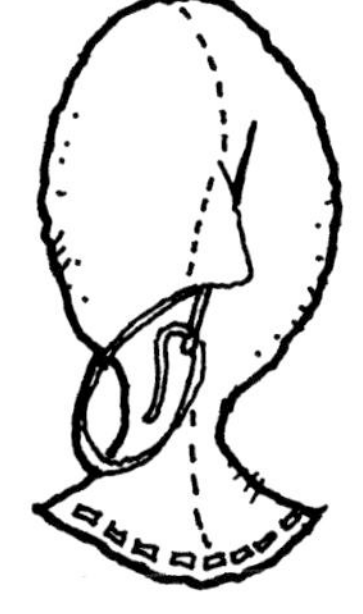

Step 2

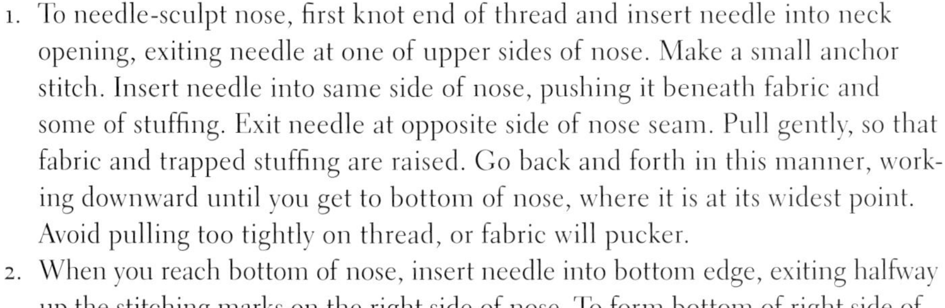

1. To needle-sculpt nose, first knot end of thread and insert needle into neck opening, exiting needle at one of upper sides of nose. Make a small anchor stitch. Insert needle into same side of nose, pushing it beneath fabric and some of stuffing. Exit needle at opposite side of nose seam. Pull gently, so that fabric and trapped stuffing are raised. Go back and forth in this manner, working downward until you get to bottom of nose, where it is at its widest point. Avoid pulling too tightly on thread, or fabric will pucker.
2. When you reach bottom of nose, insert needle into bottom edge, exiting halfway up the stitching marks on the right side of nose. To form bottom of right side of nose, repeat this step and exit out left side of nose. You don't need to make nostrils; just defining the bottom of the nose makes the right impression.

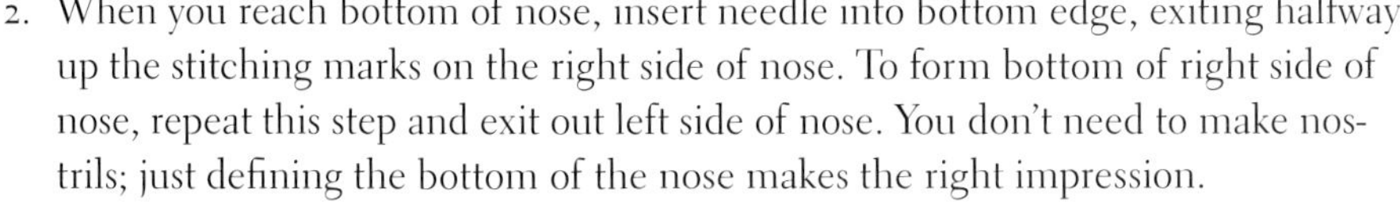

3. To form eye and cheek areas, knot thread. Enter through neck as in Step 1 and make a small anchor stitch at left corner of mouth. Reinsert needle into left corner of mouth, push it through some stuffing, and exit at inner corner of left eye. Make a small stitch, inserting needle back into same corner, exiting back at left corner of mouth. Pull slightly to allow fabric and trapped stuffing to rise. Repeat.
4. Reinsert needle into left corner of mouth, trap stuffing, and exit at outer corner of left eye. Repeat.
5. Repeat Steps 3 and 4 at right side of face. Note: If face begins to pucker, you may need to stuff head more firmly or not pull thread as tightly.

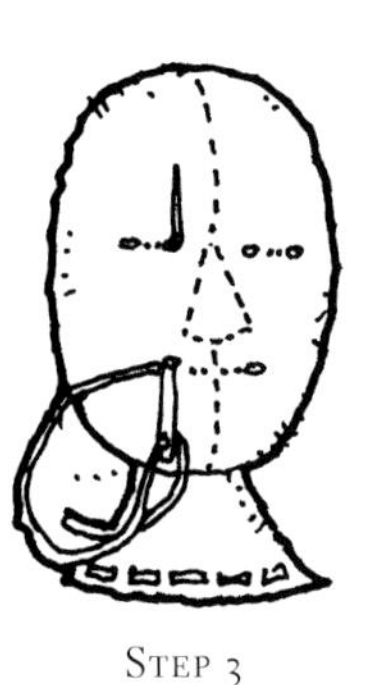

Step 3

Step 4

Sculpted Faces

Sculpting faces takes practice, and you will find that your fingers become more deft with every face you sculpt. Manipulate the muslin and stuffing with your fingers as you work and use small stitches to hold the fabric firmly in place.

Flower Fairy BY AKIRA BLOUNT, 1989.
Almost all sculpted faces utilize the same basic sculpting techniques, but Akira's dolls are especially treasured for their wonderful expressions. This is not just the sculpting, but the combination of paints and embroidery.

Hadassah (Queen Esther) BY MARY THOMAS, 1992.
Mary created this beautiful doll by using a knit fabric, which was formed into the face and body, then carefully sculpted. The features were painted, and the beautiful clothing and accessories were then added.

Cactus Cathy BY MARLA FLORIO, 1991.
Marla uses a combination of sculpting and colored pencils to create her unique doll faces. In this particular work, she has taken sculpting to new heights in creating an environment for her doll.

Face Painting

Though some doll artists use oil paints, I always recommend acrylic paints, which are water based. Acrylics have several distinct advantages over oils. Most importantly, they require minimal drying time and clean up easily with soap and water. They are also less expensive than oils and are readily available in crafts stores in an almost limitless range of colors. If, however, you like the longer drying time, allowing you to mix colors while you apply them, you can purchase drying-retardant products for acrylic paints, which makes them more like oils.

There are several quality brands of acrylic paints, and the chemical makeup of them all is the same. They vary only in terms of texture and color. I usually prefer acrylics that are specifically for crafting; acrylics designated for fabric are too thin for my style of dollmaking. The instructions in Part Two specify the paint brands each artist used to create the doll photographed, but remember that you can freely substitute other brands if you wish. The following varieties will give a range of effects when used in dollmaking.

Bowling Pin Dolls BY SUE LITTLE, 1998.
Sue Little was inspired to create these bowling pin dolls after watching an old movie. The movie included a scene in which one of the characters was playing with an old, weighted punching bag shaped like a doll. Sue thought that was a great concept for making a series of dolls, so she used a little plastic bowling pin for a pattern. She made several sizes using the basic pattern shapes and sewed the faces on separately. The faces are painted with acrylic paints, then sealed.

- Acrylic paints. Available in an ever-increasing variety of colors, these paints dry to a matte finish. When dry, the color is slightly darker than you see in the bottle. Acrylic paints with a metallic or pearl-like finish are also available.
- Gel medium. If you want to give a slightly transparent look with just a hint of color (on lips or in a shadow area), you can mix acrylic paint with a gel medium. This does not affect the drying time.
- Stain. For dollmaking, I usually select a stain that is premixed in a gel base. After the doll's features have been painted and dried, the gel stain can be brushed on, then the excess removed with a dry cloth. The stain softens or ages the appearance of the painted surface.
- Control medium. To achieve the effect of oil paints, acrylic paints may be mixed with control medium. This lengthens the drying time, thereby giving you additional time to manipulate the colors or remove some of the color.
- Textile medium. This is a water-based, colorless liquid used to thin acrylic paints. It helps prevent bleeding beyond painted lines. You can use it to lighten the intensity of strong colors. Textile medium also helps you blend and move colors more easily on fabric. There is no exact formula for mixing textile medium with paint. Some artists dip the brush in medium, then mix it a tiny bit at a time with the paint. Others paint the feature in medium first, then apply acrylic paint while the medium is still wet.
- Crackle medium. A product like Jo Sonja's crackle medium, applied over the finished face, creates "cracks" or wrinkles in the painted surface. After it dries, a gel stain is applied over it. Some crackle mediums require an additional layer of acrylic paint to activate; these are not ideal for dollmaking.

Mother Moon BY MIRIAM CHRISTENSEN GOURLEY, 2000.
This is a muslin doll with sculpted face and hands, which are painted with acrylic paint. As you can see, painted faces do not have to have human coloring. This magical little doll has "moon" coloring.

Shaker Sister BY MIRIAM CHRISTENSEN GOURLEY, 2000.
Dressed in 1850s-style Shaker summer clothing, this doll has a muslin body, which is painted with acrylic paint. After the paint dried, Miriam added a coat of Jo Sonja's crackle medium, and when dried, oak antique gel was brushed on and wiped off to give the illusion of a very old doll.

Marcella the Milliner BY MIRIAM CHRISTENSEN GOURLEY, 2000.
This doll has a perky little hairdo and hat to set off her beautiful face. Like other dolls made by Miriam, this doll is made out of muslin, which is painted and antiqued. Unlike *Mother Moon* and *Shaker Sister*, this doll's head and torso are one-piece construction.

- Glitter paints. A milky acrylic paint base is mixed with colored glitter to create glitter paints. When the paint is dry, the base is clear. Glitter paints may be mixed with other colors or thinned to create sparkly eye shadow, lip color, or cheek color.
- Metallic paints. Although these paints have a metallic sheen, there is no metal content. It is easy to thin them with textile medium for fine-line painting. Metallic paints look especially dramatic on darker fabrics.
- Sealers. When all painting is finished, the paint is greatly enhanced and protected by a sealer. Spray sealers are easiest to use, but should be applied in a well-ventilated place or outdoors. The sealer may be purchased with a matte or gloss finish. Liquid sealers may be brushed onto the painted surface.

Face-Painting Techniques

When working with sculpted faces, it is almost impossible to paint before stitching. The painted surface will crinkle up when you try to stitch it. Make sure the head is stuffed firmly to prevent problems.

Before you begin, make a sketch of the face you wish to draw onto the fabric and decide on color choices. Cover a tabletop with newspaper to protect against spills. Collect the following supplies, plus any that are on the materials list of the doll you wish to make.

- Mixing tray or palette (plastic-coated plates are fine)
- Paper towels (to remove excess water or color from brushes)
- Selected paints, plus paint-enhancing products and sealers (see pages 23–25)
- Water for rinsing brushes
- Brushes in varying sizes, including very fine brushes and stiff stencil brushes
- Blow-dryer to lessen drying time

Helen Pringle is one of the few dollmakers who use oil paints to create doll faces. Helen likes the soft, old look that oils give a doll.

Magic BY HELEN PRINGLE, 1992.

Rhino Boy BY MIRIAM CHRISTENSEN GOURLEY, 1996.

Base Paint

The base coat is painted in whatever flesh color you plan to use for the doll's skin. There is a broad range of colors available, including some that are designed for creating shadows on the face. You can use any color you like—bright green, for example, is a wonderful color for a wicked witch! Generally, you will paint the surface of the face, arms, and legs if they are going to show.

When the base coat is completely dry, you can use a very fine sanding pad to smooth the painted surface. The paint raises the nap of the fabric and tends to make it seem rough when it is dry. This light sanding helps create a smoother surface.

When you have finished sanding, apply a second coat of paint. This will ensure that you cover the surface thoroughly and don't leave spots uncovered.

Adding Shadows by Dry Brushing

The technique of dry brushing is great for adding subtle color to highlight features like the cheeks or shadowing around the eyes. You will need two or three round stiff stencil brushes in different sizes. The brush is dipped into the desired color, then rubbed onto an old rag or paper towel until most of the wet paint is removed, leaving just enough in the brush to achieve a powderlike effect. For example, when a terra cotta or barn red paint is applied with the dry-brush method, it makes a good cheek color. Apply the dry brush before doing any detail work, such as the eyes, so the color will not accidentally cover the wrong feature.

Primitive-style dolls, with simple embroidered faces, may be stained by painting strong coffee directly onto the face. The face should be wet first, and the coffee will stain some areas a little darker than others. This will give the doll an authentic "old" appearance.

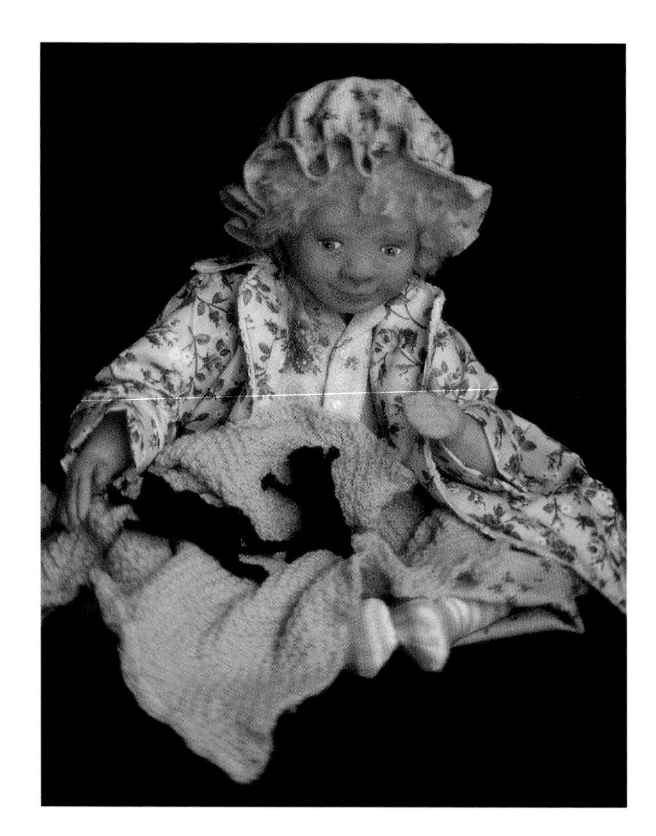

Polly Pinks BY HEDY KATIN, 1992.
This little doll is made from a knit fabric, with painted facial details. Hedy created the kittens from bits of stuffing with string wound around them to keep their shape. The kittens were then painted black.

Painting Facial Detail

Each of the patterns in Part Two includes instructions on face painting specific to the doll you are making. Here are some general guidelines to follow as you learn face-painting techniques. As with any other skill, practice as much as you can. For your first dolls, I recommend creating several heads, stuffing them, and painting them. You can then stitch the best one onto your doll's body.

If you are in doubt about a color, apply it to a scrap of muslin so that you can see how it will look. Be sure to apply the flesh-color paint to a scrap to see how the other colors will look when painted over it.

Use a small brush (#000 to #0) for painting facial details. If brushwork is difficult for you, you can use a fine-tip permanent marking pen, such as the Itoya or EK Success brands. Caution: When using sealer on marking pens, use only matte sealer. Spray just a little bit, let it dry, then apply more. If you spray too much sealer on the ink, it will run. Gloss (shiny) finishes can be applied after you've used the matte sealer.

Follow the face-painting directions for your pattern carefully, and start at the top of the face unless directed otherwise. If you start at the lips, for example, and work toward the eyes, you may accidentally brush your hand on the wet paint and smear your work.

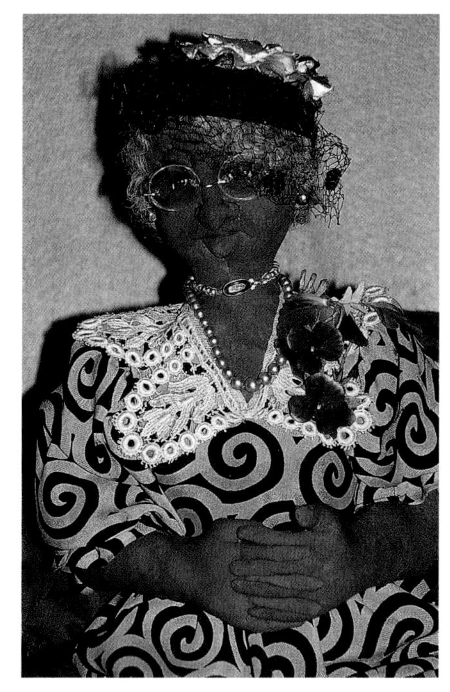

Black Aunt Cora BY VIRGINIA ROBERTSON, 1996.

Virginia uses colored pencils and fine-tip pens to create the color for the eyes, cheeks, and lips of her dolls. Paint is occasionally used for highlights. Her technique is detailed in *How to Draw and Sculpt Cloth Doll Faces*, Robertson's Quilting and Cloth Doll Supplies, Dolores, CO, 1996.

Painting Renaissance Woman

Renaissance Woman is painted in a very conventional manner, with flesh tones and natural colors for the features. You can use this simple color scheme to paint the face for any doll. If you decide to make *Renaissance Woman*, directions for the doll body are provided in Chapter 2.

SUPPLIES

- Acrylic paints. *Renaissance Woman* uses Delta Ceramcoat® paints, but you can adapt this list to use paints you already have:
  - Medium Flesh
  - AC Flesh
  - Dark Flesh
  - Bambi Brown
  - Light Ivory
  - Rainforest Green
  - Black
  - Palomino Tan
- Neutral gel
- Variety of brushes, ranging from very small (#000) liner brushes to ½" (1.5 cm) flat nylon brushes
- Spray matte sealer
- Small sanding pad (manicure supplies)
- No. 2 lead pencil

1. Base face, neck, arms, feet, and ankles with equal mixture of AC Flesh and Medium Flesh. Base legs and body, if desired, with colors of your choice. If you plan to dress doll, you may leave body unpainted.

Detail of *Renaissance Woman*. Full doll is shown on page 8.

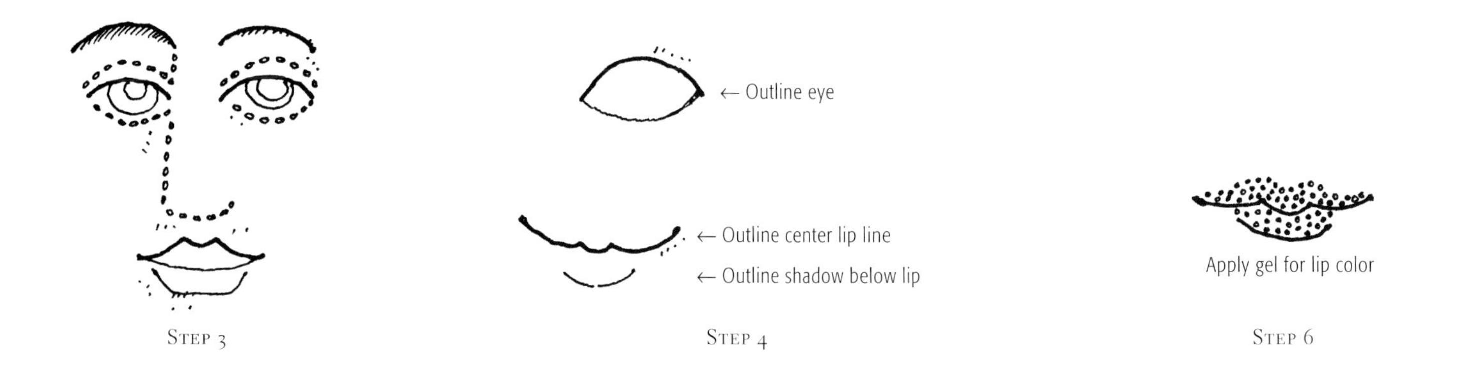

STEP 3 STEP 4 STEP 6

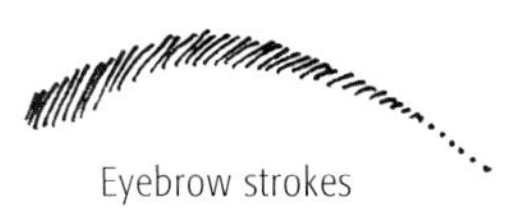

STEP 7

2. Use finest side of sanding pad to lightly sand painted surface until smooth. Apply a second coat of paint.
3. Very lightly sketch eyes, eyebrow shape, and lips with a pencil. (See "Before You Begin, Practice" on page 22 for help marking features.)
4. Use Bambi Brown to define outline around eyes, center lip line, and shadow below lower lip. Use a tiny brush, and dilute paint slightly with a small amount of water to create a finer line. Let dry thoroughly.
5. Dry brush cheek area with Dark Flesh, as detailed on page 26. Apply color to cheek in a circular motion until you decide there is enough. Apply a small amount of color just below eyebrow.
6. To create lips, mix neutral gel with a little Dark Flesh and apply with a small brush. Apply several layers until lips look dark enough.
7. Apply Rainforest Green to iris of each eye. Apply Black to pupil area. Use Light Ivory for white of eye and a tiny dot in each pupil to create a highlight. If you need to, apply a tiny line of Bambi Brown to redefine lower eye line. Use Palomino Tan to cover upper eyelid. With a tiny liner brush, apply Black to define upper eye line. Apply a tiny dot of Dark Flesh in corner of each eye. Use Bambi Brown and a tiny brush to paint eyebrows with small, thin strokes.

Painting Medieval Jester

This doll was inspired by Barbara Chapman's *Whimsical Personage* (see page 108) and has the same basic body.

Supplies

Detail of *Medieval Jester*. Full doll is shown on page x.

- Acrylic paints. *Medieval Jester* uses Americana® paints. Feel free to substitute if these paints are unavailable:
  - Base Flesh
  - Raw Sienna
  - Lt. Buttermilk
  - Mink Tan
  - Sable Brown
  - DeLane's Dark Flesh
  - Ebony Black
- Spotter brush, #000
- Spray matte sealer
- Hair fiber

1. Base coat face and neck with Base Flesh twice, as described on page 26.
2. Draw eyes and mouth outline with a pencil.
3. Use spotter brush to paint in white area of eyes using Lt. Buttermilk. Iris is painted with Raw Sienna, pupil with Ebony Black, and top lid with Mink Tan.
4. To outline eyelids, mouth line, lower lip shadow, and wrinkles below eyes, use Sable Brown diluted with a small amount of water. Test first. Dot highlight in pupil with Lt. Buttermilk. Let face dry completely.
5. Dry brush cheeks and lip area with DeLane's Dark Flesh. (See page 26 for help with dry brushing.) Spray with matte sealer when dry.
6. Twist a small strand of hair fiber, using wet fingers, to create eyebrows. Use a toothpick to paint a line of white craft glue on eyebrow line. Press strand of hair fiber in place and let dry completely. Don't worry about stray hair fibers. You can trim them when glue is dry.

Step 2

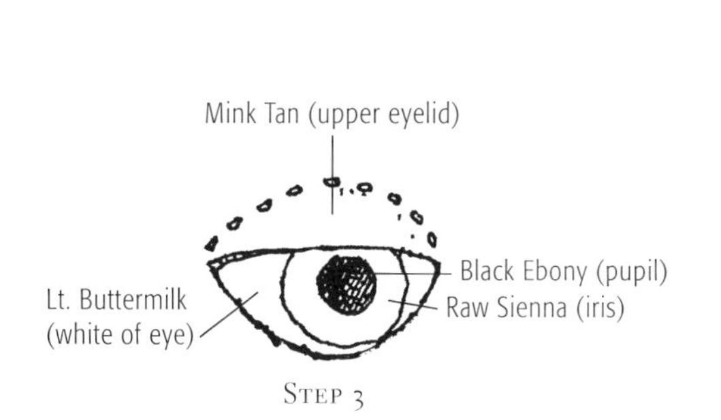

Step 3

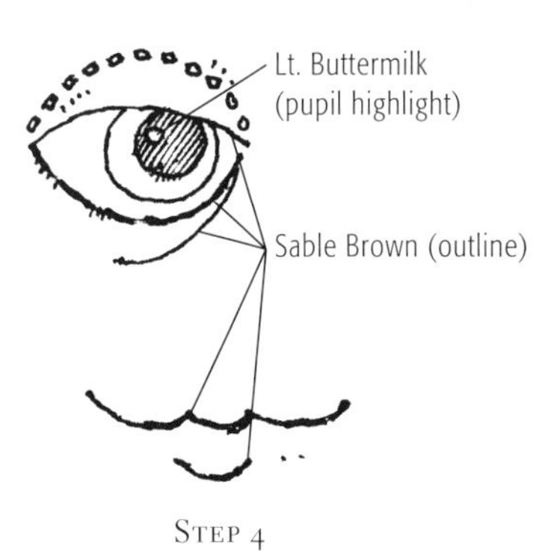

Step 4

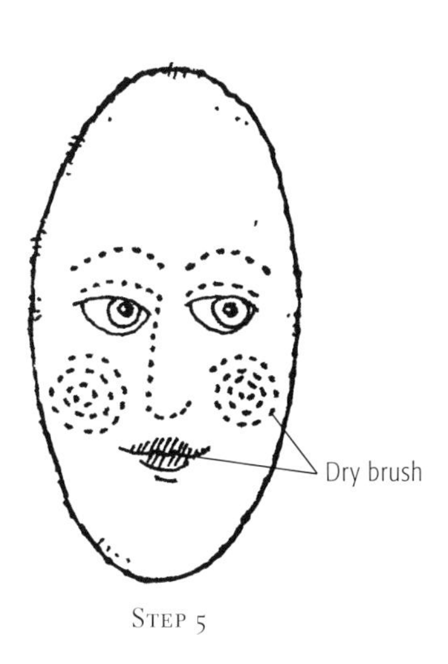

Step 5

Detail of *Frida Kahlo* by Virginia Robertson. See full doll on page 34.

Other Coloring Methods

There are some wonderful dolls whose faces are decorated, not with paint, but with other kinds of markers. Permanent-ink, fine-tip marking pens, for example, are excellent for creating fine features and for outlining or giving definition to eyes or lips. Markers are readily available in a range of colors in crafts stores. If you are unused to handling a paintbrush, fine-tip pens may be an easier option for you. *Tulip*, on page 65, is done in this way. If you use fine-tip markers, try to draw quickly and accurately. If you rest the pen too long in one spot, the line may bleed into the fabric. It's always worth taking the time to sketch out the facial features lightly in pencil first, then draw over the lines in marker.

Crayons and colored pencils are very effective tools for achieving a soft look. Many dollmakers use them to add color to cheeks, for example. The secret to using crayons for cheek color is to use a light hand. If you press too hard, your doll will end up with waxy cheeks.

Embroidering the Face

Embroidery is a very traditional way to create a doll's face. It may be used in combination with other methods to extraordinary effect. *The Woman with Too Much on Her Mind* (page 20) and *Midnight Ride Through Fairyland* (page 57) both have finely embroidered features.

Embroidery can be done before the face is stitched and stuffed if it is a flat, unsculpted face. By working on a flat piece of muslin, you are able to use an embroidery hoop to keep the fabric taut, ensuring more even stitching. Before you embroider, line the face with a second layer of fabric. This keeps the knots and tails on the underside from showing through after the doll is stuffed. When you wish to embroider a sculpted face, you may hide the knots at the top of the head where the hair will cover them. Note: You can use colored skin-tone fabric or paint afterward, if you are careful.

To begin, lightly draw the outline of the face on the fabric. You can use a No. 2 lead pencil or a disappearing-ink quilting pen to draw the features to be embroidered. Select a fine rather than a coarse-weave fabric. If you wish to embroider the face first, you will not cut out the face from the fabric until the embroidery is complete. Use a hoop that is large enough to encompass the entire design. Place the screw or clamp of the hoop in the ten o'clock position (or the two o'clock position, if you are left-handed) to keep the threads from catching on the fastener.

Choose the smallest needle possible to prevent large needle holes that can weaken the fabric. Needle size will also depend on the number of threads you will be using at one time. Most dollmaking can be done with sizes 5 to 8 embroidery needles.

A length of embroidery floss is made up of six individual strands. Cut the floss into 18″ (45 cm) lengths, and run them over a damp cloth before you separate all six strands (to keep from tangling). Reassemble the number of strands needed in the pattern you are following or the number you wish to use. For example, outline stitching of fine lines usually requires only one strand; a satin stitch can be done with two or more. As you stitch, avoid the temptation to carry the floss over from

Peppermint Tea Party BY MIRIAM CHRISTENSEN GOURLEY, 2000.
Peppermint and *Tea-Cozy Doll* are both created using the popular "red work" method. The bodies are created from muslin and the faces embroidered with a single thread of turkey-red embroidery floss. The clothing is also embroidered with the same color of thread.

Too Hot for Shoes BY SUSIE M. ROBBINS, 1988.
This wonderful dollmaker doll is concentrating on her work while the "imps" she is creating come alive and make mischief. The face is embroidered, the eyelashes are made of thread. Note the body construction—a full figure with detailed fingers. You can adapt the basic pattern on page 13 to bend at the knees. By widening the templates (using trial and error), you can create a full figure like this one.

Embroidery Stitches

Of all these embroidery stitches, only the first four—French knot, straight stitch, outline stitch, and satin stitch—are suitable for faces. Use the others for decorating doll clothing.

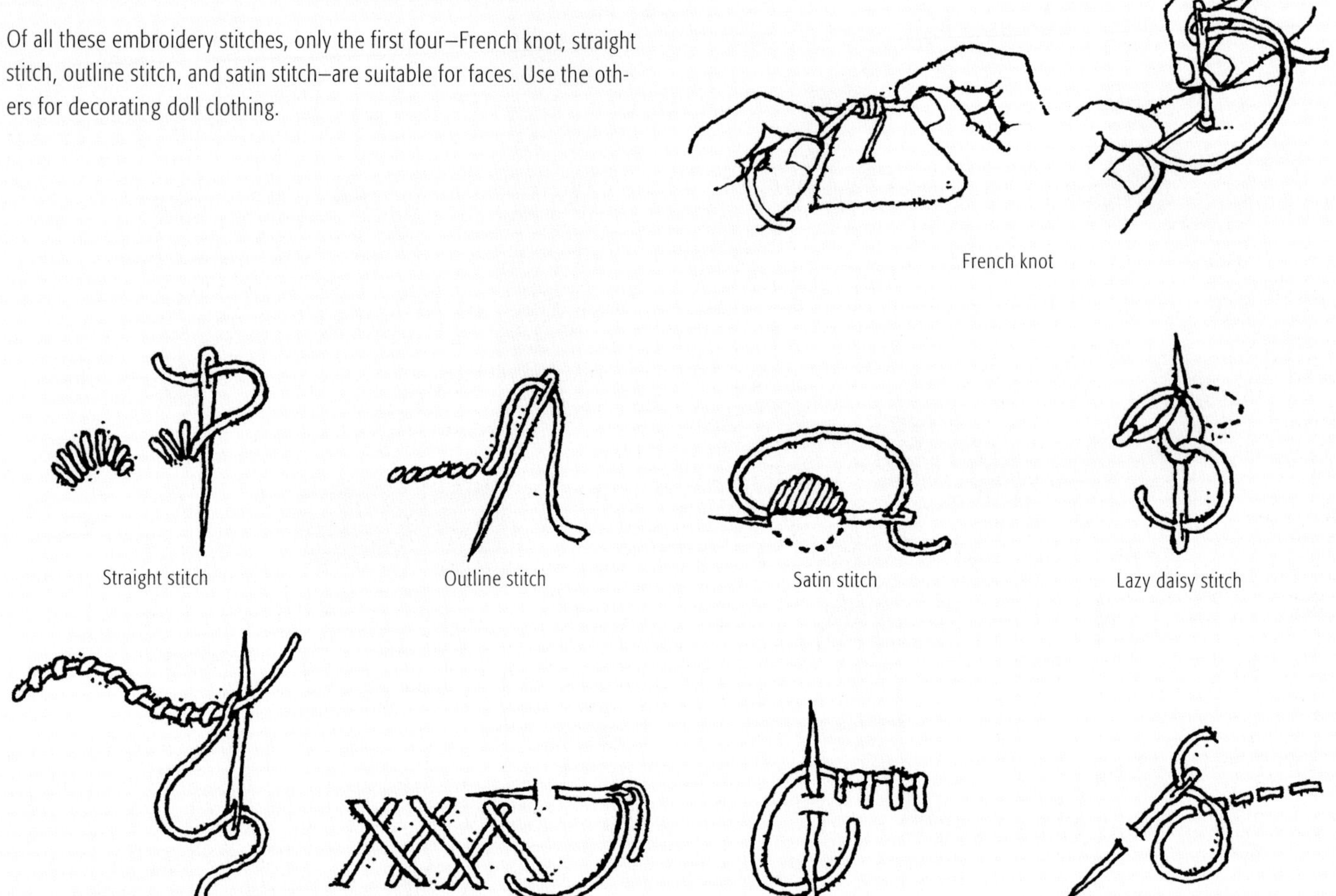

French knot

Straight stitch

Outline stitch

Satin stitch

Lazy daisy stitch

Couching stitch

Herringbone stitch

Buttonhole (or blanket) stitch

Running/quilting stitch

one feature to the next. Instead, knot and cut the thread after each feature is complete, unless you are embroidering a completed head. Dark threads are especially noticeable and may show through the fabric. The embroidery stitches most commonly used in dollmaking are shown here. If you have not embroidered before, be sure to practice the stitches you choose on a scrap piece of fabric before trying them on your doll's face.

The Face: A Portrait Gallery

Each artist here has chosen a method of creating a face that makes her doll unique. Some of the more intriguing are a combination of techniques. Use these portraits for inspiration as you select designs and techniques for dolls of your own creation.

If Some Is Good, More Is Better BY ELINOR PEACE BAILEY, HAYWARD, CALIFORNIA, 1991.
This doll's torso is constructed of fabric cubicles, which are filled with the things that clutter up our lives. The five fabric heads are painted with glittery paint. She has huge, exaggerated hips and thighs and seems to be going in seventeen different directions. She is a study in the unrealistic; yet realistic, because we all overextend ourselves. Embellishing a doll with things that have meaning to you is one way of making a statement about yourself.

The Jewel Merchant's Daughter BY KAREN BALDING, SAN DIEGO, CALIFORNIA, 1989.
Although this face is flat with no sculpting, the line along the nose gives the illusion of dimension. Some people make the mistake of putting two hard lines along each side of the nose bridge. This tends to make the nose look piglike. Facial features on this face are embroidered, although painting is an alternative.

Quality Time BY CARL AND LYNN PENDERGRASS, 1990.
Sculpting muslin cannot always give you the details you want, such as lips, chin, eyebrows, and other facial areas. You can use paper clay, wetting it and rubbing it right into the fabric, then building up dimensional areas, such as the ones I've already mentioned. Once the clay is dry, use a manicure sanding sponge to buff the areas so they are smooth. You can then base paint the flesh color over the top of the clay and fabric.

Frida Kahlo BY VIRGINIA ROBERTSON, 1996.
Virginia, a well-known doll and quilt designer and a former art professor, uses fine felt-tip pens and colored pencils to create her wonderful doll faces.

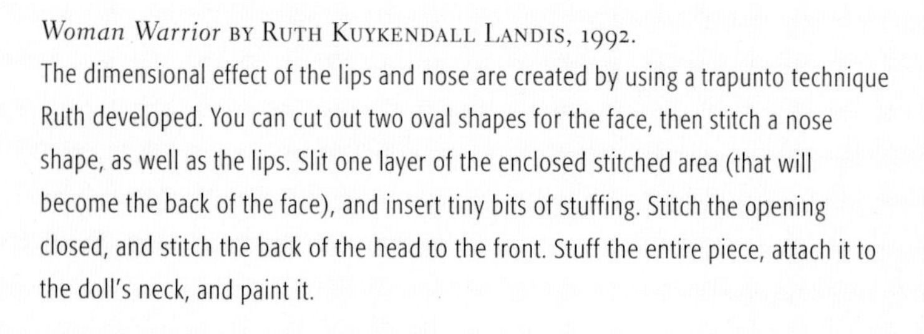

Woman Warrior BY RUTH KUYKENDALL LANDIS, 1992.
The dimensional effect of the lips and nose are created by using a trapunto technique Ruth developed. You can cut out two oval shapes for the face, then stitch a nose shape, as well as the lips. Slit one layer of the enclosed stitched area (that will become the back of the face), and insert tiny bits of stuffing. Stitch the opening closed, and stitch the back of the head to the front. Stuff the entire piece, attach it to the doll's neck, and paint it.

Dragon Lady BY JAMES FAULKENBERG, MILWAUKEE, WISCONSIN, 1989.
The face and body are constructed from felt. A clay mask forms the base to which the felt is glued. The doll is wigged with a commercial synthetic wig. The features of the face are painted with exotic Oriental features. As a youngster, James was an avid Barbie® fan, which is apparent in his creation of this fashionable lady.

D.G. Fairy BY SUE LITTLE, 1998.
Sue used her computer to create the digital graphic face for this doll. You can achieve a similar effect by taking a photograph to a copy center and having it made into an iron transfer which can then be used to impose the image onto fabric.

Aurora BY VIRGINIA SARGENT, 1990.
Virginia, a former designer for Mattel, made a clay mask and glued the muslin onto the mask to create this face. The face is then painted with acrylic paint.

CHAPTER 4

THE CROWNING GLORY: HAIR AND WIGS

FOR MANY DOLLMAKERS, THE most enjoyable part of making a doll is choosing and forming the hair. Fortunately, there is a wonderful range of fibers and colors to choose from, and styling options are limitless. I find it easiest to add the hair or wig last, even after costuming the doll. However, I recommend that you decide which fibers and style you will use before making the doll's clothes, since the look of the hair and the way it falls can influence your costuming decisions.

Rapunzel BY ROXANNE BECKER, 1990.
This beautiful maiden, whose long tresses inspired the story of true love eventually realized, is wigged with rope purchased from the hardware store. You can untwist the rope and stitch it onto the doll's head. Like other natural fibers, it can be dyed easily, if you prefer red or brunette hair.

Hair Fibers

Doll hair can be made from almost any fiber, including human hair. Synthetic fibers, such as acrylics and nylon, come in a variety of colors, and they retain their original curl and color even after a lot of handling and washing. Most contemporary dollmakers prefer to work with natural fibers which, they feel, enhance the overall appeal of the doll. A popular choice is raw washed fleece, sheared from sheep, goats, alpaca, or camels. Fleece is available in a variety of natural colors and is easily dyed. The length, of course, varies according to the breed. Natural fleeces that have been washed and carded by hand or machine to even the fiber lengths and form a batt are known as *roving*. Roving lacks the interesting curl and texture of some raw fleeces, but is readily available at crafts stores and makes beautiful doll hair. It is easy to braid. Wool fibers from natural fleeces also are available woven into twine. This *crepe wool* is perfect for curly doll hair. Simply unbraid it and pull it apart slightly to fluff the fiber. It can then be stitched directly onto the doll's head. Crepe can also be ironed to relax the curl (use a wool setting with steam).

Knitting yarn also makes wonderful doll hair and comes in a wide range of colors and textures. Natural-fiber yarns are usually a little more expensive than man-made yarns, but both are excellent choices for doll hair. Other good choices include flax, which dyes easily but is difficult to curl; hemp, which has a somewhat wiry texture; and silk, which is soft but very strong. Silk tends to tangle easily and can be difficult to work with, but it dyes well and the texture is exquisite.

Making the Hair for Renaissance Woman

The hair for *Renaissance Woman* is created in a very simple manner, in a classic styling that would suit many kinds of dolls.

Supplies

- Wool roving (I used curly wool roving braid from All Cooped Up.)
- White craft glue
- Scrap of muslin
- Gold twine
- Floral wire

1. Remove strings from roving. Set iron to wool setting (with steam), and stretch roving out on ironing board as you press it. This will straighten out curls and give a smoother hairdo.
2. Cut four or five lengths of hair long enough to drape over your doll's head and long enough for the hairdo you want. Place four lengths on muslin scrap and machine stitch down center of fibers and muslin.
3. Fold fibers in half along stitching, with muslin on outside. Machine stitch folded fibers, as close to original stitching as possible.
4. Open fibers, and trim muslin into a football shape. Press with iron to flatten.
5. Fluff fibers by pulling them apart, starting at ends and working upward. Apply white craft glue to doll's head to make fibers adhere to head. Place hair on doll's head, with a center part, and press fibers and muslin into glue until it sets. Let glue dry thoroughly.
6. Use last length of wool roving to create a braid. Twist a tiny bit of floral wire around one end of hair fiber. Divide hair into three sections and braid until there is enough to go around doll's head with about 1″ (2.5 cm) extra. Apply white glue to braid and, starting at center back, apply braid to doll's head, pressing in place.
7. Tie a piece of gold twine to secure wired end of braid underneath other remaining piece of braid and make a knot. Crisscross cord down braid about 1½″ (4 cm), leaving enough hair to match length of other doll hair. Trim hair with scissors.

Step 1

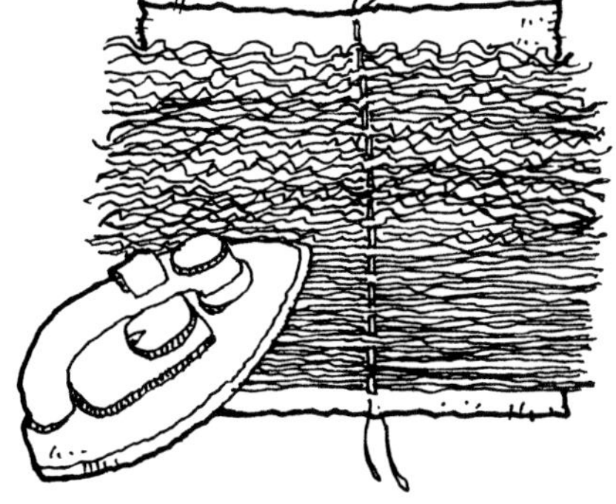

Steps 1 to 2

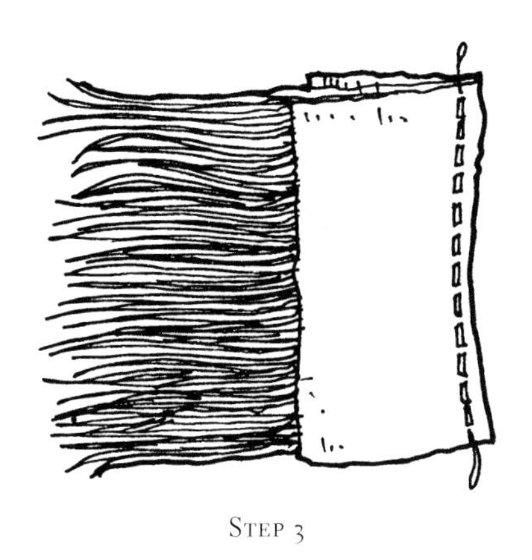

Step 3

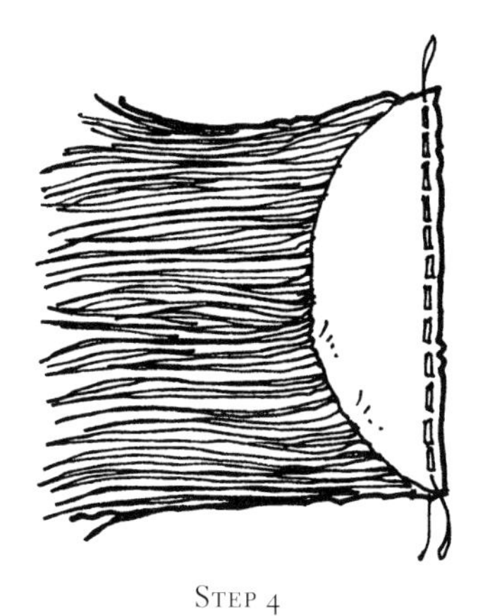

Step 4

Step 7

Curling Hair

To curl natural fibers, dampen them and wind them around a wooden dowel, pencil, or cocktail stick, depending on the size of curl you are making. Do not wind too much fiber at a time: the greater the thickness, the looser the curl. Let the fiber dry thoroughly overnight. Clip off the length you need and glue or stitch the curls to the doll's head. Synthetic fibers typically do not curl well. Test a small sample by wrapping the fiber around a dowel very tightly and immersing it in boiling water for about 30 seconds. Let it dry completely before unwinding the curl.

Dyeing Doll Hair

Man-made fibers do not absorb much, if any, color and are not good candidates for dyeing. Dyeing is far more successful with natural fibers. Take special care with silk—it absorbs color very quickly and is sensitive to hot dye solutions.

It is easy to make subtle color changes by simple tea- or coffee-dyeing. Lighter shades of wool, flax, or mohair stain nicely; pale yellow or gray fibers take on a rich brown hue. Color small quantities of fiber at a time; about a yard (meter) of natural fiber is ideal. Bring a strong tea recipe to a boil (see page 7) and then reduce it to a simmer. Wet the fiber before adding it to the tea. Do not stir the fiber, as this may cause matting. Simmer for 10 to 30 minutes, depending on the color intensity desired. Gently lift the fiber into a colander and let it drain and cool naturally, without squeezing. Avoid the temptation to dunk the hot fiber into cold water to cool it off—it will lose its natural resilience. When it is cool, rinse the fiber in warm water and drain it again. When most of the water has been drained, spread the fiber on a piece of stretched fabric, turning it from time to time so that it drys evenly.

Commercial dyes work well on hair fiber. Follow the manufacturer's directions to dye fibers effectively.

Isabella AND *Olivia* BY PATTI MEDARIS CULEA, 2001.

Doll artist Patti Medaris Culea uses many unusual fibers for hair, but her favorites are animal hair—mohair, Tibetan goat, lamb, and even yak. These come either on the hide or off. They also come in natural colors, including tan, white, off-white, and brown, just to mention a few. Patti also uses human hair—she loves the silky sheen it gives her dolls.

For her whimsical dolls and fairies, Patti often uses primary colors, so when shopping for hair dye she looks for bright, unusual colors that will complement the hues in her dolls and their costumes. She begins by washing the fiber with ordinary shampoo, rinsing it thoroughly and toweling it dry. She then applies ready-to-use hair dyes, available from any drugstore. For bright colors, Patti uses brands like Manic Panic® or Punky Colors®. She wraps the fibers in plastic wrap and lets the dye set for about 30 minutes. She then rinses the fibers in warm water until the water runs clear and hangs them up to dry.

Wig Making

Shadow Dancing BY ANTONETTE CELY, 1988.

Wig making is an easy alternative to gluing hair in place on the doll's head. It allows you flexibility, since you can change the wig from time to time if you wish. It also makes costuming the doll a little simpler, because the wig can be removed during costuming or rearranged once the costume is in place. A wig cap is similar to a swimming cap and fits snugly over the doll's head. Here, Antonette Cely shares her method for making a simple wig. When the wig is complete, you can cut and style it using small heated curlers and styling gel, just as you would for your own hair.

Supplies

- Stiff fabric, such as woven cotton, for wig cap
- Stretch fabric, such as nylon stocking
- Fiber for hair
- Tissue paper
- Thread to match hair fiber
- Pencil, chalk, or disappearing marker

If you are wigging a cloth doll for which you have a pattern, simply use the same template as for the doll's head to create a wig cap. Just add a little bit at the seams to give the cap room to slip over the head. If you have no pattern, begin by making a wig cap, as in Steps 1 to 4.

Making Wig Cap

1. Using finished doll's head as a guide, cut a strip of fabric for center, plus two semicircles for sides of head. Make pieces large enough so you can pin seam allowances together as shown.

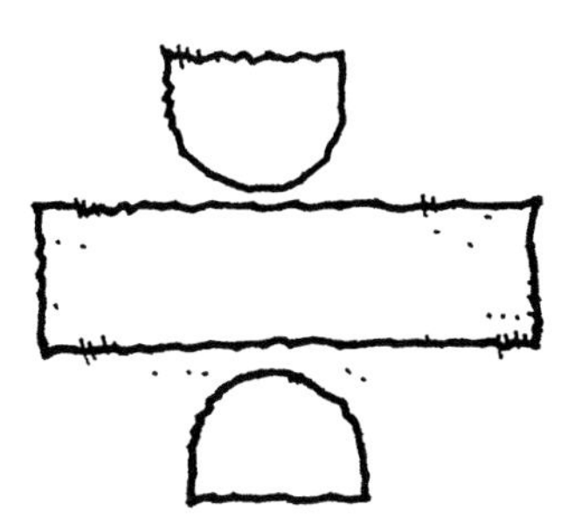

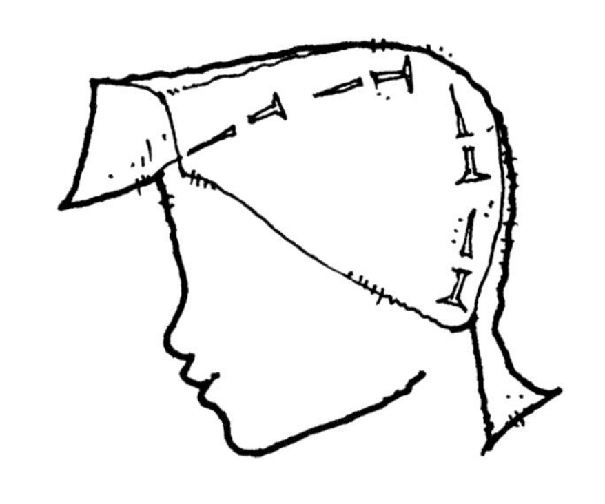

STEP 1

2. With pins in place, draw along pin line on each of three fabric pieces to create seam lines. Remove pins. Hand baste pieces together along seam lines. Fit cap to doll with seam allowances on outside. Pin and baste again, if necessary, to form a smooth-fitting cap. Machine stitch. Clip curves and trim away excess seam allowance. Topstitch seams to make them lie flat.
3. Turn seams to inside. Using pencil or disappearing marker, draw hairline directly on wig cap. Cut cap along this line.
4. Pin strip of stretch fabric and sew one raw edge around edge of wig cap. Wrap other raw edge over to inside of wig cap and topstitch in place. Cut away any excess stretch fabric.

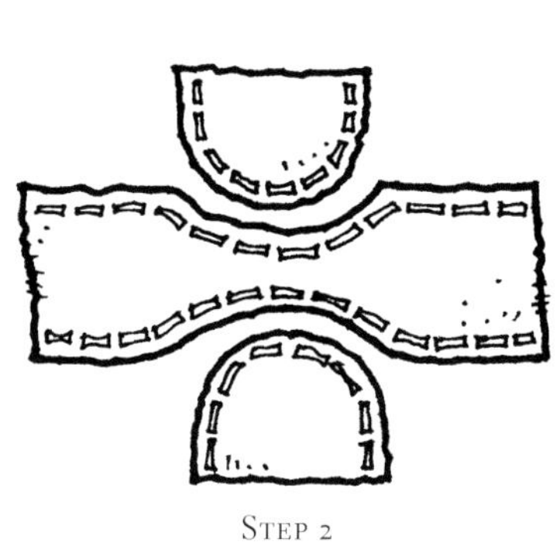

STEP 2

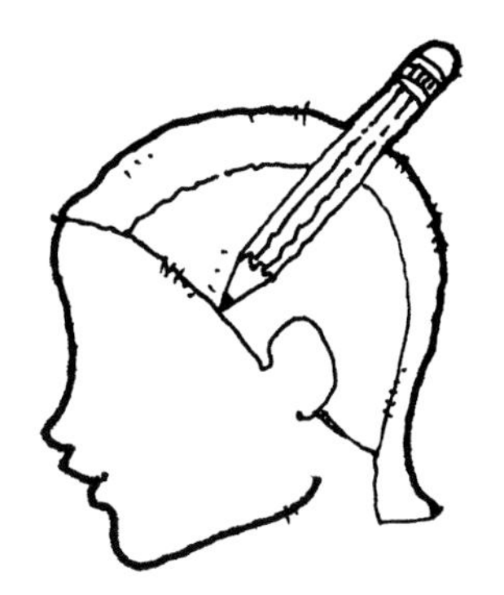

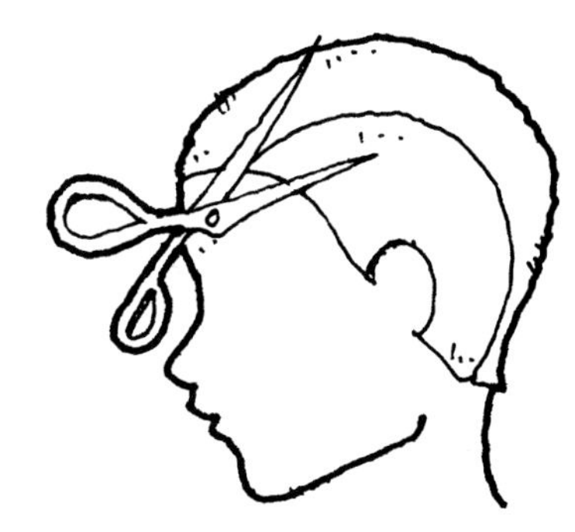

STEP 3

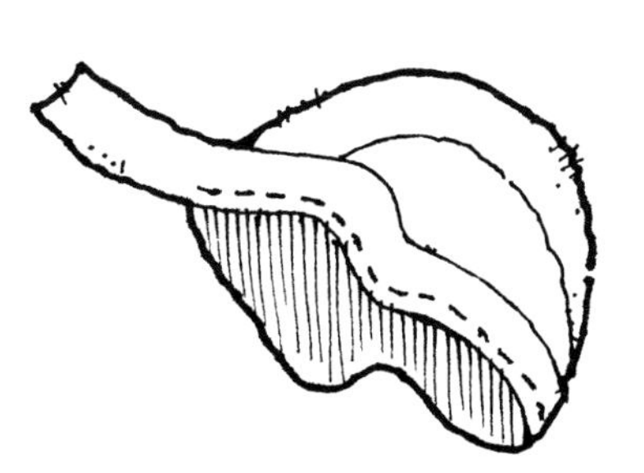

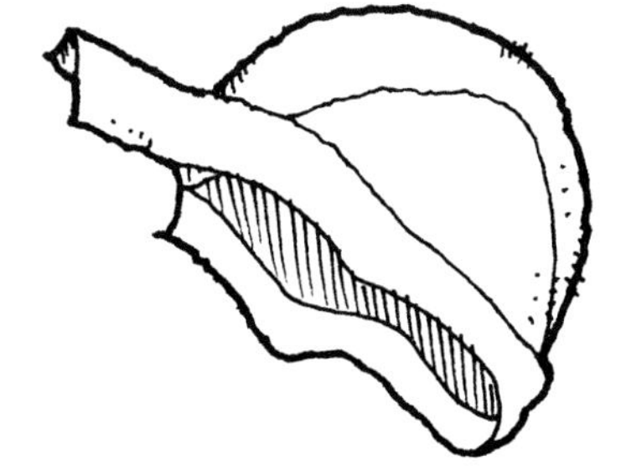

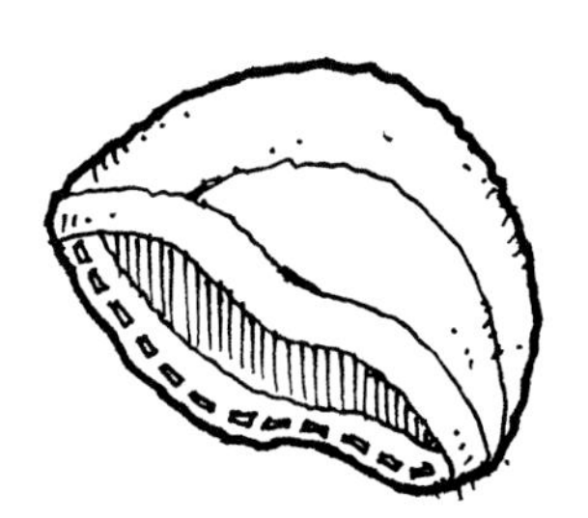

STEP 4

Wefting Hair

5. The easiest way to attach hair to a wig cap is first to sew it into wefted strips. Begin by separating hair fiber or fleece into thin bunches and laying them side-by-side on a long strip of tissue paper. Make sure there are no gaps between bunches of hair.
6. Cover hair with a second strip of tissue paper. Use pins to hold sandwiched layers in place.
7. Thread machine with thread to match color of fiber and sew small stitches—about 15 to 20 to inch (6 to 8 to centimeter)—along one side of strip lengthwise, about 1″ (2.5 cm) from edge of hair. Sew two more lines, parallel to first, about 1/4″ (0.75 cm) apart. You should have three rows of stitches.
8. Carefully remove top layer of tissue paper, pulling it sideways out of stitches. If it is too difficult to remove paper from between rows of stitches, leave it there.
9. Fold strip along center row of stitches with hair on inside and tissue paper on outside. Now machine stitch over two rows of stitches that are lined up.
10. Remove top layer of tissue paper, pulling it away from stitches as before. Fold folded edge over to meet row of stitches, and machine stitch one last time between stitching and new folded edge. Cleanly remove all tissue paper that you can.
11. Repeat Steps 5 to 10 until you have enough wefted strips to cover doll's head. Pin strips onto doll's head, one at a time, in concentric circles until you think you have enough. Brush wefted hair to remove unattached hair. If your stitching is small enough, you can safely brush hair without it falling out.

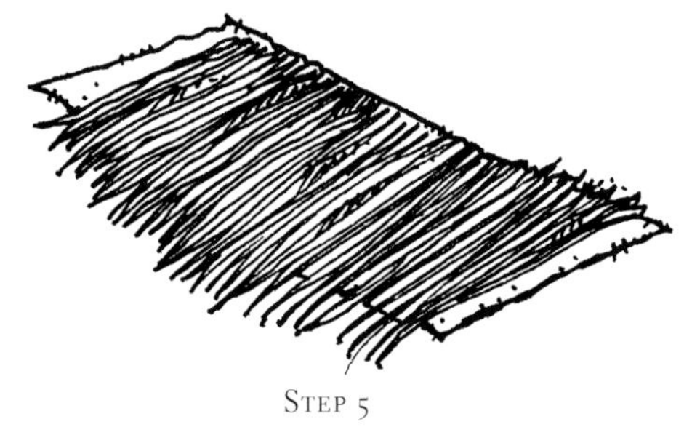

Step 5

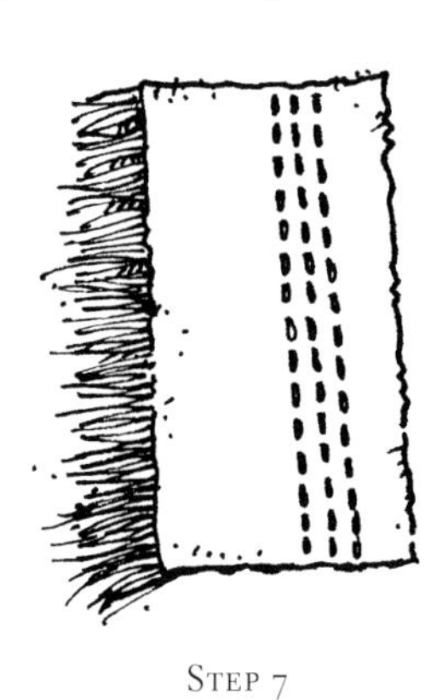

Step 6

Step 7

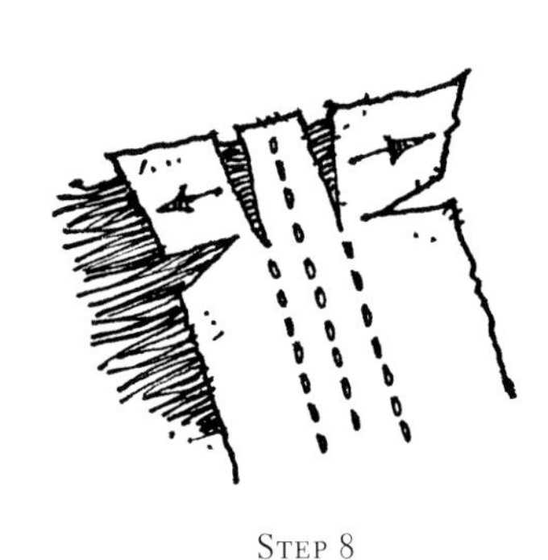

Step 8

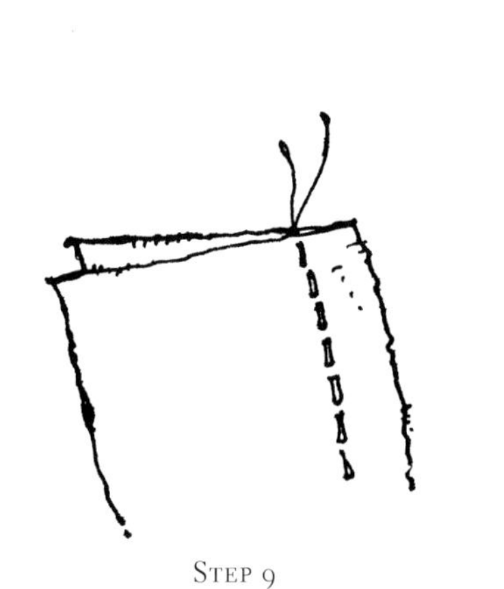

Step 9

Step 10

Attaching Hair to Cap

12. Draw lines around cap with pencil, chalk, or disappearing marker as shown.
13. Lay one row of wefting around edge of wig. Sew to wig cap by hand, then by machine.
14. Add more strips, spaced evenly apart, stopping about 1″ (2.5 cm) from crown of wig cap.
15. Place another strip of wefting next to strip closest to crown, but position so that hair falls in opposite direction. Sew in a double circle, stitching second circle on top of first. Twist this hair to form a ponytail.
16. Add final wefted strip over twisted hair and sew in a spiral that tightens over twist.
17. Brush hair that comes out on top, twisting it once, and it will lie down without a visible part.
18. If you want to pull hair up or back into a bun or ponytail, add one more strip of wefting under edge of wig, so that edge of wig cap will not show.

Step 12

Step 13

Step 14

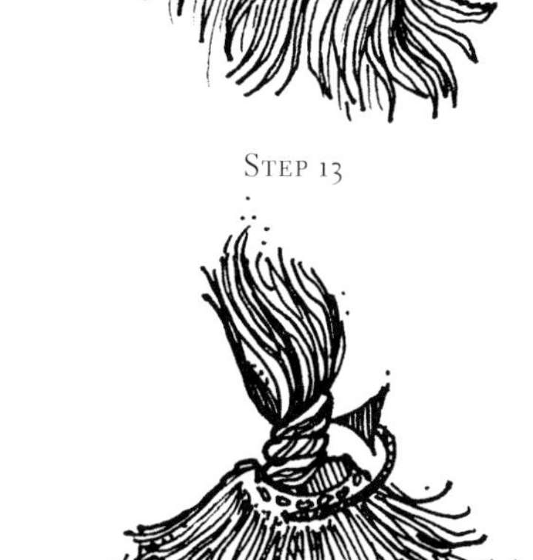

Step 15

Step 16

Step 17

Step 18

Ten Creative Wig-Making and Embellishment Techniques

The ten delightful hairstyles shown here were created by doll artist Bonnie Hoover. All are made using materials that are readily available from crafts stores or quilt shops. You can mix and match ideas to come up with a syling that is perfect for your doll.

1. **Perle cotton hair.** A loosened braid of perle cotton is glued lightly to the doll's head. Begin at the nape of the neck, working in a circle and gluing as you go, until the head is covered. Make a ribbon bow and glue or stitch it to the doll's head. For the doily embellishment, first wet the doily and toss it in the dryer to give it a crinkled look. Position it at the center of the ribbon, and add a pearl button on top.
2. **Raveled sweater wig.** Cut a piece of knitted yarn from a sweater. Separate the strands of yarn by unraveling. Glue or hand stitch in place around the doll's head, starting at the base of the neck and working in a circular direction. Create a hairstyle by clipping the strands as desired. Embellish with two bows made from rat-tail cording and a piece of grosgrain ribbon. Stitch the two bows together and position a button in the center. Glue the embellishment to the doll's head.
3. **Burlap hairdo.** Unravel a few strands of burlap. Tie together and wrap evenly around a hair loom or a piece of wire hanger bent into a U shape. Place a strip of paper underneath the loom and machine stitch down the center. Remove the paper and slip the loops from the loom. Clip the loops with scissors. Starting at the nape of the neck, hand tack to the doll's head. Make more sections of the burlap, and cover the entire head. Twist the ends to unravel slightly. Embellish with a bow and glue a bead to the center of the bow.
4. **Yo-yo hair.** To make the yo-yos, cut a small circle from a piece of cardboard. Draw around this template on the wrong side of a piece of fabric and cut out. Gather around the entire circle, stuffing the raw edges to the inside as you pull the gather stitches tight. Secure and knot. Sew a button to the center. Make enough yo-yos to cover the doll's head. Hand tack the yo-yos to the head, creating the hairstyle as you go. Make a large yo-yo and gather it in the center to create a bow. Sew a button to the center and glue to the top of the head.
5. **Button wig.** Take one plain button and cut a circle of fabric about ¼″ (0.75 cm) larger. Using a double thread, gather the circle with a running stitch, ⅛″ (0.4 cm) from the raw edge. Place the button in the center of the gathered circle. Pull tight, secure, and clip the thread. Cover several plain buttons the same way, and hand tack or glue them and other decorative buttons all over the doll's head. Embellish with two bows made from wired ribbon. Wrap small-gauge decorative wire around a small dowel to curl, then stitch the curled wire to the head. Glue small gold metal leaves in various places.
6. **Nylon stocking and cheesecloth wig.** Tea-dye nylon stocking and cheesecloth (see page 7). Cut off a piece of nylon stocking and pull it so it will ravel. Do the same for the cheesecloth. The amount you need will depend on the size of the doll's head. Combine these two pieces and stitch to the doll's head. Add more pieces until you achieve the style you want. Clip and glue to create the style. Cut one rectangle of fabric and another one of contrasting fabric using the same measurement. With the right sides together, stitch around the

rectangle. Make a horizontal slit at the center of one of the rectangles and turn right side out. Whipstitch closed and press the rectangle. Twist the bow and wrap a strong thread around a few times to secure. Turn over opposite corners of the bow and sew a button to each one. Make a bow out of rat-tail cording and sew to the bow center. Glue to the top of the doll's head.

7. **Fabric-strip hair.** Tear several ¼″ (0.75 cm) strips of fabric. Tie them together end-to-end. Wrap the strips evenly around your fingers, slip them off, and bind them together around the center with strong thread. Make as many as you need to cover the doll's head. Hand tack the bundles to the head. Clip the loops. For the embellishment, make a bow out of garden raffia. Sew a yo-yo from a scrap of fabric (see yo-yo hair above). To change the look of the yo-yo, pull a small amount of fabric from the wrong side of the fabric through the center, and wrap thread around it a few times, then knot and clip the thread. Turn the yo-yo to the other side and sew some seed beads to the center. Tack to the middle of the raffia bow and glue it to the doll's head.

Hairstyles by Bonnie Hoover.

8. **Shell-trim hairdo.** Gather a length of wire ribbon into a V with tightly pulled quilting thread, thus creating an attractive scalloped look. Turn under a small hem by finger-pressing the raw edges of the ribbon ends before you begin gluing the shell trim to the doll's head. Begin at the nape of the neck, working in a circular pattern, hand tacking the ribbon to the doll's head until it is covered. Pull up the loops of one row at the crown of the head to make them stand up. Make a silk-ribbon bow and hand tack in place. Cover a plain button with fabric to embellish the center of the bow. Stitch several beads in a random pattern over the wig.
9. **Curly wig.** Wrap bulky yarn around your fingers to make a bundle. Slip off your fingers and wrap the center with a strong thread. Hand tack the bundles to the doll's head until it is covered. Wrap crinkled yarn around a knitting needle. Prepare the curls by applying fabric stiffener. Let it dry completely. Slip the yarn off the knitting needle and cut it into short sections. Glue it to the doll's head to embellish the hairstyle. For extra sparkle, curl a few pieces of metallic ribbon with a sharp pair of scissors and tie them into a bundle. Glue the bundle to the top of the head.
10. **Curly wig using a loom.** Pair strands of yarn with strands of metallic thread and wrap them together around a loom (or a wire hanger bent into a U shape). The wider the loom, the wider the curls. Place a strip of paper underneath the loom, and machine stitch down the center of the yarn. Remove the paper, slip the curls off the loom, and stitch to the doll's head, starting at the nape of the neck and working in a circular direction to cover the head. Embellish the wig with covered buttons (see button wig above).

Tribal Woman by Christine Shively, 1995.

Untitled by Miriam Christensen Gourley, 1999.
This is an adaptation of the wired ribbon head wrap.

Embellishing the Hair: Wired-Ribbon Head Wrap

Tribal Woman by Christine Shively was inspired by a photograph in a fashion magazine. The head wrap is cleverly made by manipulating wired ribbon. I love working with wired ribbon—it is easy to use, comes in wonderful colors, and can be shaped almost any way you wish to give your doll a delightful hair embellishment. Here, Christine shares some of her secrets for attaching and manipulating wired ribbon.

Supplies

- 1″ to 1½″ (2.5 cm to 4 cm) wide wired ribbon
- Needle and strong thread
- Sharp scissors

1. Find midpoint of ribbon by folding in half lengthwise.
2. Tie one side of ribbon over other, pull and leave an opening large enough to fit over upper part of doll's head.
3. Place opening around doll's head and tighten enough to be close to head but not too tight. Folds of ribbon are slightly off-center, toward one side of doll's forehead.
4. Make sure you have a knot in end of thread when you thread needle.
5. Position doll so her back is to you (ribbon should be grazing back of neck). Insert needle at back of neck, popping knot into stuffing. Take a few small stitches and tack ribbon to doll's head all around. Work your way around front and hide some of your stitches in some front folds. Tacking down ribbon enables you to manipulate two tails of ribbon.

Step 2

Step 7

6. Think of ribbon candy you see at Christmas time, and fold one side—one wave after another—to form a wavy pleat, as loose or as tight as you please. Trim excess ribbon if there are too many loops.
7. Tack ribbon at every point where a ribbon wave touches head. You may want to arrange loops and pin them down before stitching. Repeat on other side. (In *Tribal Woman*, loops on one side point up; on the other, they point down.)

Pictures at the Salon

Each of these lovely dolls has a new hairdo that frames her face and adds to her individuality. Like a hairdresser in a beauty salon, you can clip, shape, and curl your doll's hair into any of these styles.

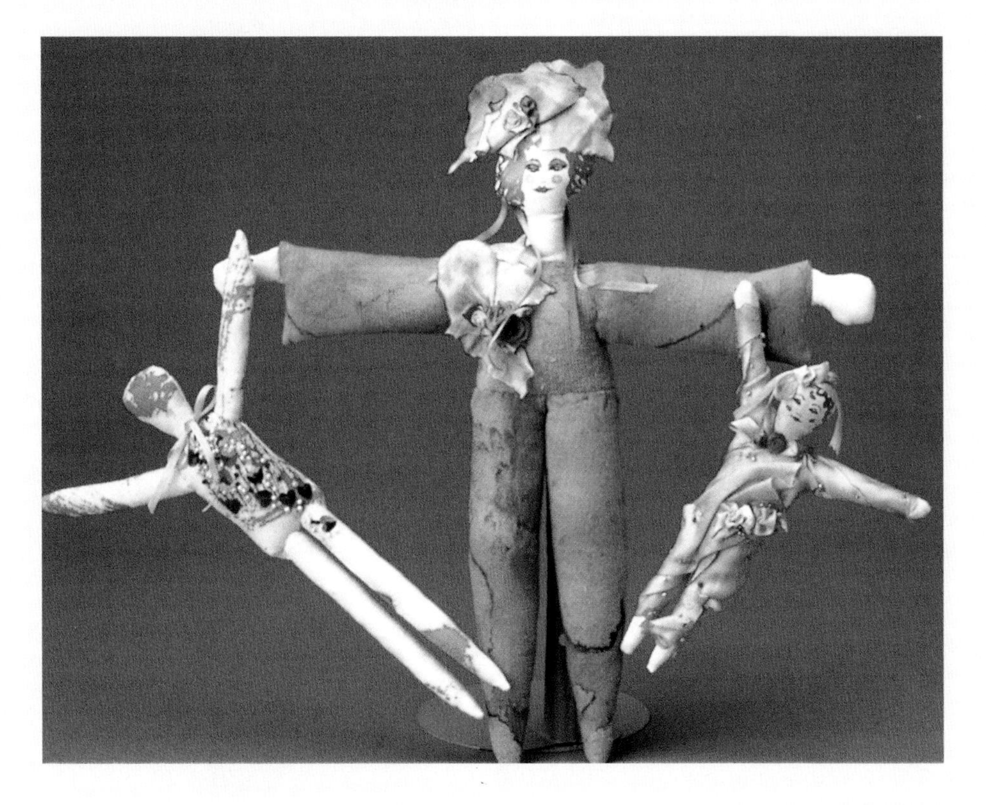

Honey, Mintie, and Sweetie by Yvonne Porcella, 1988.
Yvonne has, for many years, played with silk fabric. You'll notice that she "cut" the silk for the headgear on the center doll by burning it with a candle. Who says you have to use scissors?

Dora—No More Worries BY JANE CATHER, 1990.
I love Jane's dolls because she never follows any conventional rules. Sometimes, hair is painted on. Sometimes, it is made from an old stocking. Here, it is embellished with a bit of tinsel from the Christmas decoration box.

Scraps BY EVELYN SPILLAN, 1990.
This doll was inspired by the adventures in the book *The Patchwork Girl of Oz* by L. Frank Baum. Pipe cleaners are used to create the hairdo for this unusual doll.

Eliza with Flowers in Her Hair BY JAN FARLEY, 1990.
This wonderful doll is designed to replicate some of the antique dolls of Izannah Walker. The doll's hair, which can be of yarn or cotton string, is painted to look molded. The face is painted and antiqued.

Noah: Quick, Open the Ark! BY MARGERY CANNON, 1994.
Noah's hair, beard, moustache, and eyebrows are all made from mohair. Photograph by Jan Schou.

Birdwatching on Stargaze BY PATTI MEDARIS CULEA, 1992.
This doll has a muslin face with a center front seam. The head is then sculpted and finally painted. Patti used an old hairpiece from the 1970s for the doll's wig. Dollmaking is always a self-portrait, whether we intend it or not.

CHAPTER 5

Costuming the Doll

Puppy Kisses BY MARGERY CANNON, 1998. Margery Cannon has been featured in numerous dollmaking magazines and is often inspired by situations in real life. This doll is her affectionate look at a little girl and her adored puppy.

SO MUCH OF THE personality of a doll is conveyed by the way she is dressed. Your color and texture choices help you communicate not only a style, but a mood. A piece of burlap may evoke a rustic, country mood, while velvet and lace connote a rich elegance. Bold primary colors make a very different statement than delicate pastels. Each of the patterns in Part Two comes with complete instructions for costuming the doll. Here, I will share some basic techniques you can use to adjust those patterns to suit your own tastes or to create a costume that is unique to your doll.

Drafting Doll Clothing Patterns

Here, Lynda Larsen demonstrates how she fits clothes for her dolls. You can use your undressed doll as a mannequin. If you plan to use the same body type over and over, you may wish to custom-make a mannequin. Just remake the basic torso shape, and prop it on a doll stand. There is no easier way to ensure a perfect fit!

Dividing the Doll into Pattern Pieces

The first step to custom-made clothing is to divide the body into the various patterns from which your doll's clothing will be made. To begin, pin a length of tightly woven colored string or crochet thread cord on the doll body at the areas designated here. A dab of Fray Check® will prevent the string ends from unraveling. Pin straight through the string and into the doll body or mannequin.

The front and back of a doll mannequin marked with colored thread to delineate the pieces of the clothing pattern. This is just as easy to do with a finished undressed doll.

Front Bodice

- Around neckline where a strand of pearls might fall for a jewel neckline.
- Around entire waistline. Around the entire base of the body for a hipline.
- From neckline at center front to waist at center, and down to hipline.
- From underarm to waistline and down to hipline, marking side seam.
- From underarm to underarm, across bust point, and perpendicular to center front.
- From neckline cord to each shoulder tip, marking shoulder line.
- From center of shoulder line down through bust point to center point on waistline, between center front and side seam. Continue straight down to hipline. This marks princess line and dart line.

Back Bodice

- Center back from neckline to waistline and on to hipline.
- Shoulder blade line, approximately through center of back armhole areas.
- Princess lines.

Armhole

- Starting at tip of shoulder, drape and pin a length of cord under arm and back to starting point to create armhole. This will create an elliptical shape.

Making the Pattern

You may use muslin or paper to make the pattern pieces or templates. Particularly for larger dolls, I prefer muslin, since it allows you to visualize the drape of the fabric and helps you establish grain lines, which makes cutting a little easier.

The first step is to use your doll body or mannequin to determine the size and shape of each pattern piece. To do this, take a sheet of thin tissue paper and wad it up, crushing it completely. Then press it at a low temperature. This process will make the paper more pliable. Another option for smaller dolls is to use a well-used clothes dryer sheet. It is transparent, pliable, and strong.

The following directions assume that your doll is symmetrical. Several pattern pieces are "half pattern"—when it comes to cutting the fabric, you will place these pieces on a center fold line to cut out the full piece.

Bodice Front and Back

1. Begin with bodice front. Fold a piece of tissue paper, prepared as described earlier, in half. With extra tissue extending to top and bottom of bodice area, pin folded edge of tissue over center line down front of doll.
2. Smooth tissue up to neckline, across chest, and down to bustline and pin in place.
3. Smooth paper across to bust point and pin in place.
4. Continue smoothing paper across to underarm and pin in place.
5. Pin paper along line at side seam. This will leave excess tissue hanging from bust point which is to be folded into a dart.
6. Pinch excess tissue at intersection of princess line and waistline and crease to a point at bust tip. If necessary, clip tissue below princess line up to seam allowance to allow it to move more freely.

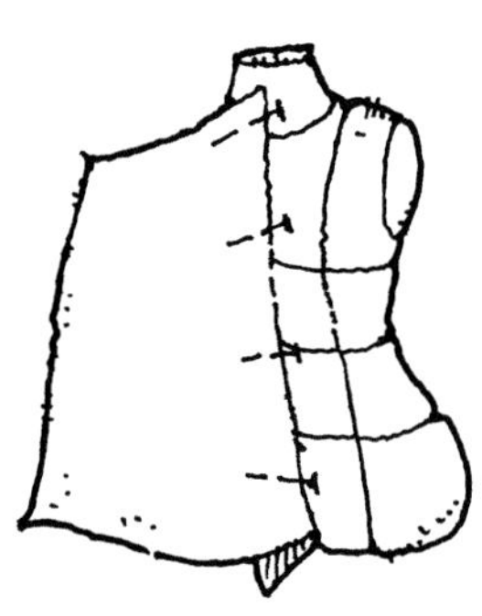

Step 1

Steps 2 to 4

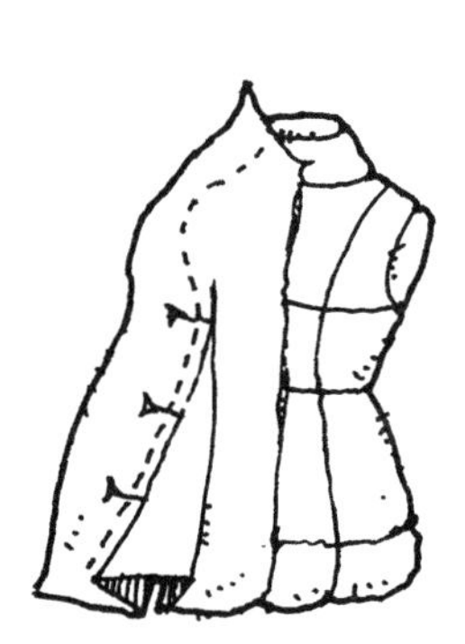

Step 5

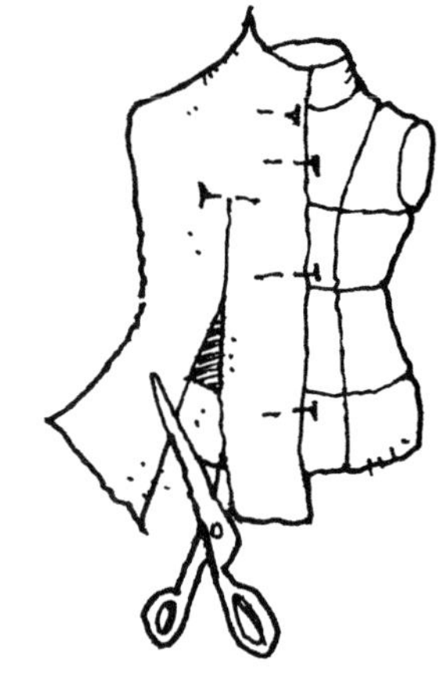

Step 6

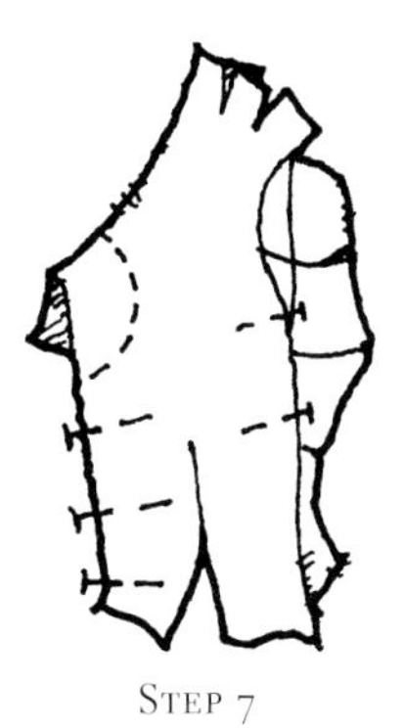

Step 7

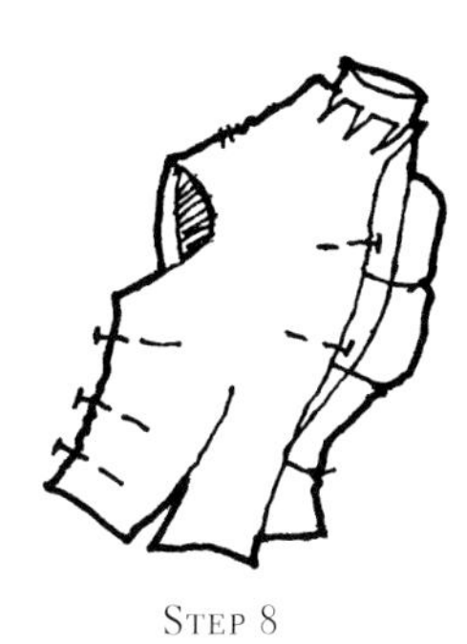

Step 8

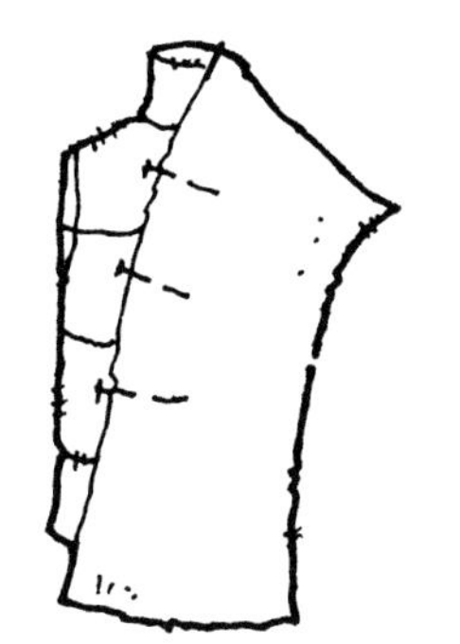

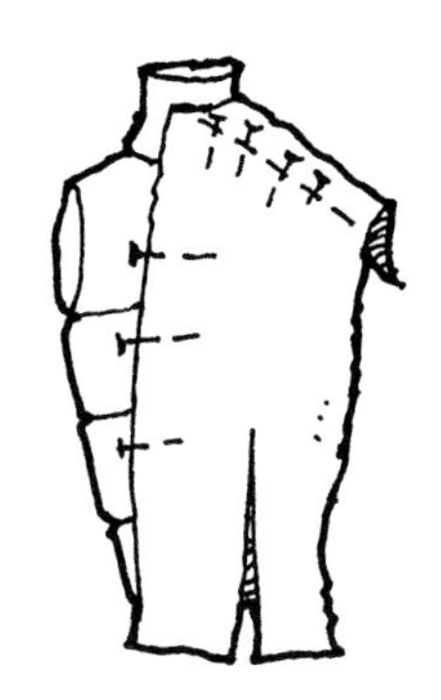

Step 9

7. To form neckline, clip diagonally in pie-shaped lines from corner of paper around neckline.
8. Smooth tissue at armhole, cutting from outer tissue edge to armhole string as necessary to allow tissue to mold smoothly to curve.
9. Repeat Steps 1 to 8 to prepare bodice back, keeping paper smooth at shoulder blade line.

Tracing the Pattern

10. With tissue paper firmly anchored, trace thread lines that are visible through tissue. Use a sharp pencil to achieve a thin, accurate line. Mark neckline, shoulder line, princess line, dart, waistline, and armhole. Remove tissue.
11. Lay tissue pattern on a flat surface and retrace on a sturdy piece of paper or muslin. Transfer marks using a ruler and a curve (such as a jar lid or a cup) to create smooth, accurate lines.
12. Add ¼″ (0.75 cm) seam allowances all around pattern pieces, except fold lines.
13. Place side seam lines of front and back bodice together to be sure they are same length. Help them match at armhole and waistline, using a jar lid or other round shape.
14. Place shoulder seams together to be sure they are same length. Match at armhole and neckline to form smooth curves.

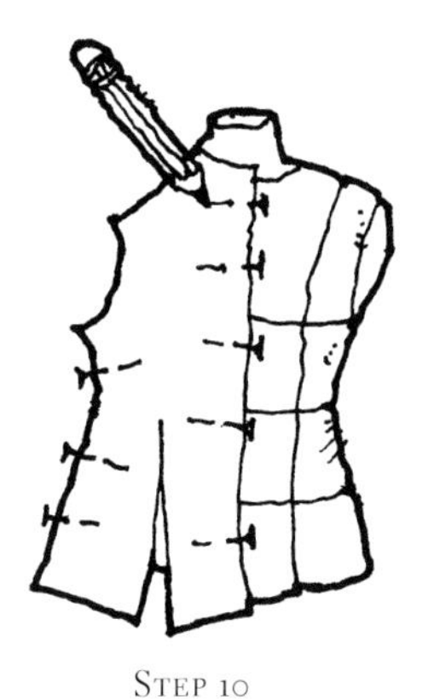

Step 10

Step 12

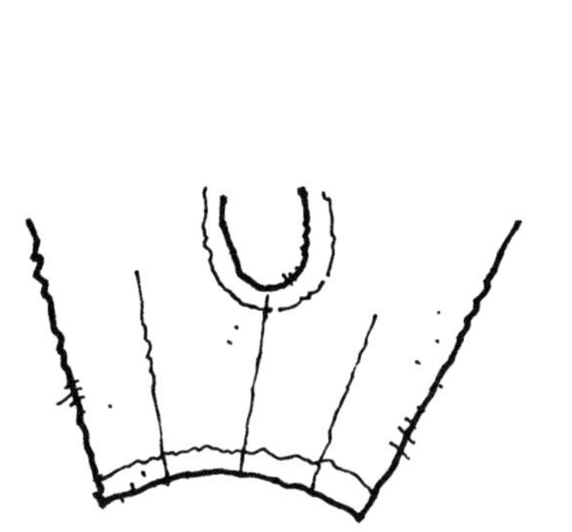

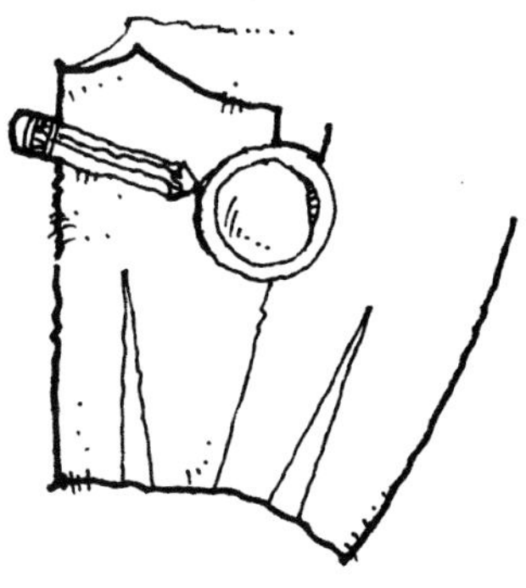

Step 13

Making the Sleeves

15. Using a tape measure, measure the circumference of the upper arm (measurement A); the circumference of the wrist (measurement B), and the length of the arm (measurement C).
16. Use the three measurements to draw a sleeve shape, as shown. Draw a gentle curve connecting side seams and extend a parallel line to match length of measurement C. Add a ¼" (0.75 cm) seam allowance around all sides of sleeve.
17. For a fuller sleeve, enlarge by drawing lines from wrist to elbow and slashing and spreading pattern. From top of each slash, cut a slit to outside edge, leaving a tiny part intact to form a hinge that will allow sleeve to be widened to any degree. Place slashed sleeve on paper and draw in finished edges.

The pattern is now ready to be positioned and pinned to your fabric. Remember to cut two sleeves. You can reuse the pattern as many times as you wish to make a wardrobe of clothes for your doll.

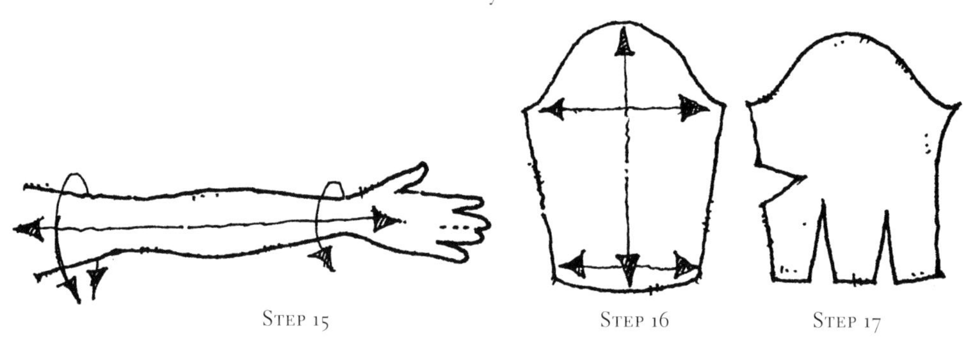

Choosing Fabrics

As the photographs in this book attest, you can use any and all fabrics for costuming your dolls. Whether you use natural fibers like cottons, wools, and silks or synthetics, each has its distinct properties.

- Cotton. Most commonly used fiber. Comes in many different weights, strengths, and textures. Can be washed and dried. Easily dyed and bleached. Must be ironed.
- Linen. One of the strongest natural fibers. Great variety, from a very rough texture to very sheer. More soil- and moisture-resistant than cotton. May be washed or dry-cleaned.
- Wool. Takes dye well, but is damaged by bleach. Very resilient. Limited range of weights and finishes, but often blended with other fibers. Some wool blends are washable and can be pressed with a pressing cloth. All pure wool should be dry-cleaned. Susceptible to moth damage, though many wools are pretreated to prevent this.
- Silk. Produced by the caterpillar of the domesticated moth, *Bombyx mori*. Available in a number of textures and weights. Very resilient. Hand washable with mild soap. Takes dye well. Only hydrogen peroxide or sodium perborate bleaches should be used.
- Acrylic. Crease-resistant and heat-sensitive. Often blended with wool; the blend is washable. May mold or shape to some degree while still warm from iron.
- Nylon. Incredibly strong, elastic, and dirt-resistant. When blended with other fibers produces fabrics with those qualities. Should be ironed on wrong side at a very low temperature setting.
- Polyester. Springy, resilient, and wrinkle-resistant. Often blended with natural fibers. Batting and sewing threads are often produced from polyester and cotton. Polyester blends are washable and not harmed by chlorine bleach. Dry quickly.

Miriam did extensive research before designing the costume for *Shaker Sister*. She decided to focus on 1850s-style clothing but added her own touches—both to simplify the construction of the clothing and to interpret it in her own style. You might want to check out a costuming book from a local library or university before creating clothing for a period doll.

How to Make Shoes

Christine Shively uses this simple method to create shoes that, with a few minor adjustments, will fit almost any cloth doll.

Detail of *Medieval Jester*. See full doll on page x.

Supplies

- Leather or Ultra Suede®
- Thick white craft glue
- Sharp scissors

1. Cut following shapes from leather or Ultra Suede®: An equilateral triangle that covers upper foot and allows two corners to fold underneath sides of foot; a rectangle that fits around heel of doll's foot. To determine width of rectangle, stand doll on a hard surface and measure from surface up to ankle. Length should go around heel to overlap sides of triangle. Round two top corners of rectangle.
2. Position triangle as shown. Be sure tip extends past toe. Glue in place on sole of foot. It is easiest to turn doll upside down. Place rounded corner rectangle piece around heel with rounded ends upward. Glue rectangle to doll's foot. If you like a pointed shoe, leave triangle at toe intact. If not, trim to an oval shape.
3. Cut a rectangle that is longer and wider than foot. Cover sole with tacky glue. Do not apply too much glue, as it will come out sides and damage surface of shoe. Use your fingers to press shoe sides and toe to rectangle. When glue is completely dry, trim excess sole away with a sharp pair of scissors.

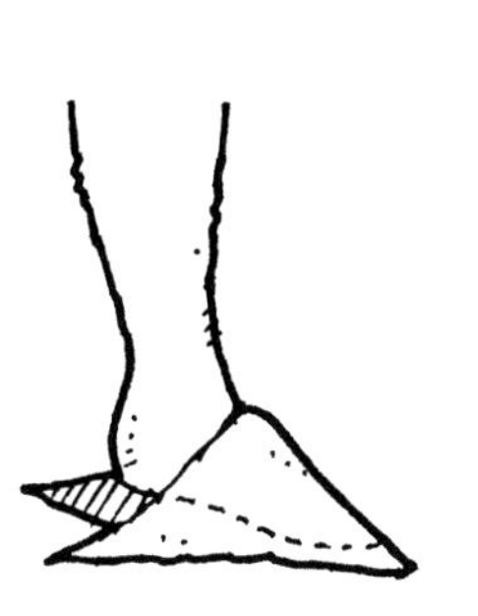

Step 2

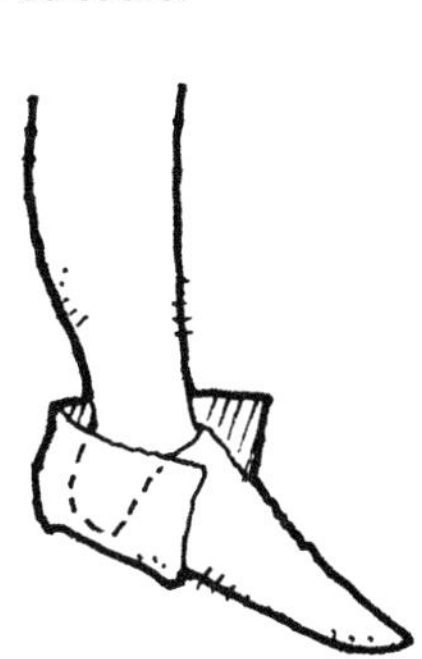

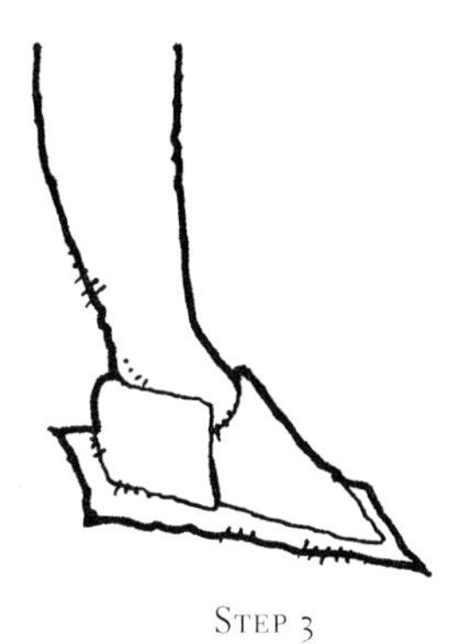

Step 3

Adding Piping

You can easily add trims such as piping. Add a ¼" (0.75 cm) seam allowance to the triangle and rectangle, then, after cutting, stitch piping directly to the right side of both, matching raw edges. Fold the raw edges under so the piping becomes the edge of the shoe; continue as in Steps 2 and 3.

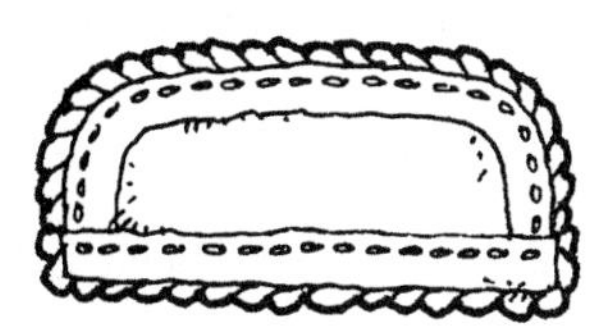

Detail of *The Midnight Ride Through Fairyland*. See full doll on page 57.

How to Make Fairy Wings

Turn your doll into an angel or a fairy by adding these wonderful fairy wings designed by Annie Wahl. I used a very similar method to create the wings for my doll, *The Midnight Ride Through Fairyland*.

Supplies

- Craft scissors
- 24-gauge wire
- Heavyweight white fusible interfacing
- Masking tape
- To add color: watercolor, acrylic, or oil paints; watercolor pens or pastel crayons
- White glue and glitter, or spray glitter

1. Draw your own wing design on white paper or trace templates A and B on page 126. Draw veins, noting how some of them fork off midway into two separate lines, forming a V shape.
2. Trace design, including veins, on interfacing, shiny side up. Leave a 1″ (2.5 cm) margin around entire wing design.
3. Measure length of each vein. Cut wire to this measurement, plus 1½″ (4 cm). Note areas where veins fork off, forming V shape. You will need to use two wires, twisting them from center point to point at which line forks. Then, separate them again to lay one strand over each fork.
4. Lay twisted wire on interfacing, shaping wire to lie on top of pencil lines. Pin wire at center of wings, and tape ends on outside margin of design.
5. Cover interfacing and wires with another piece of interfacing, shiny side down. Check manufacturer's instructions, and heat iron accordingly (usually on medium setting). Press two halves of butterfly wings together. Turn wings over, and press other side to make sure adhesion is complete.
6. Cut out wings with craft scissors, cutting off excess interfacing and wire.
7. Paint and decorate wings to suit the doll you are making. You can spray with water and a little watercolor paint. Acrylic paint, mixed with water, will also work well. You can add a little bit of white glue and sprinkle on glitter in certain areas, or spray with glitter spray.
8. Use matching embroidery floss to stitch wings together in center. Shape wings by bending halves backward a little.

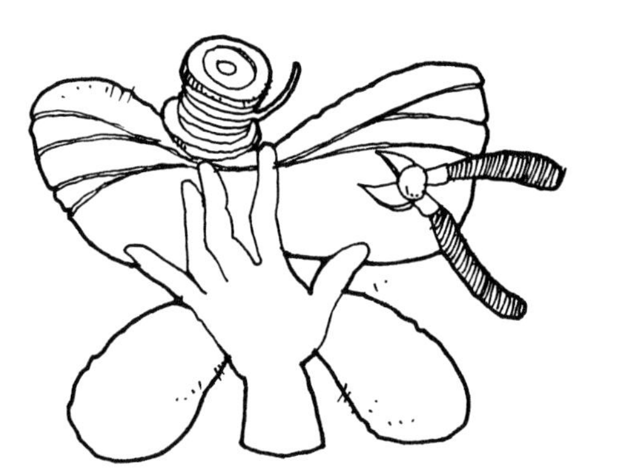

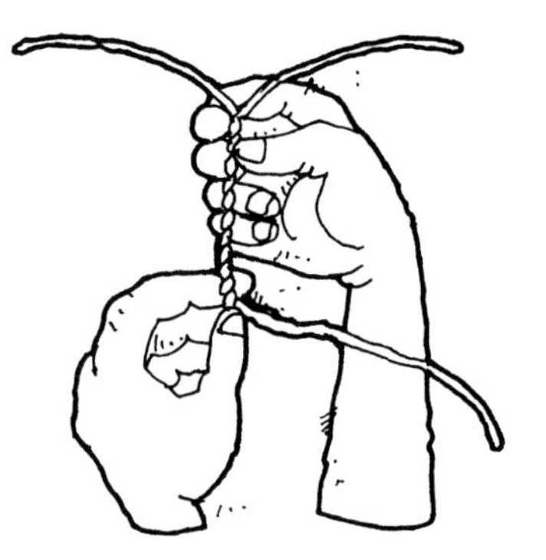

Step 3

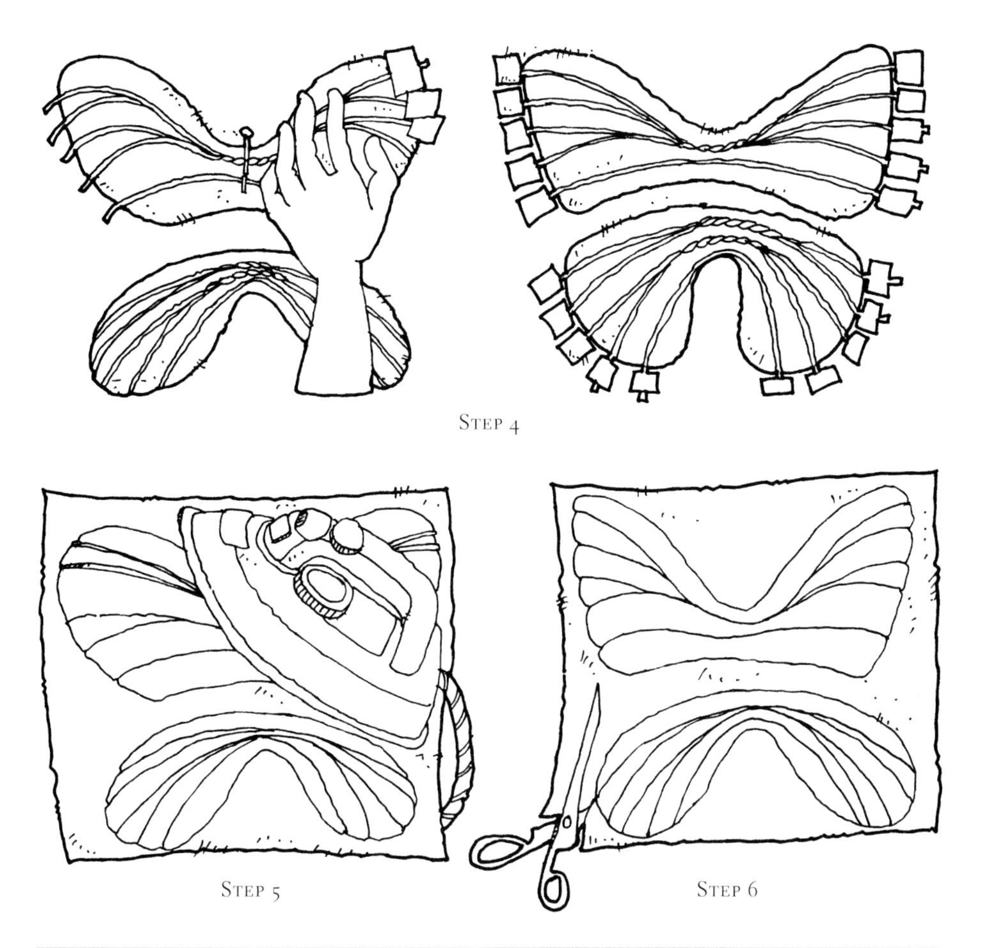

The Midnight Ride Through Fairyland by Miriam Christensen Gourley, 1989.
The wings on this fairy were painted with metallic and glitter paints.

Selena Amelia de Chocotina BY BECKY TUTTLE, 1988.
As a tribute to chocolate-lovers all over the world, Becky dressed this prim older lady in a low-waist Victorian gown trimmed with black lace. Her accessories are made from jewelry found in an antique shop and are very appropriate for her costume.

Incroyable BY LOIS BRO, 1992.
Lois observed that creating male dolls is often overlooked in dollmaking. The fabric inspired this period costume, and it is evident that Lois took great care to make the slant of the upper edge of the boot, as well as the details of the garment itself, just so. Having a costuming book is a great addition to a dollmaker's library.

Merna Bedlow BY JANE CATHER, 1989.
The bodice for this dress is embroidered; the skirt is pieced together to form the stripes and the lower edge, set off by black piping. Eccentric and elegant are a good way to describe this costume.

Earth Angel by Margot Strand-Jensen, 1988.
To dress this doll, Margot selected bits and pieces from a printed craft panel. The printed directions served as the underpants for the doll, and she mixed mesh ribbon with cotton prints, lace, and wings to create the clothing for the doll. Isn't it great to break with tradition once in a while?

Shell Woman by Susan Hale, 1988.
If you choose to dress your doll in leather, you will need to check with your sewing machine manual or dealer for assistance because you will need a different sewing needle. If your machine cannot manage the leather, take it to a shoe repair shop and pay them to stitch your seams. Susan has embellished this doll with feathers, shells, and fur. That's why dollmakers have little boxes full of stuff–you never know when you might need it!

Midnight Cat Dance by Susan McFadden and Margene Holderman, 1990.
Susan McFadden, whose doll is featured on page 102, made this doll body, and her mother, Margene Holderman, created the clothing. The coat has appliquéd cats and is quilted. Quilting is a good method to use to give clothing a little dimension or shape.

Embellishments for Doll Costumes

Each of the doll patterns in Part Two includes directions on making the costume in which the doll is photographed. By varying the colors and fabrics you can give your doll an entirely different look. You can also individualize your costume by adding some embellishments of your own. Here are some popular and easy embellishment ideas that will add a little extra sparkle to any costume.

Embellishing with Beads

You can use any type of small bead—glass, ceramic, or wooden—to dress up your doll costume. When you work with small beads, the most difficult job can be threading the needle, because beading needles are very thin. In this case, a special needle threader may be used. Needle sizes 9 to 12 are suitable for most beadwork. Thread the needle with double sewing silk, nylon thread, or thin crochet yarn. Rub the thread across beeswax for added strength.

There are many ways to bead, including weaving, stringing, and stitching directly to fabric. In dollmaking, stitching beads directly to fabric is most effective. You can do this in any of the following three ways.

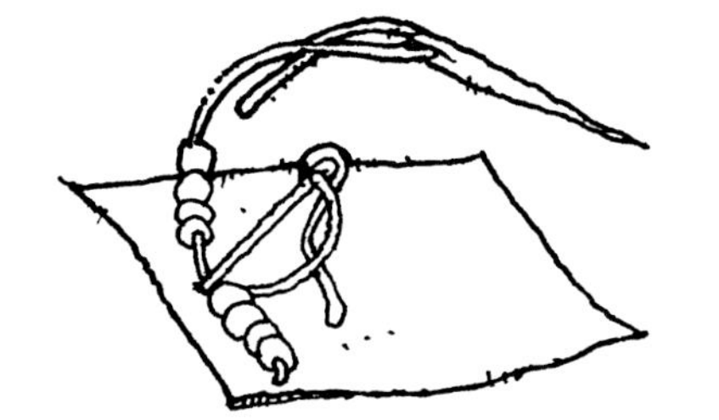
Overlaid-stitching beading

Overlaid Stitching

Sumatra, or overlaid, stitching is a technique of sewing strings of beads to fabric. You need two needles and two double threads of sewing silk. Thread one needle with beads; use the other to sew the rows of beads across the first thread with small stitches.

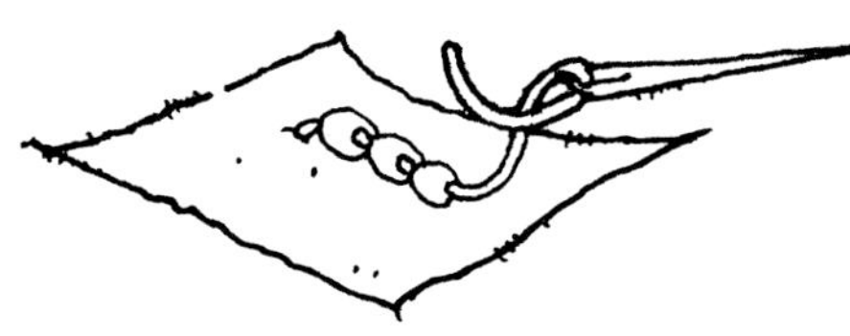
Embroidery beading

Embroidery

You can add colors and patterns to fabrics by using embroidery techniques, such as the ones used for *Mother Moon*, shown on page 24. Her clothing is embellished with felt stars and moons, stitched to the fabric with a buttonhole stitch. Running stitches provide additional patterns to the skirt of the smock, and straight-stitch stars embellish the bodice.

Using embroidery, beads can be stitched to fabric either singly or in groups. If you are sewing just one bead, it should be large enough to stand out as a point of focus. The most suitable stitch is a tacking stitch. Choose a bead with a large hole, such as a ring bead, and attach it with about six stitches. The stitching then becomes part of the embellishment. Groups of beads may be stitched on individually but placed very close to each other. Once beads are in place, thread a strand of cotton through all of them so they lie in the same direction.

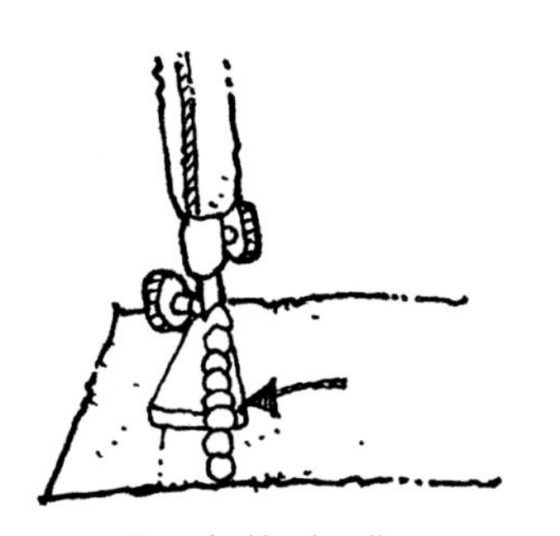
Cross-locking beading

Cross Locking

Cross-locked beads comprise a single strand of beads strung together with several interwoven strands of thread. They may be stitched to fabric either by hand or by machine. To machine stitch, draw a line on the fabric where the beads are to be attached. Use a zipper foot and zigzag the strands of beads to the fabric. The zipper foot will rest next to the beads as you stitch.

Embellishing with Laces, Trims, and Buttons

Antique laces and various trims such as cording, ribbon, antique buttons, and fringe can be beautiful as embellishments for doll's clothing or for jewelry. Just remember the scale of the doll, and don't overwhelm it with buttons that are too large.

Embellishing with Ribbon

To apply ribbon directly to the fabric, topstitch close to each side of the ribbon or machine embroider along the edges. If you machine embroider, use paper (such as typing paper) underneath to keep the fabric from puckering. If a straight stitch is used, stitch as close to the edges of the ribbon as possible. Alternatively, you may wish to use decorative machine embroidery to apply the ribbon to the fabric.

Step 2

Step 3

Ribbon Roses

Making your own ribbon roses requires patience and a great deal of practice, so practice on inexpensive ribbon before attempting the more expensive wire-edged or metallic ribbons. Use ¾″ to 1¼″ (2 cm to 3.2 cm) ribbon. The length will depend on how large you want the rose to be, so do not cut the ribbon; just unwind some from the spool.

1. Cut ribbon diagonally.
2. Make a double pleat, parallel to the diagonal end.
3. Wind ribbon around pleat several times to form stem and center of rose.
4. Turn ribbon away from you at a 45-degree angle. Continue wrapping ribbon around stem until you reach end of angle.
5. Make a new 45-degree angle each time you come to end of previous angle. In this way, you begin to form petals. When rose is large enough, softly gather ribbon at base and wrap floral wire tightly around base to secure it (use small pliers). Take a needle and matching thread and stitch through as many layers as possible at base of rose to keep it from unraveling. Wrap thread around base and tie a knot.
6. Clip rose stem close to base of rose if you will be using on a hat or lapel. If you are making a small bouquet for doll to hold, do not clip stem. Leave long wires at stem and wrap them with floral tape.

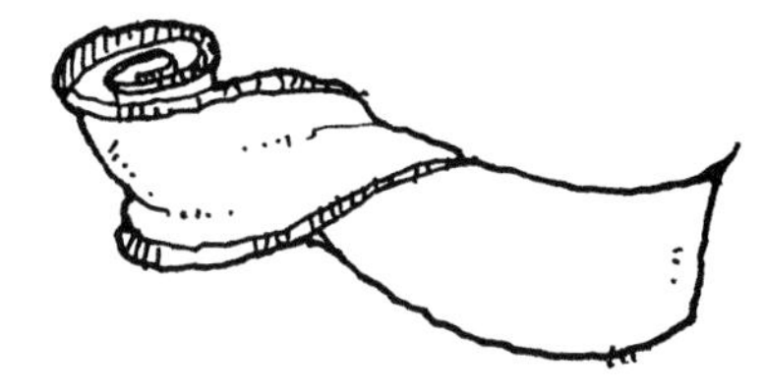

Step 4

Steps 5 and 6

Small Single Bow

1. Cut a piece of ½″ (1.5 cm) ribbon or torn fabric measuring about 3″ (8 cm).
2. Tie a knot at center. This should be rather loose.
3. Clip ends in an inverted V pattern, as shown, trimming the bow to an appropriate length. Glue in place.

Traditional Bow

1. Cut a length of ribbon or torn fabric about three times longer than width of finished bow plus about 3″ to 4″ (8 cm to 10 cm) extra for knot.
2. Form two loops and tie them together.
3. Adjust loops to make them smaller by pulling ends of ribbon, or make them larger by pulling slightly on loops.
4. Trim ends on a diagonal or in an inverted V pattern, as shown.

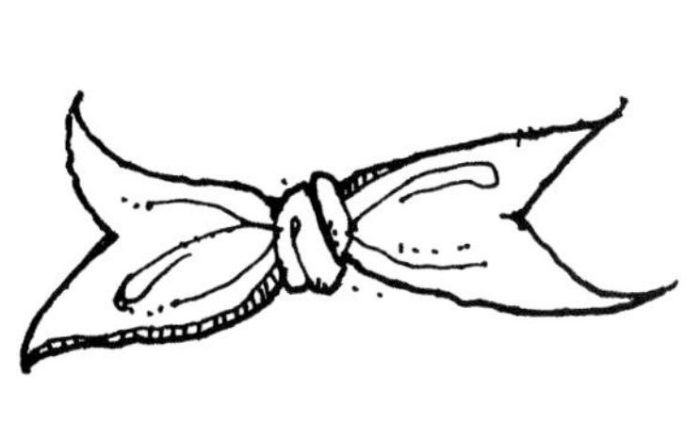

Small single bow

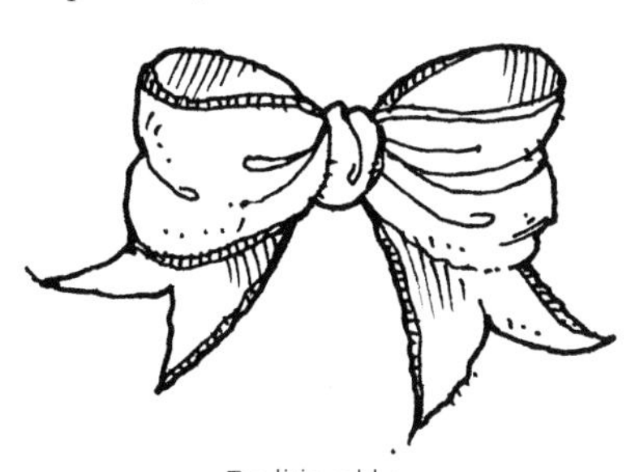

Traditional bow

Detail of *Mother Moon*. See full doll on page 24.

Vasalissa's Doll by Sue McFadden, 1995.

Part Two
A Pageant of Dolls

The ten dollmaking patterns in *Crafting Cloth Dolls* have been selected to provide projects with varying degrees of difficulty, so that you can build your skills as you create your own pageant of dolls. The dolls also reflect a range of styles. Once you become familiar with the techniques introduced in Part One and expanded upon in the individual patterns, you will be ready to tailor each doll and its costume to your own tastes.

Tulip

Tulip by Rita Carl, 1998; 13″ (33 cm).

This pretty doll body is easy to make and a delight to embellish in any way you choose. Rita has dressed her very simply and given her easy-to-make fairy wings. If you prefer an off-white or pink doll body, use Rit® dye (Tan) or tea or coffee dye to color the muslin before you begin.

Supplies

- Scraps of tea-dyed muslin for body and pantaloons
- Scraps of printed fabric for clothing
- Scraps of tulle for wings
- Yarn for doll hair (purple/brown heather mohair)
- Brown and black Micron Pigma permanent marker, size 005
- Acrylic paint: dark red and white
- Two small black or blue seed beads for eyes
- Linen thread or embroidery floss
- Fine-point disappearing ink marker
- Stuffing
- Cardboard
- White craft glue

Templates on pages 127–128. Use ¼″ (0.75 cm) seam allowance unless otherwise indicated.

Making the Body

1. Trace template A onto a doubled layer of muslin. Machine stitch together on lines with very small stitches, leaving an opening of about 2″ (5 cm) at bottom. Trim around body pieces, leaving a ⅛″ (0.4 cm) seam allowance. Clip curves, taking care not to cut stitching, and turn right side out.
2. Stuff firmly. Leave lower opening unstuffed just enough to turn raw edges inside by ½″ (1.5 cm). Hand stitch opening closed.
3. Prepare arms using template B and following Step 1. Stuff hands firmly, but leave flexible enough to enable hands to fold and grasp flower. Stuff arm very lightly at middle, as marked by opening. Hand stitch opening closed.

The Dollmaker—Rita Carl

Several years ago, Rita Carl began making crafts items for bazaars. It was a way to make a little extra money while staying home with her children. Rita couldn't seem to find patterns that appealed to her, but managed to duplicate dolls she had seen elsewhere. Once she had gained confidence by recreating the works of others, she decided she could make up her own designs and subsequently developed her own series of patterns. *Reet's Rags to Stitches* is a line of whimsical characters inspired by her daily adventures. Admirers say their favorite aspect of Rita's designs are the quirky faces she gives her dolls. All her great little characters bring a smile!

4. Attach arms to body back, just below neck, hand stitching both top and bottom edges where they attach to back. Curve arms around toward front, continuing to stitch until arms are firmly attached to sides of body. Stop just short of side seam of body.
5. To form fingers, transfer markings from template. Use tan quilting thread to make tiny running stitches along finger lines. Pull stitches slightly to indent.
6. Prepare legs using templates C and D. Follow Step 1, leaving tops open. Stuff firmly, up to top. To create toes, use a tan-colored quilting thread and make a knot at one end. On right foot (template C), insert needle on bottom of foot, very slightly to right of seam, about ⅜″ (1 cm) from end of foot. Exit needle through top of foot, and insert needle into original insertion point on bottom. Exit needle through top, slightly to left of seam. Pull thread to indent toe, and continue stitching in this manner until all five toes are formed. End on bottom, knotting twice and making a small stitch to bury end of thread in foot. Repeat for left foot (template D), beginning first stitch slightly to left of seam.
7. With toes pointing outward, stitch legs to bottom of body, leaving about ¼″ (0.75 cm) between legs.

Costuming the Doll

8. To make pantaloons, cut two pieces from muslin using template E, positioning as indicated on fold line. Right sides together, stitch both sides from waist (point A) to crotch (point B). Match points A and B and sew inside leg seam. Clip curves, turn right side out, and press. Turn a ½″ (1.5 cm) hem at waist and each leg. Sew a running stitch around waist and leg, pulling stitches to gather. Place pantaloons on doll and adjust gathers. Make a knot, and push bottom of pantaloons up so they puff out a bit.
9. Cut template F (bodice) on a double fold. Fray sleeve edges and cut out neck opening. Sew underarm seams, clip curves, and turn right side out. Place on doll.
10. For skirt, cut a 5½″ × 24″ (14 cm × 60 cm) piece of fabric. Find center point and mark. Right sides together, stitch back seam (shorter edges) and press open. Turn right side out and cut some jagged V points along bottom of skirt, cutting up into skirt by 1″ (2.5 cm) or less. Use a piece of linen thread or embroidery floss to stitch along top edge of skirt, beginning and ending at center front. Put skirt on doll and pull up gathers. Tie thread in a tiny bow.

Making the Hair

11. Cut a piece of cardboard 4½″ (11.5 cm) wide. Wrap yarn around cardboard, approximately 24 times. Slide off cardboard and find center of hair. Tie two pieces of yarn around center, and knot firmly. The four ends of the yarn used to knot hair will be bangs. Rip a long, very thin strip of fabric. Leave about 2″ (5 cm) of strip free and begin tightly winding strip around top of hair, beginning at the knot. Continue for 1″ (2.5 cm), then tightly wind it back down and tie both strip ends in a square knot.
12. Locate bangs. Spread other yarn loops apart below knot and place hair on doll's head, with top knot at center. Pin in place. Spread hair around doll's head to cover back. Apply white craft glue to doll's head and press hair into place. Trim bangs about ¾″ (2 cm) long. Clip loops at top of topknot, and play

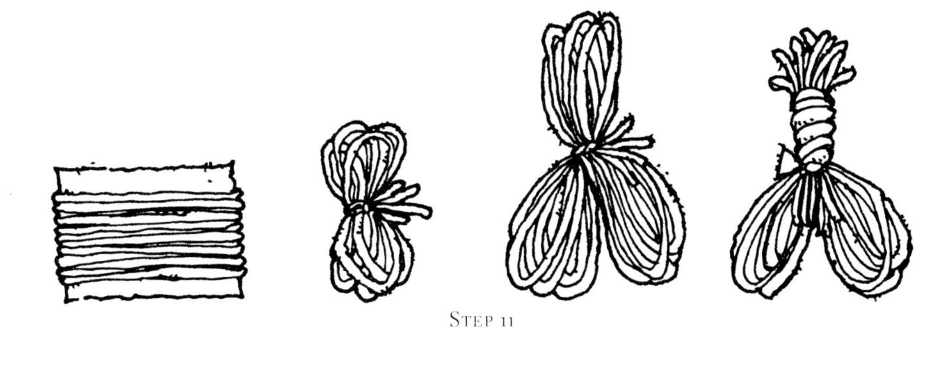

Step 11

Step 14

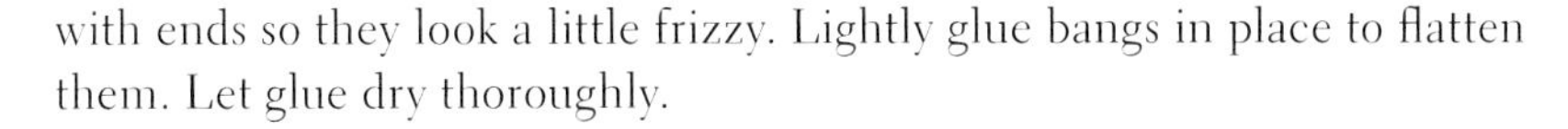

with ends so they look a little frizzy. Lightly glue bangs in place to flatten them. Let glue dry thoroughly.

Creating the Face

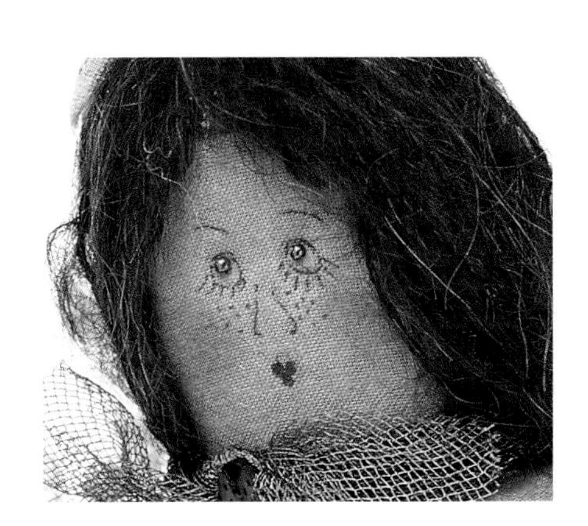

13. There is about 1″ (2.5 cm) of space between bottom of bangs and top edge of bodice. Use a fine-point disappearing-ink marker to draw face as shown. Dry brush cheeks with a dark red paint. (See page 26 for help on dry brushing.)
14. Use black marker to lightly draw nose, eye outline, and eyebrows and eyelashes. Use white acrylic paint to paint eyes within outline. Use a beading needle to stitch pupils. Sew them toward top of eye so it looks like doll is looking up. Dot some freckles with brown marker. Use dark red acrylic paint on a very fine brush or top of a round toothpick to make lips. Apply three dots and blend together to form lips.

Embellishment

15. To make wings, cut two 8″ (20 cm) lengths of tulle. Trim ends in pointed V shape, as you did skirt. Tack centers of two strips together to form an X. Stitch or glue wings to doll's back.
16. Stitch a loop of twine or strong thread at base of doll's neck to use as a hanger. Fold ends of hands around tiny watering can, tulip, or other decoration and stitch in place. (You will find tiny accessories like these in crafts stores.) Tie a tiny scrap of tulle around Tulip's neck and stitch a tiny ladybug button at center of tie.

Tom Mato

Nothing could be simpler! Pose this little doll any way you wish.

Tom Mato by Sue Little, 1998; 14″ (35 cm).

Supplies

- Poster board for templates
- Stuffing
- Fabric (three prints)
  - Arms: 10″ × 14″ (25 cm × 35 cm)
  - Legs: 12″ × 20″ (30 cm × 50 cm)
  - Body : 7″ × 8″ (18 cm × 20 cm)
- 7 pipe cleaners (chenille stems)
- Pigma pens: black regular tip; brown regular and brush tips
- Acrylic paint: white, yellow, red, and brown
- Matte spray sealer
- Vinyl coat hanger for stand
- Styrofoam vegetable for head, about 2½″ (6.5 cm) wide
- Needle-nose pliers

Templates on page 129. Use ¼″ (0.75 cm) seam allowance unless otherwise indicated.

Making the Head

1. Using ice pick or awl, gently twist a hole in neck area (opposite stem) of your Styrofoam vegetable. Make hole 1″ (2.5 cm) deep. Cut one pipe cleaner in half, and bend one of these pieces in half again. Fill neck hole with glue and insert cut ends of bent piece as far as you can. Allow to dry for 24 hours.
2. Painting on a slick surface will be a different experience than painting on cloth. Keep a wet cloth handy and you'll be able to start over if it's looking—you know—untomatolike.
3. Start with basic outline of features with your brown Pigma pen. For a tomato that is 8″ (20 cm) around, or about the size of a tennis ball, use a 1″ × 1¾″ (2.5 cm × 4.4 cm) face.

Step 3

Step 5

4. Mix a little red with a little yellow to get a color slightly darker than your tomato. Test it on back and wipe off quickly until you get right shade.
5. Shade basic face around eyes, down left side of nose, around cheek, across upper lip, and below lower lip. Use your brown Pigma brush if you like. Any mistakes can be erased with a wet cotton swab.
6. Paint in whites of eyes. Add a little white to your shade color and paint bottom lip. After white in eyes has dried, paint in iris (brown) and pupil (black). You should also paint in nostrils at this time. When all is dry, use your black pen to outline eyes and middle of lips. Add "sparkle" to eyes with white paint. Lightly spray with sealer. When dry, spray again. Then, set head aside.

Making the Body

7. Transfer templates A to D to poster board and cut them out. There is no seam allowance included on arm and leg templates. Set templates aside.
8. Use a pencil to trace arms and legs directly on wrong side of a doubled piece of fabric. Stitch penciled lines, completely around each arm and leg. Cut out, leaving a ¼" (0.75 cm) seam allowance. Clip curves and small X on shoulder and thigh for turning right side out. Be sure to cut X on one side of fabric only. To determine which side, place arms on table in a mirror image of each

The Dollmaker—Sue Little

Sue Little has a sense of humor when it comes to dollmaking—and cooking. Some of her other creations include *Melon E* (a cantaloupe doll), *Chili*, *Gourdy*, *Hot Stuff* (green onion), *Elberta Clingstone*, *Yam What I Yam*, and *Banana Man*. Inspired by a purchase at a crafts show in Hot Springs, Arkansas, Sue began making life-size baby dolls, puppets, and teddy bears in 1982. For a time she lived near Frankfurt, Germany, where she began creating her own patterns and selling her work at crafts shows throughout Germany.

Back in Texas, Sue joined Ditzy Doll Tarts in Dallas, where she discovered an amazing group of kindred spirits. Her dolls have been displayed at Dollmakers Fiesta in Austin, Texas, and other quilt and doll shows. Sue's studio is a large old metal army desk purchased for $10. She says it has all kinds of room and pull-out writing surfaces. Her creations are displayed on three shelves over the desk, which is in the guest room. She harbors fantasies of getting rid of the bed so she can spread out a little.

other. When stuffed, X sides will be next to body where they will not show. Turn all pieces right side out.

9. Topstitch hands as shown on template. Fold pipe cleaner in half and cover raw ends with a little bit of tape. Put folded end into hand, and bend to fit elbow. Insert tiny bits of stuffing around pipe cleaner and continue stuffing up to shoulder. Repeat for other arm.
10. To make legs, tape two pipe cleaners together after folding tips down. Push into toe which has a tiny bit of stuffing in it. Use a hemostat to insert tiny bits of stuffing around pipe cleaners. Bend wire at knee and continue stuffing up into thigh area. Bend ends of pipe cleaners together and tape ends. Finish stuffing and repeat for other leg.
11. Cut out body piece D on doubled fabric. Stitch around piece with a ⅛″ (0.4 cm) seam allowance. Leave an opening for neck and a small opening for crotch. To make a boxed bottom, pinch bottom seam and a side seam together, forming a point. Stitch about ½″ (1.5 cm) from point, and repeat for other side. Clip tips off and turn right side out through neck opening. Stuff body and neck to firmness of a ripe tomato. Hand gather small neck opening.

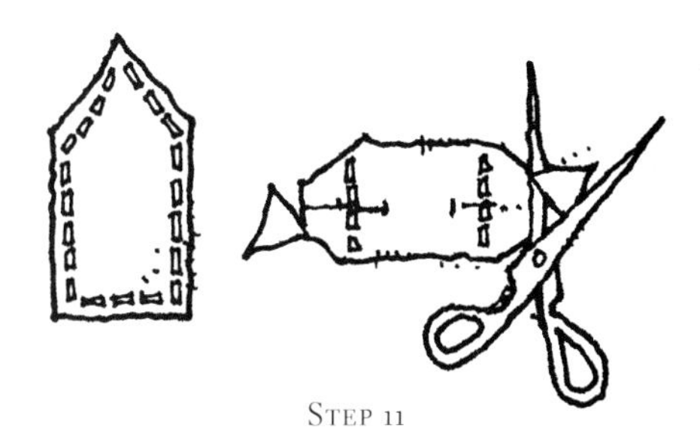

Step 11

Posing the Doll

12. To attach head, use ice pick or awl and gently push into neck of body. Work into stuffing the length of pipe cleaner that is attached to head. Be careful not to push stuffing down—just form a hole for pipe cleaner. Try head on body, and if it's the way you want it, remove head. Insert glue into hole and put head back on. Let dry thoroughly.
13. Position arms and legs with pins on body until you achieve the look you want, then stitch them on.
14. To make a stand, cut a piece of coat hanger 19″ (48 cm) long and bend in half using needle-nose pliers. Bend 2½″ (6.5 cm) of each end to a 45-degree angle and bend ends around to form a small C. This will leave a 7″ (18 cm) stand. Use ice pick or awl to poke up into body, and insert wire into hole to make Tom Mato stand up.

Step 14

Constable Shoes

This helpful, friendly constable is inspired by an illustration in *The Tale of Two Bad Mice* by Beatrix Potter. It also reminds me of a policeman I met in England, who goes by the nickname "Shoes."

Constable Shoes by Miriam Christensen Gourley, 1998; 37″ (94 cm).

Supplies

- ¼ yard (25 cm) muslin
- Scrap of black fabric
- Scrap of felt for bottoms of shoes
- Stuffing
- ½ yard (45 cm) blue felt
- Dark blue grosgrain ribbon, ⅝″ (1.8 cm) wide
- ½ yard (45 cm) black satin-face ribbon, ¼″ (0.75 cm) wide
- ⅓ yard (30 cm) black satin-face ribbon, ⅛″ (0.4 cm) wide
- Small silver buckle, ½″ (1.5 cm)
- 7 silver military-style buttons, ⅝″ (1.8 cm) or smaller
- Large military-style button for helmet, 1″ (2.5 cm)
- Scrap of cinnamon plush felt for hair
- Americana® paints:
  Flesh Tone, Medium Flesh, French Gray Blue, Lamp (Ebony) Black, White Wash, Lt. Cinnamon, Dk. Chocolate, Antique Maroon, Brush 'n Blend
- Delta Ceramcoat® paints: Prussian Blue, Oyster White
- Acrylic varnish
- Jo Sonja's® Crackle Medium
- Deco Art-Gel Stains™ (Oak)
- 2 covered buttons, 5/16″ (0.8 cm)
- Scrap of thin cotton batting
- Matte spray sealer
- Sculpting needle and strong thread

Templates on pages 130–134. Use ¼″ (0.75 cm) seam allowance unless otherwise indicated.

Making the Body

1. Cut out templates A, B, C, D, F, and H from muslin. Cut out template E from scrap of black fabric and template G from scrap of felt.
2. Place back head gusset (template A) and one face piece (template B) with right sides together, matching neck edges, and pin in place. Stitch up to 1/4" (0.75 cm) from gusset point. Repeat to attach other face piece.
3. Pin face pieces together and stitch, starting from gusset stitching, all around nose and mouth to neck edge, leaving it open. Trim seam allowances to 1/8" (0.4 cm), clip curves and angles, and turn head right side out.
4. With right sides together, stitch torso (template C) together, leaving neck open and one side open for turning. Clip curves. Place head inside torso, and pin neck edges together. Backstitch neck edges together using very small stitches. Turn torso and head right sides out and stuff firmly. Stitch opening closed.
5. With right sides together, stitch arms (template D) together, leaving an opening for turning. Trim seam allowance to 1/8" (0.4 cm) and clip curves. Turn arms right side out and topstitch fingers, using template for placement. Carefully stuff fingers, using very small pieces of batting and pushing batting in firmly. Finish stuffing arm and stitch opening closed.
6. With right sides together, stitch shoes (template E) to legs (template F). Press seam allowance toward shoes. With right sides together, pin legs pieces together and stitch around them, leaving an opening at upper thigh (as indicated on template). You will also leave bottom end open. Clip a scant 1/4" (0.75 cm) around bottom edge of shoe, about 3/8" (1 cm) apart, and pin clipped edges of shoe to felt soles (template G); wider part of sole is at heel. Stitch shoes to soles, trim seam allowance, clip curves at ankle, and turn right side out. Stuff legs firmly and stitch opening closed.
7. Place ear pieces (template H) on a piece of thin cotton batting, and stitch around entire ear. Trim seam allowance to 1/8" (0.4 cm). Make a slit in one layer of muslin in each ear and turn right side out. Press and use a needle and quilting thread to stitch around outside perimeter of each ear, about 1/16" (0.2 cm) from outer edge.
8. Attach ears to head using a sculpting needle and some strong upholstery or quilting thread. Insert needle into ear from wrong side to hide knot, make a small stitch to catch thread in fabric, and push needle through ear and head,

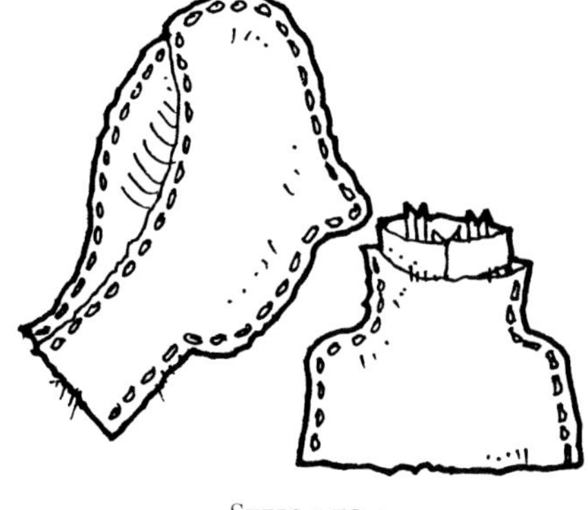

Steps 2 to 4

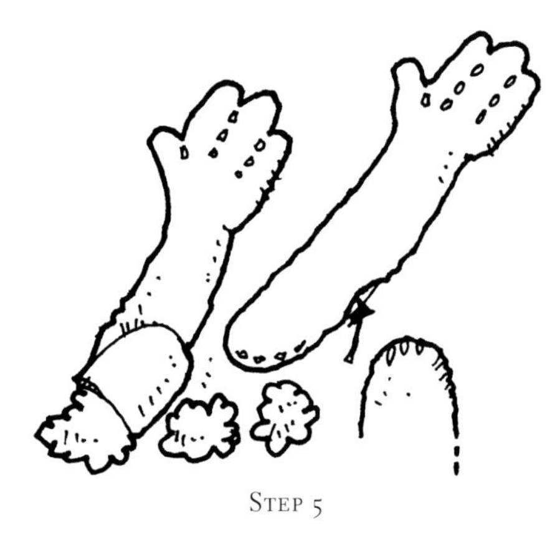

Step 5

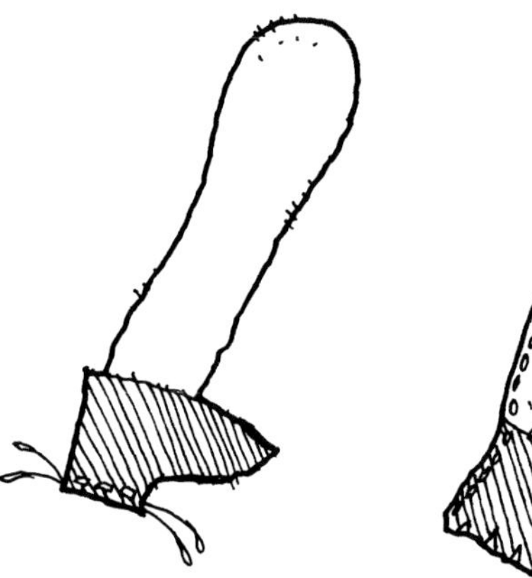

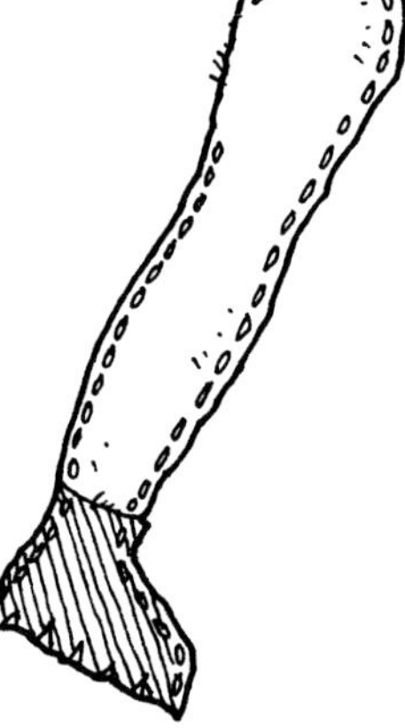

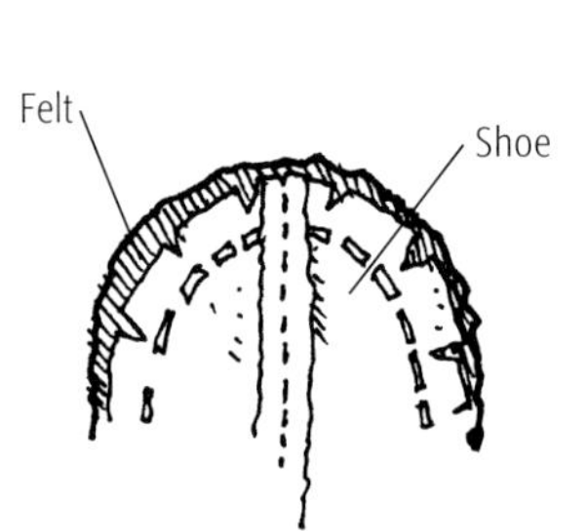

Step 6

out other side through other ear. Make a small stitch through ear and return through ear, head and first ear, indenting just slightly. Return needle back through all layers, and make a knot in opposite ear. Do not pull too tightly or ears will be very wrinkled.

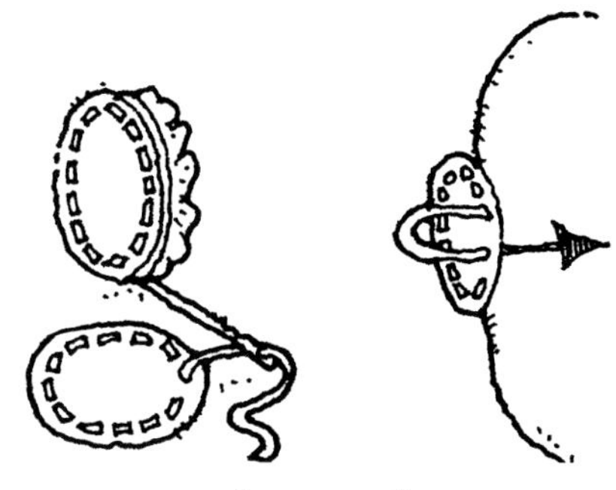
Steps 7 to 8

9. For eyes, cover two 5⁄16″ (0.8 cm) buttons with muslin, and use sculpting needle and thread to attach buttons to head. Push needle through button loop and into knotted end of doubled thread. Pull tightly and knot will be hidden behind button loop. Push needle into area marked for eye, and out back of head at gusset seam. Go through seam with needle to catch some fabric, and push needle back to button loop, through it, and back out same hole. Pull to indent button a little in eye area. Repeat this procedure one or two more times until button is indented enough. Push needle out back seam, make a knot to secure, and repeat procedure for other eye.

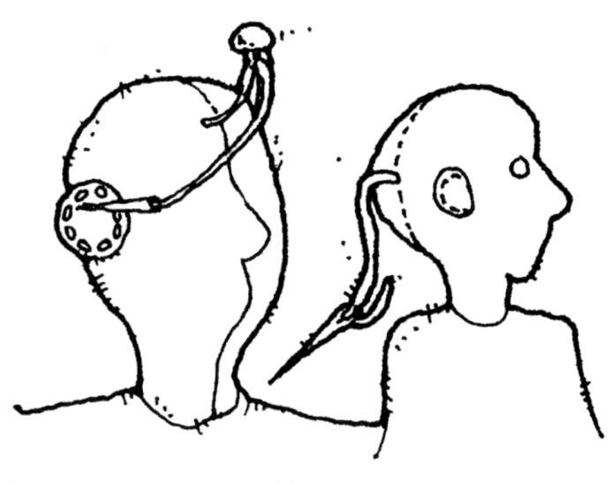
Step 9

10. Sculpt mouth by entering head at back, a little below knots for eyes. Bring needle out through front at corner of mouth, over to other corner, and back out other back gusset seam. Enter at same beginning point, back out corner of mouth, pulling slightly, and repeat procedure. Pull threads to indent mouth area, and tie a knot at back of head. Repeat this procedure to make indentation at bottom of lip. This stitch will be much shorter than mouth.

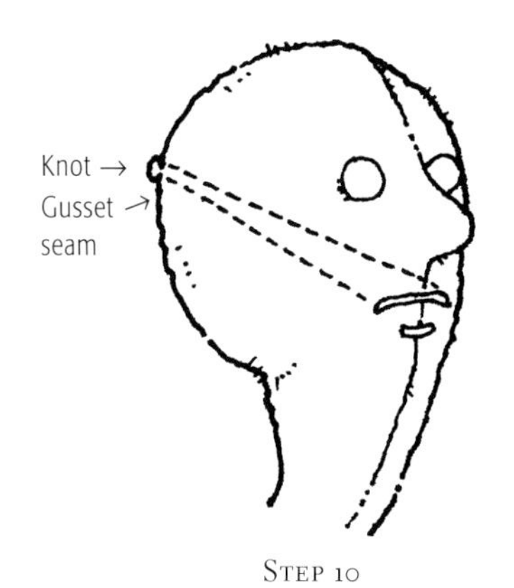

Step 10

11. Base coat face and hands of doll with two coats of Flesh Tone, letting each coat dry thoroughly. Use a pencil to sketch eyes. Apply Medium Flesh to upper eyelids in a quarter moon shape. Apply French Gray Blue to iris area, and Lamp Black to pupils. Apply White Wash to whites of eyes, and add a tiny dot in upper right side of each pupil for a highlight. Use a small brush to add Dk. Chocolate to lid line—this should be very thin. Add a small amount of Brush 'n Blend to thin Lt. Cinnamon a tiny bit, then use a small brush to apply short strokes of paint across top of eyes to form eyebrows. Use a few strokes of Dk. Chocolate to add a little "texture" to eyebrows. Let paint dry thoroughly. Thin a small dot of Antique Maroon with Brush 'n Blend to subdue color. Dry brush cheeks, inner ears, lower lip, and area from eyelid to brow. Let paint dry.
12. Apply crackle medium over all painted surfaces of hands and head. Let dry thoroughly, then brush on gel stain and wipe off immediately with a paper towel. Spray painted surfaces with matte spray sealer. Note: Hands are painted with Flesh Tone, then crackled and antiqued like face. Stitch arms to shoulders of torso. Set legs aside until trousers are finished.

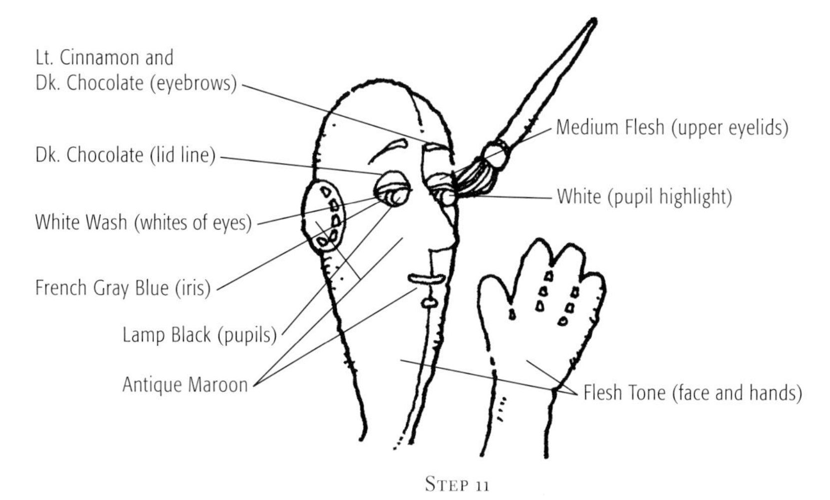

Step 11

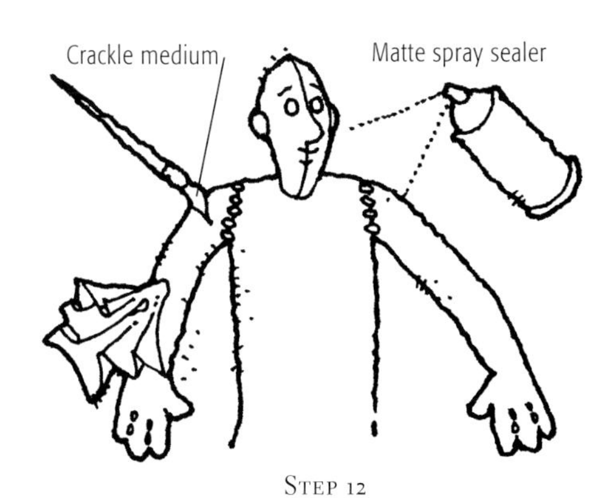

Step 12

Steps 13 to 14

Making the Hair

13. Place two hair sides (template I cut from felt) with right sides together and stitch around back of head. Trim seam allowance and turn right side out. Place on doll's head to see whether it fits. Since felt has a little "give" to it, you can sometimes use your fingers to stretch it out a little to fit curve of head. Trim sides of hair, if necessary, and glue on doll's head.
14. Cut mustache (template J) from felt and glue under nose.

Costuming the Doll

15. Cut trousers from blue felt (template K). Pin grosgrain ribbon down center of trouser legs and stitch in place.
16. With right sides together, stitch front and back center seams. Clip curves and pin legs together. Stitch inseam and turn up ½″ (1.5 cm) for lower hem. Hand stitch hem in place. Turn trousers right side out and hand gather upper waist ½″ (1.5 cm) from raw edge.
17. Insert legs, thighs first, into lower end of trouser legs. (The feet will not fit through trousers in normal manner.) Pull trousers down toward knees while you stitch legs to torso. Feet should face straight forward. Use heavy-duty thread to secure legs to body.
18. Pull trousers up and pull thread to gather trousers around waist. Tie threads in a square knot and cut off excess thread. Tuck raw edges into gathered waist of pants.
19. With right sides together, stitch jacket back (template L) to jacket fronts (template M) at shoulder seams. Clip neck angle, and press seams open.
20. With right sides together, pin sleeve (template N) to jacket and stitch, easing jacket to fit sleeve. Felt can be stretched a little to accommodate curves. Stitch grosgrain ribbon to lower edge of sleeve, ¾″ (2 cm) away from lower edge.
21. With right sides together, stitch side and underarm seams. Turn up ½″ (1.5 cm) and hand stitch lower hem of sleeve.
22. With right sides together, stitch lower jacket (template O) to jacket, matching front raw edges. Turn under ¼″ (0.75 cm) of front and bottom edges of lower jacket and hand stitch hem in place.

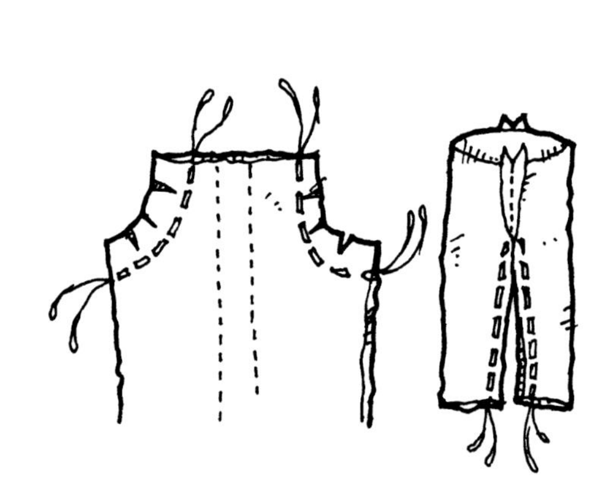
Steps 15 to 16

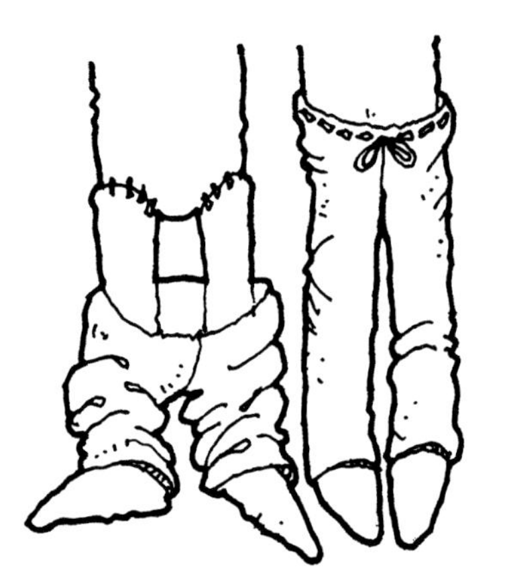
Steps 17 to 18

Steps 19 to 22

23. With right sides together, stitch upper collar (template P) to jacket. Collar should overlap hemmed edges ¼″ (0.75 cm) on each side. Fold collar in half, lengthwise, matching raw edges, right sides together. Stitch ends of collar, trim seam allowance, and turn collar right side out. Stitch raw edges of collar to inside of jacket neckline. Press jacket.
24. Stitch buttons on left side of jacket, spacing them about ½″ (1.5 cm) apart. Place jacket on doll, overlapping button edge on top of right edge, ¼″ (0.75 cm), and stitch or glue front opening closed.
25. Make a belt by placing a piece of black ¼″ (0.75 cm) satin-face ribbon around lower seam line. Overlap ends at front and glue them to jacket. Cut 1½″ (4 cm) ribbon and wind around center of a small buckle. Glue to keep it from slipping, then trim ends of ribbon at a 45-degree angle. Glue buckle to front to cover raw ends of belt.
26. Cut helmet pieces (template Q) from blue felt. Right sides together, stitch around top of helmet. Clip angles, turn hat right side out, and turn facing toward inside of hat. Stitch facing to hat.
27. Stuff hat firmly with batting to help form rounded shape.
28. Apply two coats of varnish, allowing each coat to dry thoroughly. Mix Prussian Blue paint with a small dot of Oyster White, just to lighten it a little (paint should be color of felt uniform). Apply one coat of paint to helmet and let dry. Remove most of batting and place hat on doll's head to determine proper fit. Remove or add batting as needed, so front of helmet barely covers top of eyebrows.
29. Cut a 6½″ (16.5 cm) length of ¼″ (0.75 cm) black satin-face ribbon, and stitch to helmet for a chin strap. Note template for placement. Glue ⅛″ (0.4 cm) black satin-face ribbon around lower quarter, at widest part of front of helmet. Note template for placement. Stitch button to front center of helmet, about ¼″ (0.75 cm) above ribbon. Place helmet on doll and tack chin strap to upper front collar to hold in place.

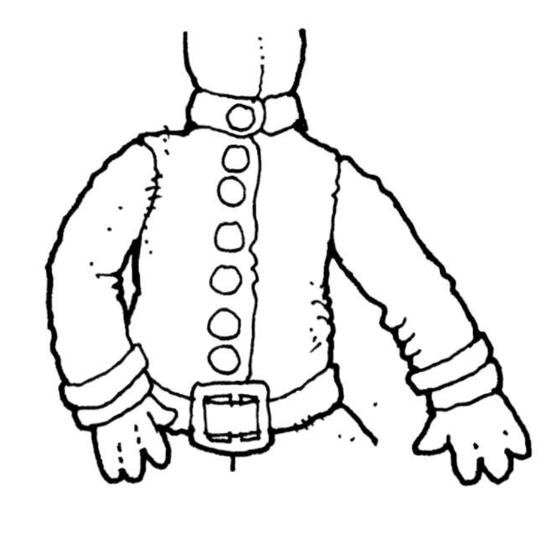

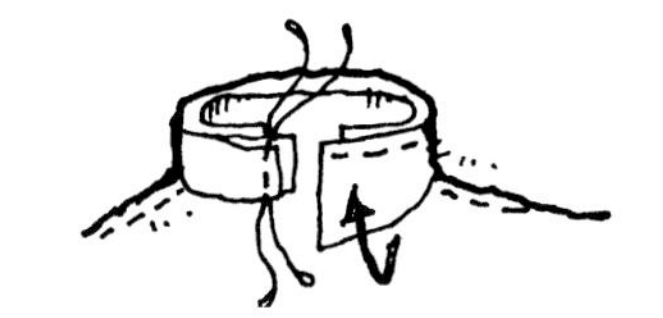

Steps 23 to 25

Steps 26 to 28

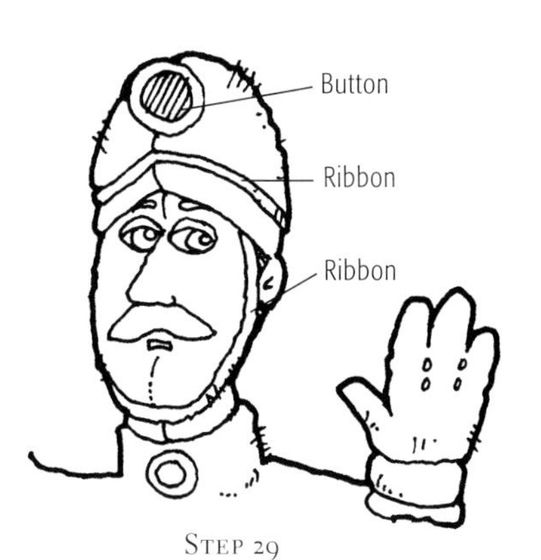

Step 29

Medieval Knight

With the increasing popularity of Renaissance costumes, this little knight is the perfect accent to your home.

Medieval Knight by Brenda Gehl, 1999; 15″ (40 cm).

Supplies

- 1 yard (90 cm) muslin for head, body, and armor
- 1 yard (90 cm) crushed red velvet for garments
- 7½″ × 17″ (19 cm × 43 cm) piece of metallic gold fabric for garments
- 1 yard (90 cm) of ½″ (1.5 cm) gold trim for garments
- 2½ yards (225 cm) narrow rope braid (black)
- 8″ (20 cm) length 1½″ (4 cm) crochet lace edging for mail collar
- 6″ × 6″ (15 cm × 15 cm) black felt for back of shield
- Stuffing
- Long dollmaking needle
- Perle cotton (black)
- 2 buttons, ½″ (1.5 cm)
- Glass seed beads (black or dark gray)
- 10 round gold beads, ¼″ (0.75 cm)
- Acrylic colors by Plaid:
  Apple Barrel® color—English Navy; Folk Art Metallic colors—Gunmetal Gray and Inca Gold; Folk Art® colors—Santa's Flesh, Thicket, Licorice, Cherokee Rose, Cherry Royale, Warm White
- Clear gloss liquid acrylic
- #3 and #6 round paint brushes
- #8 round stiff bristle brush
- Brown pencil
- 17″ (43 cm) wooden dowel, ⅜″ (1 cm) diameter, for spear handle

Templates on pages 135–138. Use ¼″ (0.75 cm) seam allowance unless otherwise indicated.

The Dollmaker–Brenda Gehl

As a child, Brenda learned to knit and sew—and her grandmother did beautiful crewel and embroidery work, which she attempted to imitate. By the time she was in fourth grade, she was making wonderful doll clothes out of her mother's cleaning rags and her grandmother's scrap yarns.

From this charming beginning, Brenda continued her education: in high school, she studied painting and sculpting; in college, she completed her degree in art at the University of Wisconsin in Milwaukee. She dabbled in several things, but when she discovered dollmaking, she knew she had found something really good. Her designs have been seen in several publications, including *Better Homes and Gardens* special-interest magazines. She exhibits and teaches her unique construction methods, including creating a figure that stands without the use of an internal armature or external stand. She uses figures as a dimensional canvas and enjoys painting the surfaces of her dolls.

Steps 6 to 11

Making the Head

1. Cut two head pieces (template A) from muslin. Sew darts. Place front and back pieces right sides together and sew, using ¼″ (0.75 cm) seam allowances. Turn right side out and stuff firmly (but not solid as a rock). Hand stitch opening at top of head closed.
2. To needle-sculpt head, use strong thread and doll needle to stitch through back of head at neck and come out through an eye. Insert needle ¼″ (0.75 cm) over from first stitch and go out through back of head, at neck. Repeat, pulling thread tightly and positioning stitches to form a square. Do this for both eyes. Knot and clip thread end at back of head.

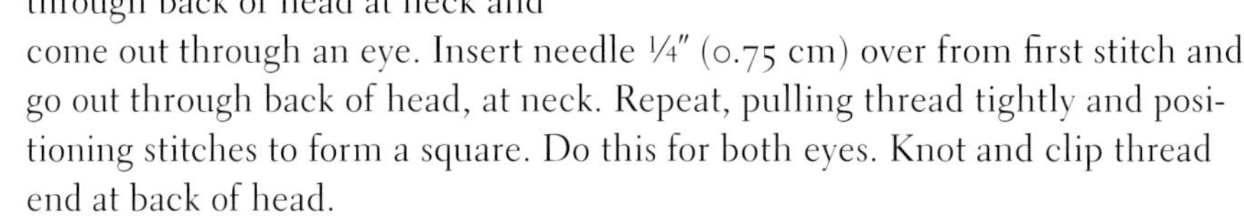

Steps 1 to 4

3. To form jaw, needle-sculpt back and forth through head along side seams of face, pulling stitches tight. Knot and clip thread end at back of head.

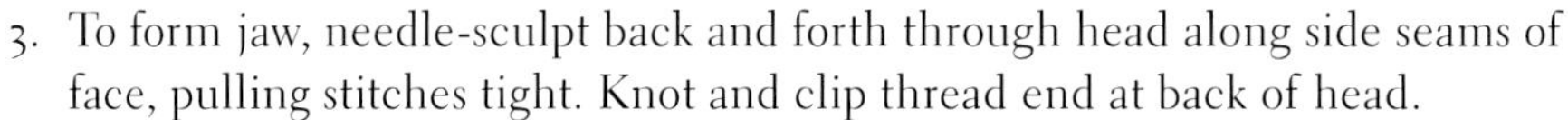

4. To make mouth, insert needle through back of head and come out front of head at one side of mouth. Insert needle through other side of mouth and come out back of head. Pull stitch just enough to give mouth definition. Repeat this stitch, then knot and clip thread end at back of head.
5. For eyes, cover ½″ (1.5 cm) buttons with muslin. Using strong thread, stitch them in place through head from back to front, pulling button down tightly against face. Knot and clip thread end at back of head.

Making the Body

6. To make body, trace templates B, C, and D on doubled muslin. Do not cut yet. Sew around traced lines, leaving an opening at bottom of body and at tops of legs and arms. Cut out pieces, trimming ¼″ (0.75 cm) or less from stitching. Clip curves where needed.
7. Place center top and center bottom seams of each foot together and sew each toe as indicated by template markings. Do this on body for both shoulders. Trim seams and turn all pieces to right sides.
8. Stuff body and legs firmly. Turn in raw edges by ¼″ (0.75 cm). Using strong thread, baste around folded edge of body. Pull basting thread to gather stitches and close opening. Knot and clip thread end. There will still be an opening in bottom of body. Whipstitch opening closed.
9. Baste around folded edge of each leg, pulling thread tightly to close openings. Knot and clip thread ends.
10. Stuff hands and arms firmly to stitch line indicated on pattern. Machine stitch across each arm where indicated. Turn in raw edges at top of each arm by ¼″ (0.75 cm), and machine stitch openings closed along folded ends.
11. Position head, arms, and legs on body. Ladder-stitch in place, using strong thread.

Costuming the Doll

Making the Armor

12. To make mitten gauntlets, sew two gauntlets (template E), with right sides together, using ¼″ (0.75 cm) seam allowance and leaving open where indicated for turning. Clip curves and trim corners. Turn each piece to right side and press. Stitch openings closed.
13. Referring to pattern markings and using a double strand of perle cotton and dollmaking needle, stitch through gauntlets to create long vertical stitches on facing sides. Do not pull stitches tight, just allow them to lie evenly on surface of fabric. (The back of each gauntlet will not be visible.) Glue rope braid along top and bottom edges of gauntlet. Allow braid to extend ½″ (1.5 cm) beyond ends. This can be trimmed away later.
14. In same manner, stitch tops of each mitten, referring to pattern markings. Remember that back of mitten can be seen, so stitch in a neat and creative manner.
15. Make sabatons (foot armor) in same way, referring to pattern markings. Stitch through feet using a double strand of perle cotton and dollmaking needle. Beginning on bottom of each foot, glue rope braid in place by going over and around heel, then back under foot. Go over top of foot and end on bottom. Allow glued areas to dry for several hours.

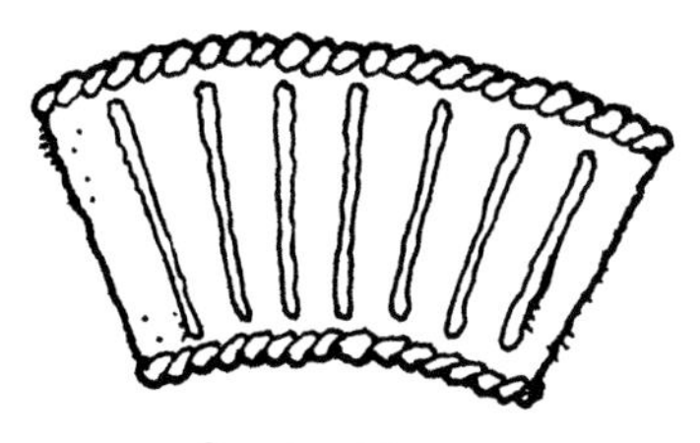

Steps 12 to 13

Step 14

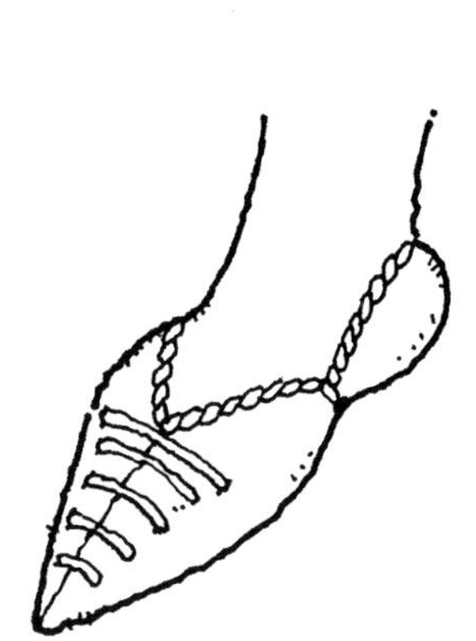

Step 15

Painting the Face and Armor

16. Base paint front of head using Santa's Flesh. Paint each button eye with Warm White. Allow paints to dry. Paint irises Thicket, making circles about two-thirds size of button. Paint pupils Licorice, and highlight each eye using Warm White. Allow paints to dry.
17. Draw upper and lower lids on button eyes using brown pencil. Paint lids Santa's Flesh, allowing pencil lines to show. (The pencil gives edges of lids a nice, finished look.)
18. Brush Cherokee Rose paint mixed 1:1 with water on cheek area and around eyes to give skin color and texture. Allow paint to dry. Paint lips using Cherry Royale. Allow face to dry completely. Paint over irises and lips using clear gloss acrylic.

Steps 16 to 18

Steps 19 to 20

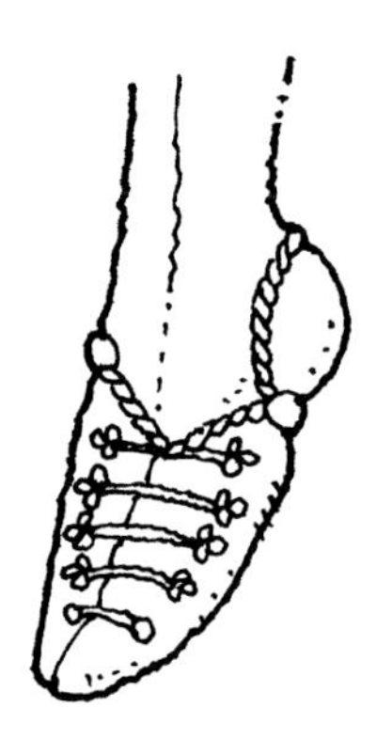

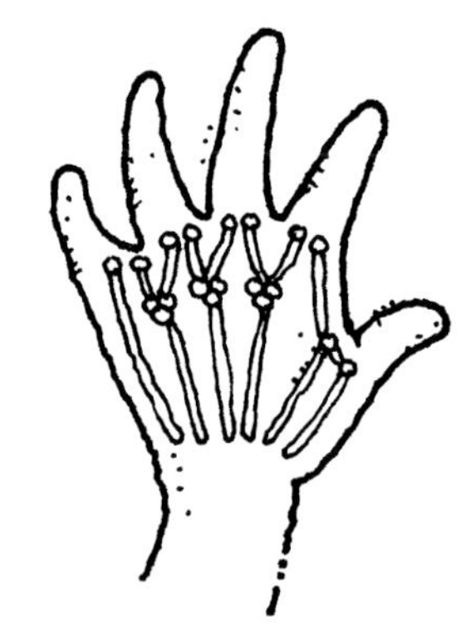

Steps 21 to 22

19. Base paint body using English Navy. Paint both sides of each gauntlet, arms, legs, and back of head. Work slowly, painting over seams, topstitching, and braid. Allow paint to dry for a few hours before applying gray coat that follows.
20. Using a stiff bristle brush and a small amount of Gunmetal Gray, work paint into bristles of brush until it is nearly dry, then scrub paint into blue surfaces of body, arms, and legs. (This is called dry brushing.) This will give armor a metallic shine with blue depth. Allow paint to dry.

Beading

21. For sabatons, sew 1 seed bead on each end of first stitch at toe. Sew three beads on each end of remaining stitches. Sew gold beads on inside and outside edges of sabatons.
22. For mittens and gauntlets, sew seed beads in place. Cut excess braid from ends of gauntlets and glue in place around arms so ends meet where they will not be visible when doll is posed. (Use straight pins to hold gauntlets in place.)

Completing the Costume

23. On bias, cut one velvet skirt, 12″ × 38″ (30 cm × 95 cm) and two collar pieces (template F). Cut one gold fabric piece 7½″ × 17″ (19 cm × 43 cm). Sew velvet skirt piece, with right sides together, along short sides to make center back seam. Hem bottom edge with a 2″ (5 cm) hem. Machine stitch two rows of gathering stitches along top edge.
24. Place skirt on doll with seam at center back and pull stitches to gather skirt tightly around torso, under arms of doll. Tie ends of gathering threads together. Hand stitch skirt to doll around gathered edge.
25. Baste a 17″ (43 cm) length of gold trim along bottom edge of gold skirt piece. Hand stitch it securely in place. With right sides together, sew short sides of skirt together to make center back seam. Machine stitch two rows of gathering stitches along top edge. Place gold skirt over velvet skirt, matching center back seams, and pull stitches, gathering skirt evenly around doll. Hand stitch gold skirt in place on doll.
26. With right sides together, sew around edges of collar, leaving open where indicated. Clip corners and trim seams where needed. Turn right side out. Baste gold trim around outer edge of collar, then stitch securely in place. Position collar on doll so ends meet at center back. Hand stitch in place on doll body.
27. To make helmet, cut two helmet side pieces (template G) and two helmet crowns (template H) from muslin. Trace one nose guard (template I) on doubled muslin and sew on traced lines. Cut out nose guard, trimming seams

close to stitched line. Slash back of nose guard and turn to right side through opening. Whipstitch slashed opening shut.

28. Sew helmet sides, right sides together, along bottom edge using ¼″ (0.75 cm) seam allowance. Clip seam allowance along curve, turn right side out, and press. Open piece and match back seam, right sides together. Sew and finger-press seam open. Turn piece right side out and baste layers together along top edge.
29. Place helmet crown pieces together and baste around outer edge. Match center back seams together and machine stitch. Turn crown right side out. Pin crown and helmet sides right sides together, matching center back seams and center front markings. Machine stitch in place. Glue rope braid in place along bottom edge of helmet and around seam on crown. Set nose guard aside.

Accessories

30. To make shield, cut two inner shield circles (template J) and two outer shield circles (template K) from muslin. Place circles right sides together and sew all around outer edges. Slash back of each circle, turn right side out, press, and whipstitch openings closed. Trace five shield markings (template L) on doubled muslin and sew through both layers on traced lines. Cut out pieces, trimming seams close to stitched lines. Slash back of each piece, turn right side out and press.
31. Glue inner circle centered on outer circle. Glue rope braid around edge of outer and inner circles. Allow glue to set, then glue five shield markings with narrow point toward center, evenly spaced around circle. Allow several hours for glue to dry on helmet and shield.
32. Sew markings on shield with a double strand of perle cotton, using technique described in Step 13.

Step 32

33. Base paint both sides of helmet, nose guard, shield, and 8″ (20 cm) length of crochet cotton (mail collar), using English Navy. Allow paint to dry completely. Using dry brush method (described on page 26), apply Gunmetal Gray paint to outer surfaces of helmet, nose guard, shield, and crochet mail collar. Allow to dry.
34. Sew seed beads in place on shield. Sew one gold bead to center of shield. From black felt, cut a circle, ⅛″ (0.4 cm) smaller than shield, and a 3″ × ½″ (8 cm × 1.5 cm) strip for shield handle. Center handle on felt circle and sew in place along short ends. Glue felt circle to back of shield to finish.

Step 34

35. To complete mail collar, sew five gold beads, spaced 1″ (2.5 cm) apart, starting with center front bead. Glue mail in place, centered under chin and around sides of doll's face. Position helmet on head and glue in place.
36. To make spear, wrap rope braid around bottom of wooden spear handle six times, and glue in place. Allow glue to dry. Base paint entire handle using English Navy. After paint has dried, apply Gunmetal Gray to blue handle using dry brush method. Set handle aside.
37. Cut two spear head pieces (template M) from muslin. Stitch with right sides together, leaving open where indicated. Clip corners and turn to right side. Base paint both sides of spear head using Licorice. After paint has dried, apply Inca Gold to both sides using dry brush method. Allow to dry.
38. Finger-press spear point through center, forming a crease on both sides. Glue spear head to wooden handle. Glue gold trim in place over raw edge of spear head. Position spear and shield in knight's left hand to finish.

Momotaro (Little Peach)

Momotaro is a charming Japanese fairy tale about an old couple who longed for a child. One morning, the old woman found a large peach in the stream outside their house. She brought the peach inside to eat for breakfast, but as soon as her knife touched the skin, the peach opened. Inside, she found a tiny baby boy—Little Peach.

Momotaro (Little Peach) by Shauna Mooney Kawasaki, 1998; 19″ (48 cm).

Supplies

- ⅓ yard (30 cm) bleached muslin for body
- Plastic manufactured armature (optional)
- ⅓ yard (30 cm) fabric for pantaloons
- ⅓ yard (30 cm) fabric for kimono
- ¼ yard (25 cm) fabric for skirt panels
- Scraps of fabric for clothing accents
- Beads, buttons, trims
- Fine black yarn, cord, or crochet thread for hair
- Stuffing
- Red, black, and white acrylic paint for face
- Decorative thread, embroidery floss
- Scraps of black fleece (lightweight) for shoes and shoe tops

Templates on pages 139–143. Use ¼″ (0.75 cm) seam allowance unless otherwise indicated.

The Dollmaker—Shauna Mooney Kawasaki

Shauna Mooney Kawasaki was born in Provo, Utah, educated in Orem, Utah, and graduated from the "school of hard knocks." She was art director for a children's magazine for seventeen years; married her boss and his seven children; and has happily retired to a world of writing, drawing, sewing, sculpting, and borrowing children. She has written and/or illustrated more than thirty books for children and is just getting started. She has done murals for children's exhibits, had one-person doll shows, and worked on high-pressure projects no one in her right mind would take on. She loves monsters, aliens, and scary things—and she hates cats!

Making the Body

1. Placing templates on fold, trace two legs (template A), and two arms (template B) on doubled muslin. Do not cut yet. Stitch front leg seam, leaving top, toe, and bottom of foot open. Trim seam allowance to ⅛" (0.4 cm) and clip curves.
2. Stitch ¼" (0.75 cm) from lower edge of heel area, starting about 1" (2.5 cm) from center back, and ending 1" (2.5 cm) from center back on other side. Clip to stitching, every ¼" (0.75 cm). Cut two soles (template C). Right sides together, pin leg and sole. Stitch, leaving toe open. Turn leg right side out, and set aside.
3. Stitch around arms, hands, and thumb, leaving top open. Trim seam allowance to ⅛" (0.4 cm), clip curves, then turn right side out. Lightly stuff fingers, and topstitch them with sewing machine, or topstitch fingers first, then insert pipe cleaners to allow hands to be posed. Set arms aside.
4. Trace head (template D) on doubled muslin. Cut out head sides, adding ¼" (0.75 cm) seam allowances. Stitch front seam, starting at dot above forehead and ending at bottom neck front. Cut out head gusset (template E). Place head gusset with right sides together, matching dots on gusset to dots on head. Stitch to one side of head at a time.
5. Stitch remaining length of neck, trim seam allowance to ⅛" (0.4 cm), clip curves, turn right side out, and stuff head very firmly. Neck piece will be stuffed up into head.

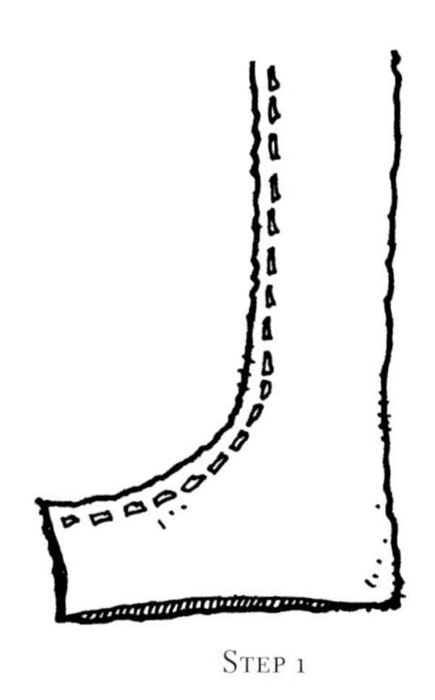

Step 1

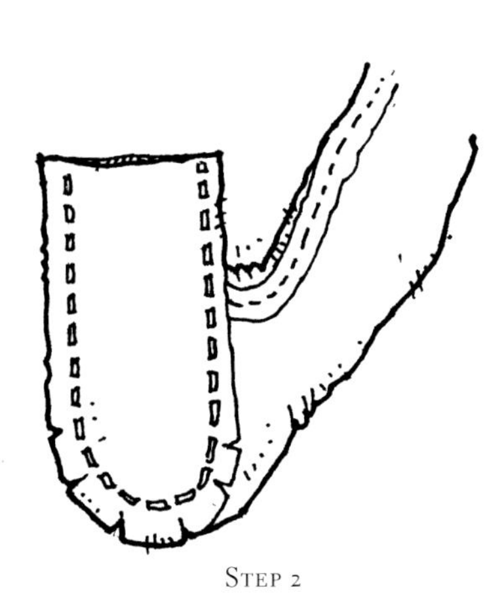

Step 2

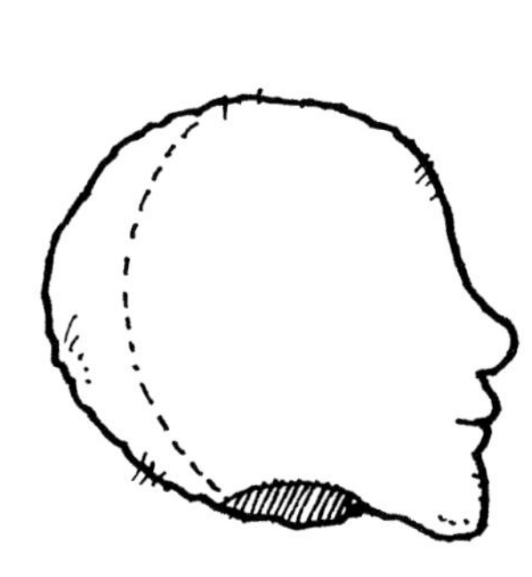

Step 5

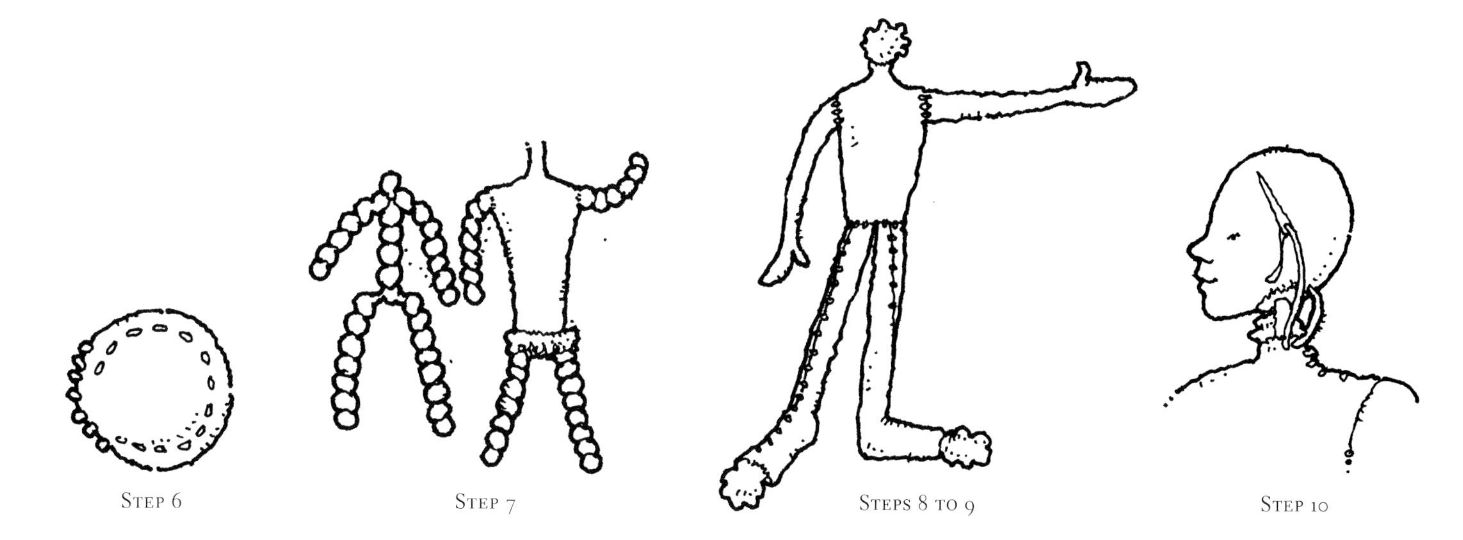

Step 6 Step 7 Steps 8 to 9 Step 10

6. Cut two ears (template F) from muslin. Baste each around perimeter and pull thread to gather. Stuff them to make them about ⅜″ (1 cm) long. Stitch them to head, using a long needle to go back and forth from one ear to other. Stitches along inside of ear (which go back and forth through head) will form a C shape.
7. Cut out body (template G) and stitch, leaving neck, arm, and lower body open. Trim seam allowance, turn body right side out, and place over armature (one you either purchase or make yourself—see page 16). Stuff body.
8. Pull legs up over ends of armature, insert them into lower body, and stitch lower body and legs together. Stuff legs through toe openings, making sure you stuff legs, and especially ankles, very firmly. Stitch toe openings closed.
9. Slip arms over armature and stuff them firmly. Stitch arms to shoulders.
10. Slip body neck into neck opening in head, and stitch in place.

Creating the Face

11. Use template as a guide to pencil on features (eyes, eyebrows, and mouth). Use black paint and a very, very fine brush to paint eyebrow and top eye line.
12. Make a very small black dot for doll's eye, with a white pinpoint highlight. Paint lips red.
13. Lightly draw hairline in pencil. Glue 6 to 8 strands of black yarn at a time, so lengths of yarn face forward. Do several layers completely around head. When glue is dry, hold doll horizontally while you tie hair up into a ponytail, high on head. Use a dot of glue to secure ponytail to head. Trim hair bluntly, and use trimmings to pad scalp so white muslin won't show through. Glue strands in place where needed.

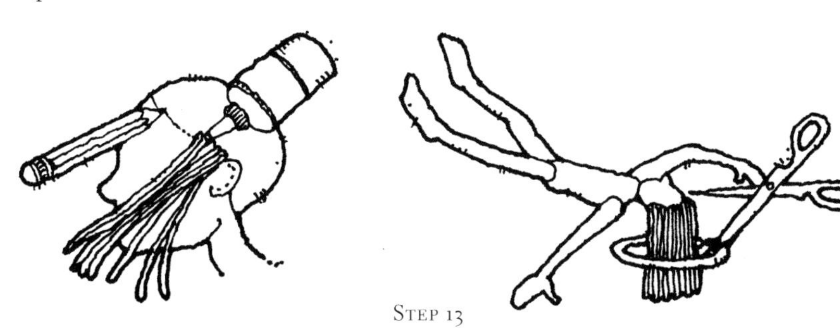

Step 13

Costuming the Doll

Note: All strips for edging (kimono, sheath, pantaloons) are torn 1¾″ (4.4 cm) wide, then halved or folded in thirds. Frayed edges are a decorative feature—the more frayed, the better.

Pantaloons

14. Cut two pantaloons (template H) on fold. With right sides together, stitch inseam and outside seam, leaving open where indicated on pattern. Clip curves, turn right side out, and press. Tear two strips of contrasting fabric, 1¾″ × 18″ (4.4 cm × 45 cm), and press in half, with right sides out, frayed edges together. Pleat front and back of pantaloons with about four pleats for each side, about 1½″ (4 cm) deep. Baste pleats.
15. Pin one of folded, torn strips over raw edges of pleated front pantaloons waist. Be sure strip is centered. Stitch strip, starting at one end and ending at other, stitching through all layers of front pantaloon and folded strip. Tie a knot in each end. Repeat for back pantaloons. Place pantaloons on doll.
16. Tear a strip, 1¾″ × 12″ (4.4 cm × 30 cm), and set it aside.

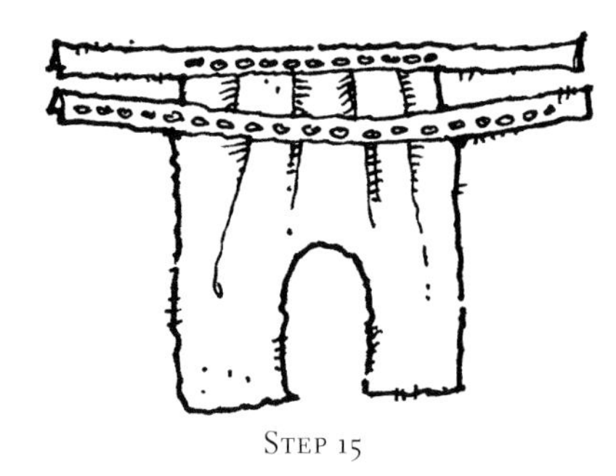

Step 15

Kimono

17. Cut kimono top front/back (template I) on doubled fabric. Cut front down center. Right sides together, stitch shoulder seams. Press seams open. Right sides together, stitch underarm seams. Turn right side out and press.
18. Tear a contrasting strip of fabric measuring 1¾″ × 36″ (4.4 cm × 90 cm) and fringe. Press in half and use it to edge neck and entire left side of front opening of kimono. Use remainder of strip to edge sleeves. Gather lower sleeve near folded edge of contrast strip. Place kimono on doll, pull up sleeve gathers, and tie to secure around doll's forearm.
19. Tuck kimono inside pantaloons, and tie front tie in back (ties inside). Bring pantaloon ties back around to front of doll and tie a square knot in center front. Fold extra fullness of pantaloon at doll's lower leg so fold is taken from outside of leg and folded around toward center front of leg. Using a needle and thread, stitch folded half of strip of fabric from Step 16 around leg, with fringed edge upward.

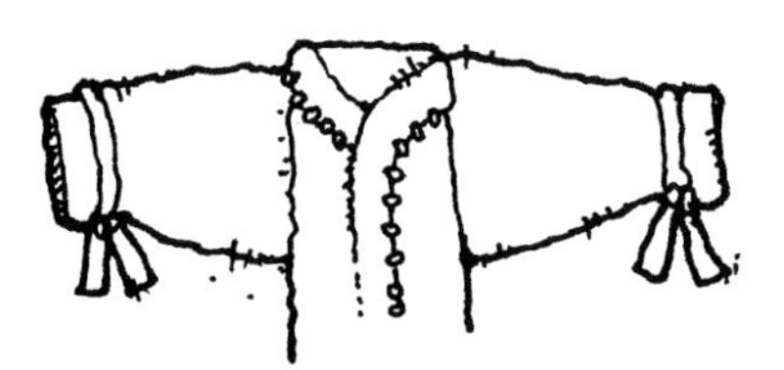

Step 18

Step 19

Sheath

20. Cut out six skirt panels and lining panels, each 5″ × 8″ (13 cm × 20 cm). Cut out six decorative strips, 1½″ × 5″ (4 cm × 13 cm). Press under ¼″ (0.75 cm) on one long side of each decorative strip. Pin strip to skirt panel, matching raw edges. Stitch folded edge to panel, either by hand or machine. Repeat for all six skirt panels.

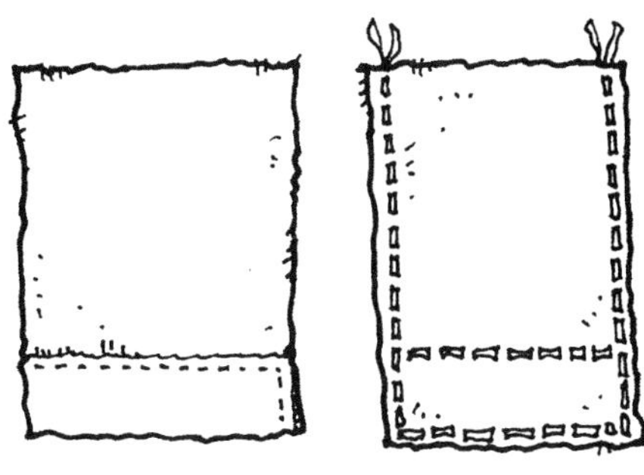

Step 20

21. With right side of skirt panel facing right side of lining, stitch sides and bottom edge of panel (the bottom edge has decorative strip). Trim seam allowance, turn right side out, and press. Use embroidery floss to make a running stitch along side edges of panel. Stitch on beads or other embellishments, including embroidery, if you wish. Front and back of sheath each use three panels. The two side panels are pleated in middle, so depth of each pleat is about ¾″ (2 cm). Each outer panel has a pleat that faces outward. Center panel has two pleats, ¾″ (2 cm) deep each. Folded edge and outer edge will line up exactly. When pleats are made, baste together to hold.
22. Cut two strips measuring 1¾″ × 18″ (4.4 cm × 45 cm) and two measuring 1¾″ × 8½″ (4.4 cm × 22 cm). Fold in half, lengthwise. Stitch one short end and long raw edge to make tubes. Turn right side out, press, and set aside.
23. Cut one front and one back sheath (template J) on fold of doubled fabric. Place folded panel with right sides together on top of batting and stitch two sides through all layers. Trim seam allowance, turn right side out, and press. Quilt, bead, or otherwise decorate.

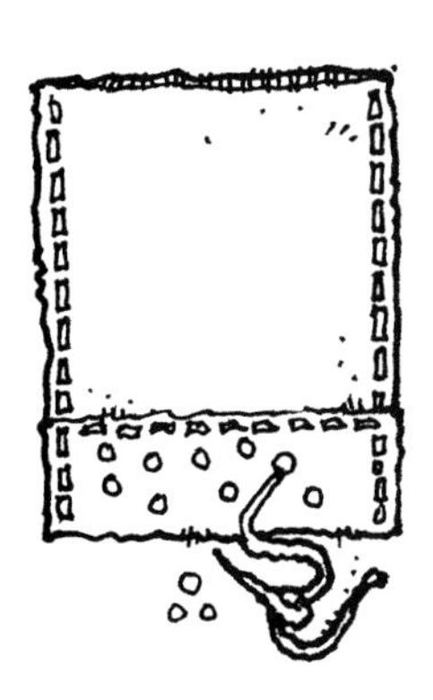

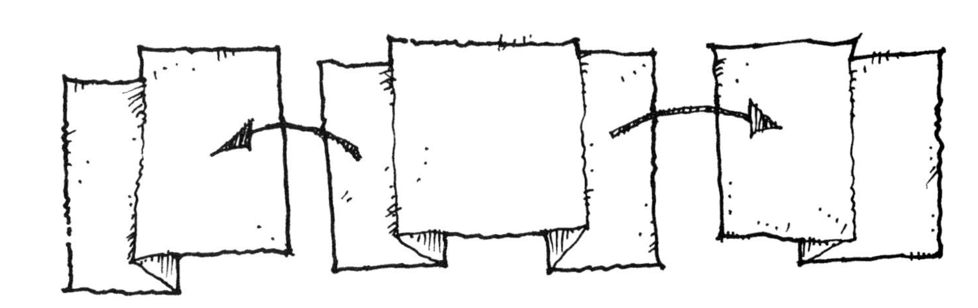

Step 21

Step 22

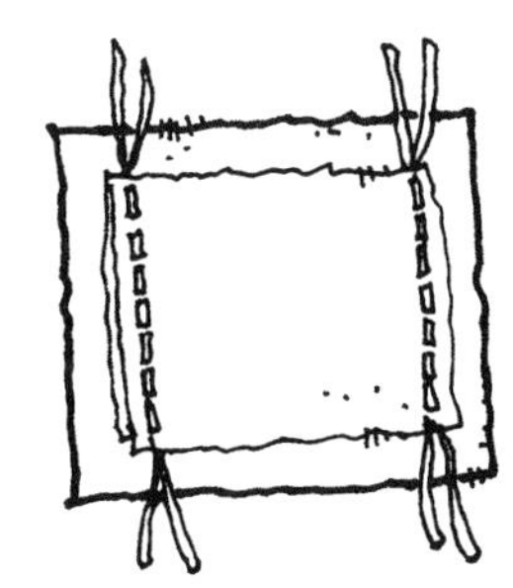

Step 23

24. Make shoulder pads using template K, following Step 23. Leave straight edge open for turning.
25. To assemble sheath, pin one long 18″ (45 cm) tube of fabric across raw edge of back panel, centering panel. Pin one short 8½″ (22 cm) tube along each edge of back panel so it is tucked underneath long tube, but on top of back panel. Hand stitch tubes to sheath. Stitch front panel to other ends of short tubes, and add long tube, as you did for other side.
26. Center each shoulder pad underneath short tubes, so rounded edge of shoulder pad is facing outward. Stitch in place.
27. Place two outer pleated panels next to each other, and center twice-pleated front panel over two side panels. Stitch panels together. Place raw edges of panels under long tubes of fabric, and stitch in place. Add any decorative stitching you like along edges of flattened tubes.
28. Place sheath over doll's head, and tie ties as you did with pantaloons.

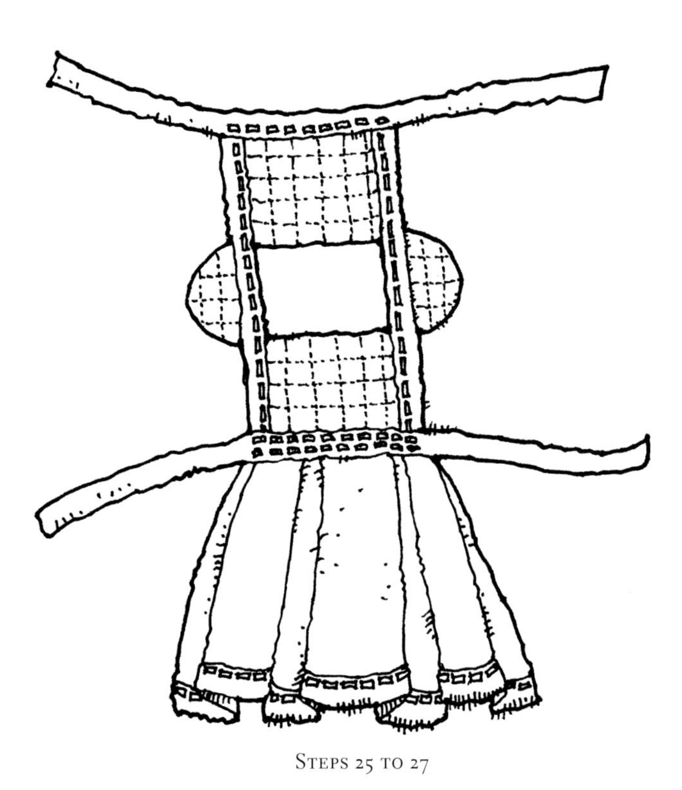

Steps 25 to 27

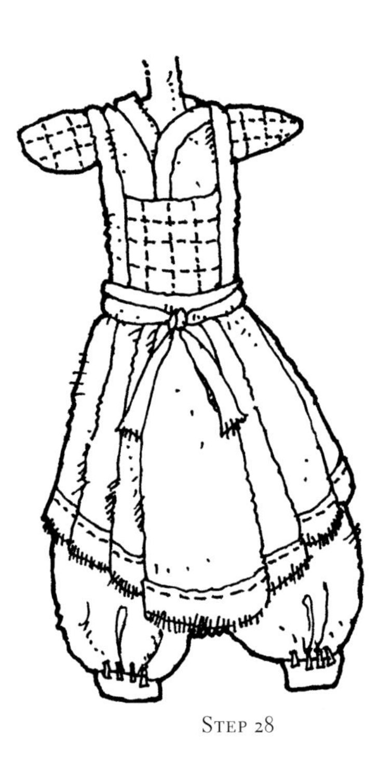

Step 28

Arm and Leg Bands

29. Make arm and leg bands by fringing both sides of a 2½″ (6.5 cm) wide strip of fabric. Arm bands are 2½″ (6.5 cm) long and leg bands are 4½″ (11.5 cm) long.
30. Cut (do not tear) a contrasting piece of fabric to same length and width as other bands. Turn under raw edges so contrasting band is narrower than fringed band and press.
31. Stitch each band together with three rows of stitching in contrast area, and two rows on each end, next to fringe. Leave long enough lengths of embroidery floss so you can gather them tight around doll's wrist and ankle area, and tie floss in knots. Trim knots, leaving about 1″ (2.5 cm) of thread. Do not place leg bands on doll until you finish shoes.

Shoes

32. Cut out two shoe tops (template L) on fold of doubled fabric. Place on doll's foot and stitch front together, with raw sides out.
33. Cut two shoe bottoms (template M). Gather ½″ (1.5 cm) from outer edge. Place cardboard sole (template N) inside and hold in place with dot of glue. Place on doll's foot and gather tightly. Stitch to bottom of foot.

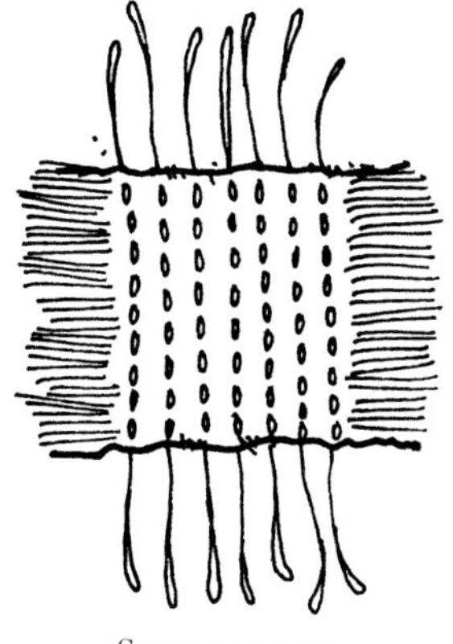

Steps 29 to 31

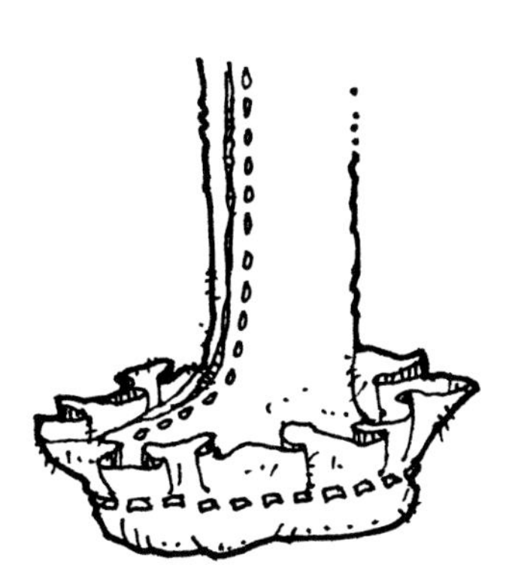

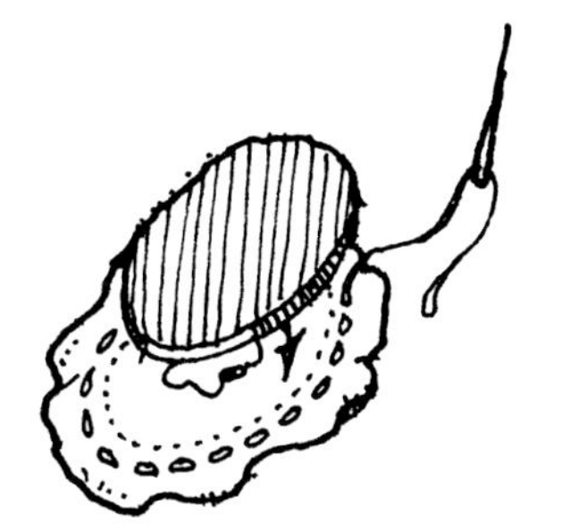

Step 33

Frens

FRENS

Frens BY ANNIE MOON, 1999; 18" (45 CM).

THESE SIMPLE RAG DOLLS are made from old woolen skirts, sweaters, and flannel shirts. Clothing is attached and the shirt is only cuffs and a tail. A second shirt or sweater can be added by making and attaching the shirt pattern a second time. You can use old clothes that mean something special to you for a really treasured piece.

SUPPLIES (ONE DOLL)

- ½ yard (45 cm) flesh-colored wool for head, body, arms, and legs
- ⅛ yard (12 cm) dark wool for shoes
- ⅛ yard (12 cm) for pants and skirt
- Scraps for shirttail, sleeves, and heart
- Old sweater for sweater and cap
- Candlewicking thread (or embroidery floss), black and red
- Tiny buttons
- Stuffing
- Crayola® crayon: Bittersweet

Templates on pages 144–147. Use ⅛" (0.4 cm) seam allowance unless otherwise indicated.

The Dollmaker—Annie Moon

Annie Moon lives on a mountaintop in rural southwest Virginia. She lives without electricity or running water, but with many dogs and chickens. Her ideas for dolls come faster than she can make them: all kinds of dolls, from very primitive rag dolls, to strange creatures on armatures mounted on wood bases, to Santas and witches, to plain old men and women.

Annie makes her living from dollmaking. Though it is not lucrative, it allows her to do what she loves all day, every day, whether it is rummaging in thrift stores or sewing all those doll parts. Her studio is her bed in her tiny mountain cabin. She had a fire in December 1997, so she doesn't have a lot of "stuff" anymore. Her favorite features of her home/work area are windows all around the house with bird feeders at most of them.

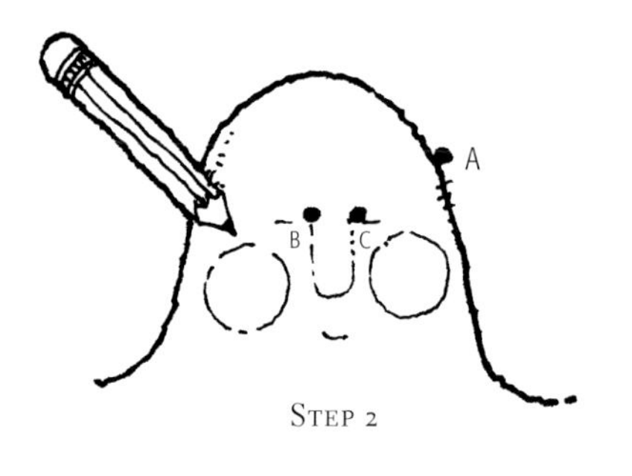

Step 2

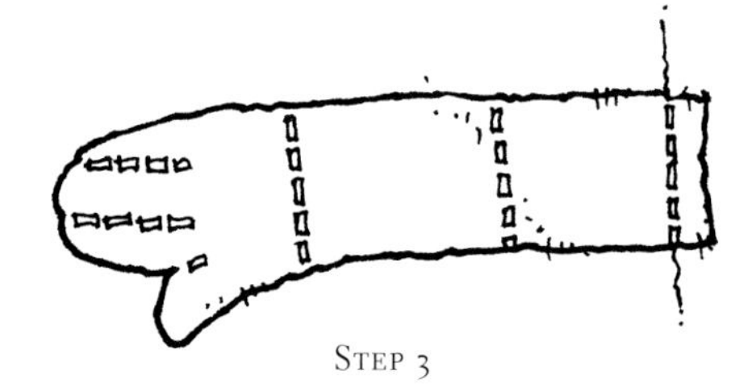

Step 3

Step 4

Making the Body

1. Right sides together, stitch body-head (template A), leaving opening for arms. Turn right side out, and stuff head and neck firmly. For a stiff, straight neck, make a single stitch, all the way through body, right below neck, and stitch back and forth a few times, pushing stuffing up into neck. Secure thread firmly and knot off.
2. Needle-sculpt nose by lightly marking nose on face. Insert needle at side of head (point A), and exit at left side of upper nose (point B). Make a tiny anchor stitch, then reinsert needle, pushing it under a bit of stuffing, and exit at right side of upper nose (point C). Reinsert needle, just a stitch below point C, following marking of nose. Pull a tiny bit and exit just a little below point B. Continue back and forth, pulling gently each time. Make a looping stitch, back and forth, to form base of nose, and work back up nose, exiting at top of head, where you will knot thread.
3. Right sides together, stitch arms (template B), leaving an opening at top. Turn right side out, stuff fingers lightly, and topstitch fingers as indicated on template. Stuff hand to wrist, topstitch at wrist, stuff to elbow, and topstitch across elbow. Stuff lightly to top, topstitch across top, and insert top of arm into body. Hand stitch arms to body.
4. Right sides together, stitch shoes (template C) to legs (template D). Press seam allowance toward shoes. Place legs with right sides together and stitch around legs, leaving open at top as indicated on pattern. Clip curves, turn right side out, and stuff to knee. Topstitch across knee, and stuff lightly to top of leg.
5. With toes pointing upward and right sides together, baste tops of legs to open end of head-body. Fold raw ends inside doll and stitch body opening closed.
6. Embroider eyes and mouth with black and red candlewicking thread. (You can use three strands of embroidery floss, if you can't find candlewicking thread.) Eyes and mouth are made by knotting thread and entering back of doll's head, making a single stitch about 1⁄16″ (0.2 cm) long for each eye, and exiting through back. Make a knot. Repeat for mouth, using red thread.
7. Color cheeks with a Bittersweet Crayola.

Costuming the Doll

8. Coat and cap are made from knitted sweaters. Take care when cutting sweater (template E) and cap (template F) so yarn doesn't unravel. With right sides together, stitch underarm seams with small, tight stitches. Carefully turn right

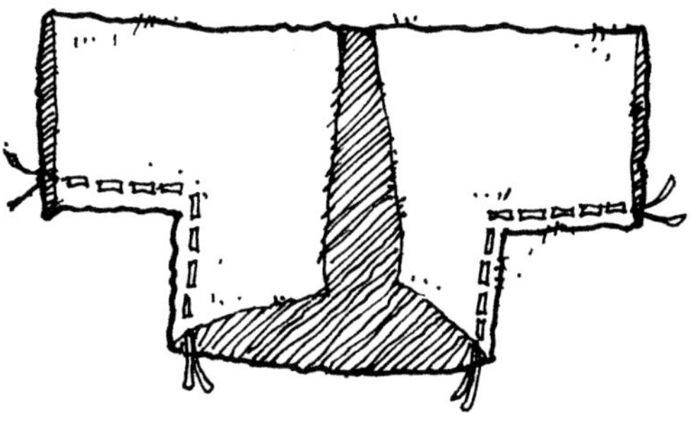

Step 8

side out. Roll under a tiny hem, and hand stitch sleeves, lower edge, front opening, and neck opening. Make cap by placing right sides together and stitching around curved edges. Turn right side out and roll under a tiny hem. Hand stitch hem.

9. Cut shirt sleeves (template G) and fold under one short side. Place on doll's hand, beginning on palm, circling wrist, with right side of fabric toward hand. Stitch to doll's wrist, about ¼″ (0.75 cm) from raw edge around wrist. Fold cuff up toward arm to form a sleeve. Stitch folded edge to sleeve, and catch doll's arm in it to keep sleeve in place.
10. Cut out shirttail (template H). Press under a ¼″ (0.75 cm) hem on bottom edge. Use a running stitch to stitch hem in place. Fold shirttail in half, wrong sides together, and stitch a running stitch ¼″ (0.75 cm) from fold. Press fold to one side and stitch buttons down front of shirttail. Set aside.
11. Right sides together, stitch sides and inseam of pants-underpants (template I). Clip curves and turn right side out. Press under ¼″ (0.75 cm) for lower hem. Use a running stitch to hem pants, and place on doll. Tack to doll's waist.
12. Right sides together, stitch side seam of skirt (template J). Press seams open and press under a ¼″ (0.75 cm) hem at bottom (wider end) of skirt. Use a running stitch to hem skirt. Use needle and thread to gather upper skirt and place on doll. Tack skirt to doll's waist.
13. Put sweater on doll, pulling sweater sleeves over cuffs, which are already sewn on doll arms. Tack sleeves in place with thread that matches sweater. Overlap sweater at neck and pin in place.
14. Place shirttail under sweater (one or two layers), over pants or skirt, and pin in place until it looks just right. Tack shirttail and sweater in place, and add many buttons—mismatched, to add a great deal of charm. Place hat on head, pulling it down low to complete the look.

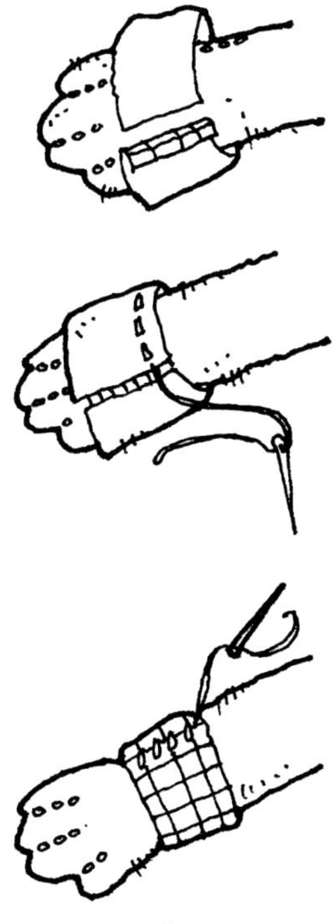

Step 9

Accessories

15. To make heart (template K), place fabric with right sides together and stitch heart, leaving an opening. Clip, turn, and press. Stuff very lightly.
16. Cut a square of muslin and embroider according to template L. Use candlewicking thread or embroidery floss to stitch rectangle to heart, using random stitches. Stitch heart to doll's hands or sweater.

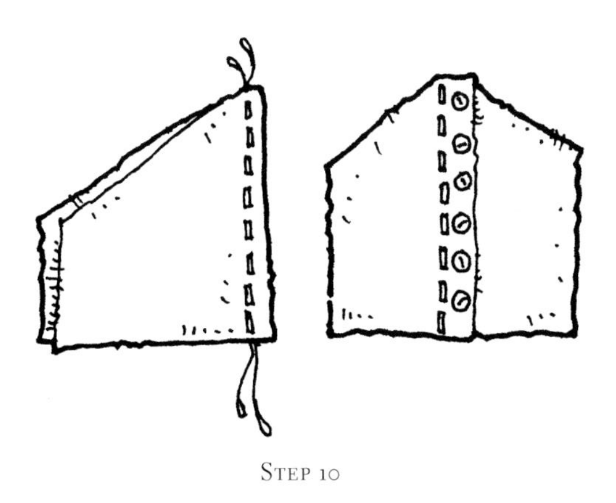

Step 10

Use different colors to create *Sno-Baby*, also made by Annie Moon.

Posey Julia

Posey Julia is a whimsical little creature, half child and half sage, old woman. She makes me think of the wisdom of children, as well as the occasional forays into childhood that adults sometimes take. This is a wonderful doll to touch, as the textures created by the cutting and stitching of handmade felt satisfy our tactile urges.

Posey Julia by Elise Peeples, 1998; 12″ (30 cm).

Supplies

- ¼ yard (25 cm) robe velour in desired flesh tone for doll body
- Stuffing
- 4 flat, 2-hole buttons, ⅝″ (1.8 cm) diameter
- 8 buttons for flowers on hat and dress
- Waxed dental floss or waxed button thread
- 3″ to 5″ (8 cm to 13 cm) long needle
- Brown Micron Pigma permanent marker, size 005
- Artist's colored pencils or fabric paints for coloring face
- Hair: small amount of mohair fiber or yarn
- Perle cotton, embroidery floss, or fine yarn
- Wool roving for felted leggings, shoes, and hat: 1 yard (90 cm) bright pink; ½ yard (45 cm) magenta; ½ yard (45 cm) bright green
- Liquid bath soap
- 12″ (30 cm) from the toe end of nylon pantyhose
- Felted wool sweaters for clothing (choose 100% wool labeled "dry-clean only." Washable wool has been treated not to shrink, so it won't felt.)

Templates on pages 148–151. Use ¼″ (0.75 cm) seam allowance unless otherwise indicated.

Felting Wool Sweaters

To shrink, either boil sweaters in hot water for 1 or 2 hours until felted or wash two or three times in machine on hot with a small amount of soap. When sweaters have felted to your liking, dry on hot in the dryer. Some sweaters are very resistant and take a few tries, others felt faster. When felting more than one sweater, do not mix colors because bleeding sometimes occurs. When dry, shake out lint. Do this outside, away from the house. You now have beautifully patterned and colored felt that can be used just like commercial felt.

The Dollmaker—Elise Peeples

Elise says her dolls are made of cloth because of the accessibility and textural quality of the medium. Her focus is the clothing—rich, unusual fabrics and varied surface design techniques are her special interest. Fairy tales, myths, and goddesses are the inspirations for many of her dolls.

Elise lives in a small town in Washington on one acre of land, which includes an herb garden. Her studio is a small, finished room in her garage. It is filled with dolls, fabrics, beads, lace, ribbons, fresh flowers, pictures, and books. She likes the fact that it is separate from the house and she doesn't have to drive to it, but wishes it were bigger. Professionally, she has several part-time jobs. She makes and sells one-of-a-kind dolls; designs a line of cloth-doll patterns which she sells through a mail-order catalog; and teaches at dollmaking clubs, fabric stores, and conventions.

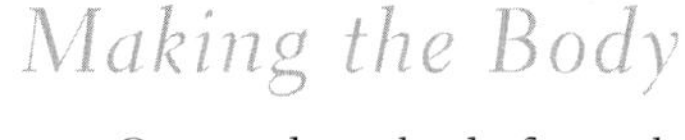

Making the Body

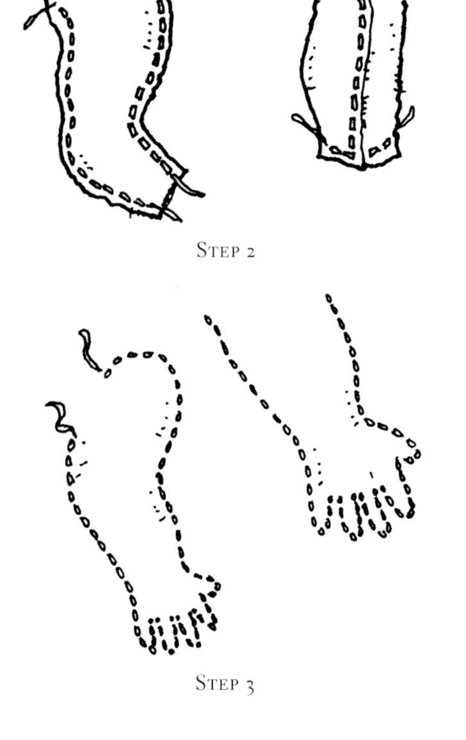

Step 2

Step 3

1. Cut out legs, body front, body back, head front, and head back pieces (templates A to E).
2. Right sides together, stitch legs (template A). Leave open between dots and at toes. Fold toes with raw edges even, matching seams. Stitch across toes, curving seam to make toe area rounded. Turn legs right side out through opening. Stuff firmly, and hand stitch openings closed.
3. Trace arms (template F) on wrong side of fabric. Use a pencil close to fabric in color so line won't show through seams. Do not cut out yet. Stitch just inside traced lines, leaving open between dots. When you stitch around fingers, take two small stitches between each finger so there is room to cut. Cut out arms, leaving a $1/8$" (0.4 cm) or less seam allowance, and turn right side out through opening. Stuff fingers and arms carefully, and hand stitch openings closed.
4. To make darts on body back (template C), fold on center line and sew on dotted line. Cut back opening slash as marked on template. Right sides together, stitch body front (template B) to body back, leaving neck edges open. Turn right side out, stuff firmly, and hand stitch back opening closed.
5. To make head, with right sides of head back pieces (template D) together, stitch center back seam, leaving open between dots. Stitch head front (template E) to head back, matching centers. Turn head right side out, stuff firmly, and hand stitch openings closed. Do not assemble body until you have made felt leggings, shoes, and hat.

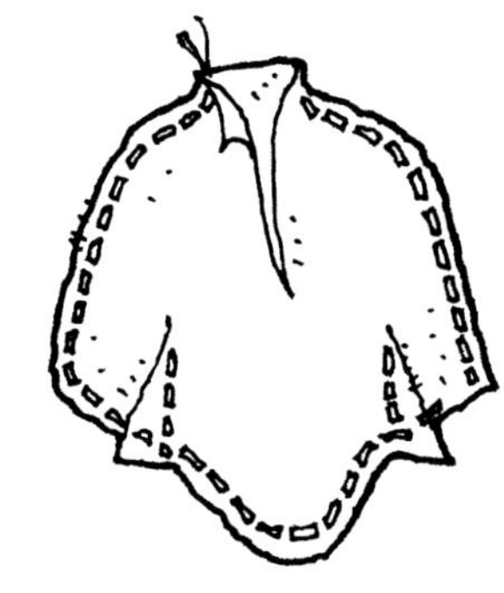

Step 4

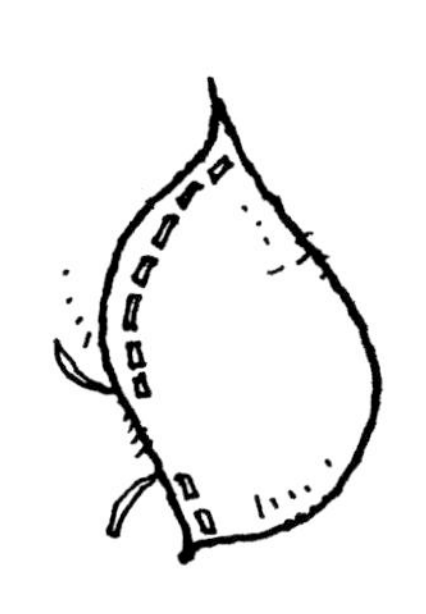

Step 5

Making the Costume

Leggings

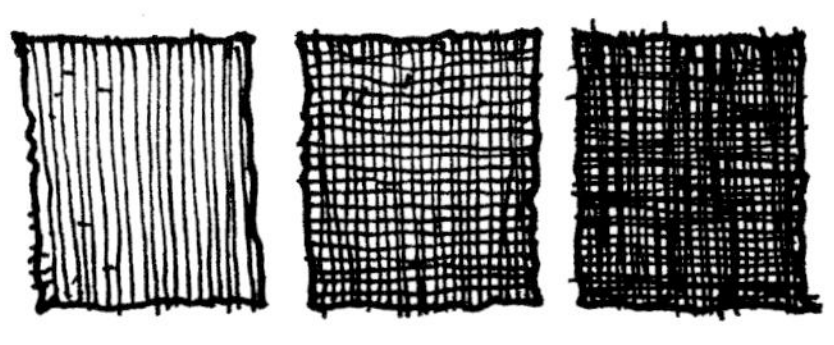

Step 6

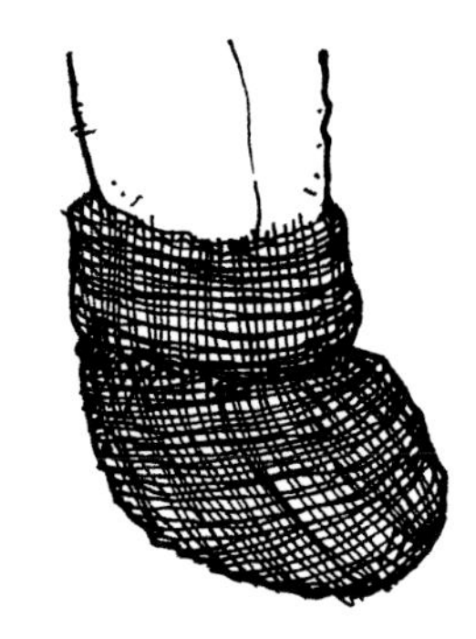

Step 8

6. Draw a rectangle, measuring 8″ × 7″ (20 cm × 18 cm), on paper. Take a 9″ (23 cm) length of pink roving. Pull off wisps of roving and lay out on paper, just overlapping edges. Lay all fibers in same direction. Make a second layer, placing at right angle to first layer. Build up alternating layers of fiber until you have used all 9″ (23 cm).
7. Pull off long, ¾″ (2 cm) wide strips of magenta roving for stripes (save a small amount of magenta to decorate hat). Lay, evenly spaced, across pink roving. Pat layers to press them together.
8. Carefully pick up wool and wrap around one doll leg. Wool should overlap on back about 1″ to 1½″ (2.5 cm to 4 cm). Press wool on leg. Carefully draw pantyhose piece over wool to hold in place and secure with knot or rubber band.
9. Fill small bowl or glass measuring cup with hot water (as hot as you can stand—not boiling). Dip leg in water and squeeze gently to saturate leg. Remove from bowl and gently squeeze out extra water. Put about ½ teaspoon (2.5 ml) of liquid soap in your palm, rub hands together to spread soap. Begin to massage soap very gently into wool using a squeezing motion. When you feel wool is saturated with soap, begin to massage in a gently circular motion, working over whole surface of wool. Continue for about a minute. Untie pantyhose and check to see whether wool is holding together. If it is still very wispy, replace pantyhose and massage for another minute. Carefully remove pantyhose from leg. Add more hot water if wool feels dry. Continue rubbing and massaging leg until wool shrinks to fit leg—about 10 to 15 minutes.
10. Rinse leg under warm running water to remove as much soap as possible. Squeeze out as much water as you can. Let leg dry. You can put it in a clothes dryer with a bath towel on medium hot for 30 to 40 minutes or until dry. When dry, check that seam up back hasn't shrunk apart. If it has, pull edges together and hand stitch.
11. Repeat Steps 6 to 10 for other leg.

Shoes

12. Divide green wool lengthwise into two pieces. Pull off thin strips, smoothing out to a flat "ribbon" of wool. Wrap around doll's foot. Keep wrapping, overlapping wool, until foot is completely covered and you have used all pieces of wool. Be sure to vary direction of wool as you overlap, so that direction of fibers changes—rather like winding a ball of yarn. Use extra wool in toe area if you want to make a turned-up toe. Carefully cover foot with toe of nylon pantyhose, securing with rubber band.
13. Felt wool following Steps 9 to 10. To shape turned-up toe, draw out a point of felt and shape as desired. Keep in mind that felt shrinks where you rub it most. Rinse. Squeeze out extra water and reshape toe. If you put leg back in dryer, toe will lose its pointed shape and become more rounded.

Hat

14. Wrap head with wisps of other piece of pink wool, building layers of alternating fiber direction. Wrap around some of front, but don't cover too much of face. When pink wool is used up, pull off thin strips of reserved magenta

wool. Wrap around your finger to form rings and position rings on hat, pressing them into pink wool.

15. Carefully cover hat with pantyhose and follow felting instructions in Steps 9 to 10. When hat is dry, trim edges to frame face. Decorate edge with buttonhole stitch, using a medium-fine perle cotton, embroidery floss, or fine yarn.

Creating the Face

16. Carefully remove hat from head. Draw face on head front, using brown Micron pen. Color in eyes, lips, and cheeks with either artist's colored pencils or fabric paints.
17. To add dimension to face, thread long needle with strong thread that matches skin tone of doll. Knot thread and insert needle into head from back. Take a small stitch to lock knot. Bring needle out at outer corner of one eye. Reinsert needle very close to exit point, go deep, behind stuffing, and come out at outer corner of mouth. With your fingers, gently squeeze two points and pull up thread to tighten. Reinsert needle very close to exit point, going deep beneath stuffing, and exit at inner corner of same eye. Squeeze two points and pull up thread to tighten. Retrace your stitches (inner eye corner to mouth to outer eye corner) and finally back through back of head. Take a few small stitches to lock thread, and cut. Repeat for other eye.
18. Stitch and glue three wisps of mohair or yarn to center front of doll's head, where it will be tucked just under front of hat. Cut five flowers from contrasting colored felted sweater. Sew to hat with buttons in center of each flower. Replace hat on head, and hand stitch in place.

Step 16

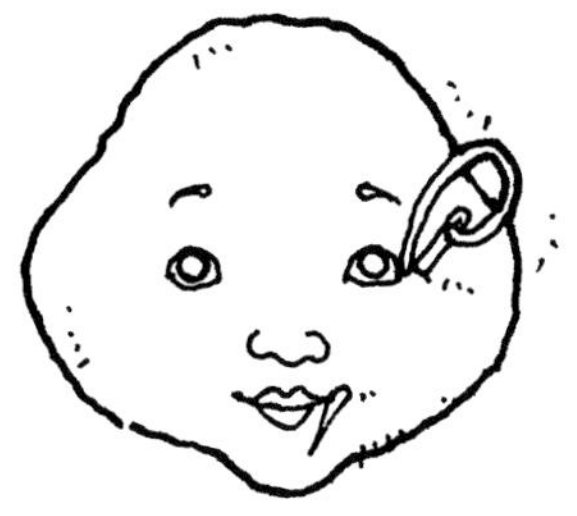

Step 17

Step 18

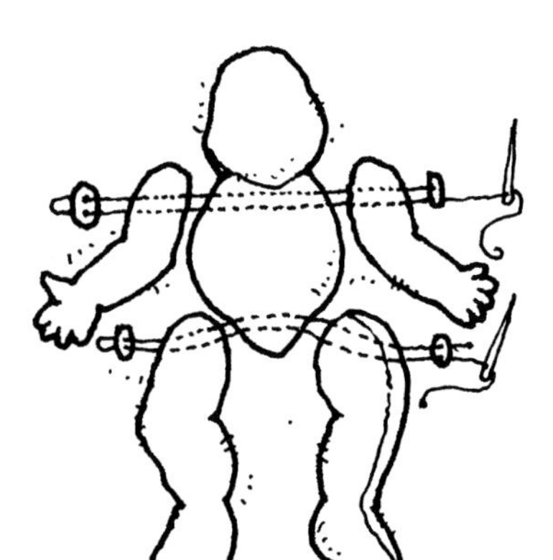

Step 20

Assembling the Doll

19. By hand, sew head to neck of body. When you position head, tilt it slightly to one side for a charming look.
20. Thread a long needle with two strands of waxed dental floss, double floss, and tie a knot in end. Hold arms up to body to determine best position. String arms to body by taking needle through arm, body (just behind side seam), through second arm, and one 2-hole button. Reverse direction, back through other hole of button, arm, body, and other arm, and through first hole in second button. Pull floss very tight, compressing arms and body (working with a buddy on this step is helpful). Tie a knot, cut off ends, and repeat for legs.

Costuming the Doll

21. Cut bloomers (template G) from felted sweater. With right sides together, stitch center front and center back seams. With right sides together, stitch leg seam, matching center seams. Turn right side out, and decorate edges with buttonhole embroidery.

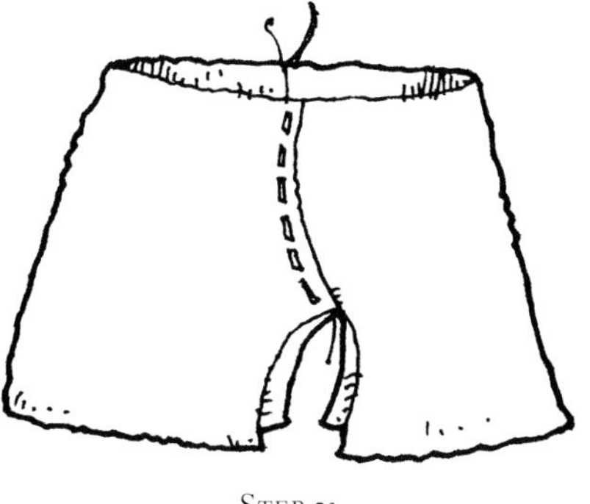

Step 21

Step 22

22. Use a needle and thread to gather legs 1″ (2.5 cm) from embroidered edges, using floss, perle cotton, or yarn. Gather waist edge, put bloomers on doll, and pull gathers to fit doll's waist. Tie thread around waist, pull up leg gathers, and tie.
23. Cut dress front and back (template H) and two sleeves (template I) from one sweater. Cut collar (template J) and two cuffs (template K) from contrasting color. With right sides together, stitch shoulder seams. Cut a back opening as marked on template. Finish outer edges of collar and cuffs with buttonhole embroidery.
24. Gather upper edges and, with right sides together, pin collar to neck and cuffs to sleeve edges, pulling up gathers to fit. Stitch, then zigzag over seam. Fold seam to inside and topstitch.
25. With right sides together, stitch side seams. Finish lower edge of dress with buttonhole embroidery. Cut three flower shapes and three leaf shapes as you desire from contrasting felted sweater, and stitch leaves to front of dress. Stitch flowers centered over leaves. Stitch a button at center of each flower.
26. Put dress on doll and sew up center back seam. If you want clothes to be removable, sew elastic to waist and leg edges of bloomers and a snap to back edge of dress.

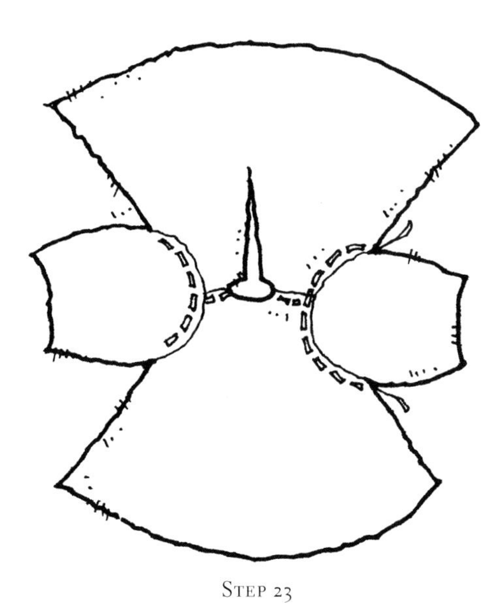

Step 23

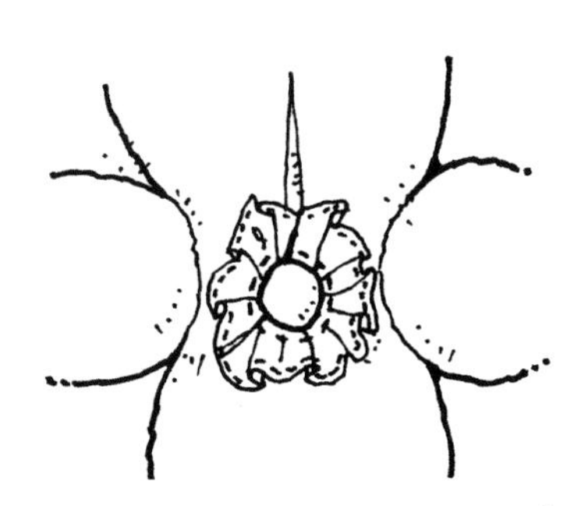

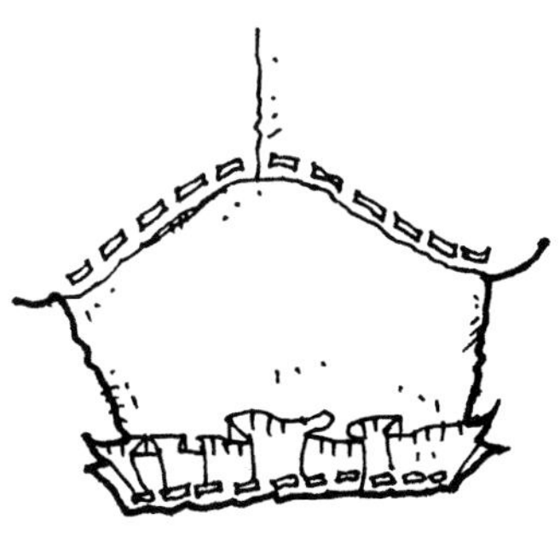

Step 24

Vasalissa's Doll

The discovery of the story of Vasalissa, in the book *Women Who Run with the Wolves*, by Clarissa Pinkola Estes, Ph.D., opened up new avenues of dollmaking for Sue McFadden—that of story. *Vasalissa's Doll* has a wonderful felt body, including a face that uses a Paper Clay mask underneath.

Vasalissa's Doll by Sue McFadden, 1995; 12" (30 cm); felt and Paper Clay®.

Supplies

- 8 oz. Paper Clay
- 2" (5 cm) Styrofoam egg (pitted surface, not smooth)
- Quilter's thread, upholstery thread, carpet thread, or dental floss
- ½" (1.5 cm) button
- 6½" × 8½" (16.5 cm × 22 cm) felt for head
- 18" × 18" (45 cm × 45 cm) felt for body
- Textile medium
- Acrylic paints for eyes, lips, and shoes
- Acrylic varnish
- Stuffing
- Buttons—2½" and 2⅝" (6.5 cm and 7 cm)
- ¼ yard (25 cm) fabric for blouse-underwear, plus felt scraps for blouse sleeves
- ¼ yard (25 cm) fabric for jumper, plus felt scraps for jumper trim
- ⅔ yard (60 cm) ribbon/trim, ⅝" (1.8 cm) width
- Crewel yarn or embroidery floss
- 1½" × 6" (4 cm × 15 cm) scrap of tulle
- Button or snap for jumper back
- Small amount of crushed pastel crayon (blush)
- Fake fur or mohair fur for wig, 4" × 4" (10 cm × 10 cm)
- Sandpaper
- Air-vanishing marker
- Sharp crafts knife
- Pipe cleaners
- Plastic wrap, plastic knife, and plastic mat
- #0 fine-point artist's brush
- #4 flat or filbert artist's brush

Templates on pages 152–155. Use ¼" (0.75 cm) seam allowance unless otherwise indicated.

The Dollmaker– Sue McFadden

Sue's dolls are constructed and primarily made of Paper Clay and felt. They reflect the expertise gained from a background in studies of portraiture, drawing, painting, and fiber arts. Currently, Sue has finished her home studio, called Daedalus Studio, where she displays her illustrations and bits and pieces of nature to inspire her work. Her fabric collection is displayed on open shelves and is readily accessible. Her favorite feature is the natural light that reflects off the cream-colored walls and floors. The room is filled with all her books and dollmaking supplies, as well as her treasures. If you make this doll, Sue asks that you tag it with the pattern name, *Vasalissa's Doll*, © 1995 by Sue McFadden, along with your signature and the date.

If you do not want to make your own mask, you can use a porcelain-doll mold. Just remember to sprinkle talcum powder inside first, roll Paper Clay out into a round shape, and press into front half of face mold. Allow Paper Clay to dry until it is leather hard, and remove from plaster mold. When clay is dry, sand it a little to remove any roughness. Move on to Step 7.

Making the Head

1. Prepare Styrofoam egg for sculpting by marking features with a felt-tip pen. Draw a line down center front, and a second line from side to side. Smaller tip of egg forms chin. Gently press in eye socket areas with finger. Dip egg into water. This prepares Styrofoam to bond with Paper Clay.
2. Place a piece of plastic wrap over a ball of Paper Clay. Gently roll out clay to a ¼" (0.75 cm) thickness on a plastic mat. Peel plastic wrap away. With plastic knife, carefully remove clay from mat.
3. Wrap Paper Clay around wet Styrofoam head form. Gently press clay into Styrofoam. Pinch off excess clay and smooth ragged edges with fingertips dipped in water.
4. Thread ½" (1.5 cm) button with a 20" (50 cm) length of carpet thread. Pull two thread ends together. Knot thread behind button and again at bottom ends of thread. Push button into bottom of head (the neck area). Allow thread to dangle. Roll out a small piece of Paper Clay. Wrap around dangling thread at base of head. This forms neck. Gently smooth clay into head area. Use water to smooth, if necessary.
5. Add pieces of Paper Clay to build up face. Always moisten surface of clay before adding new clay. Use a slab of clay for forehead and crown of head, and rolled cylinders or balls for nose, chin, cheeks, and so on. Form forehead, nose, cheeks, lips, and chin. Smooth forms together and set head aside to dry.
6. When clay head is completely dry, it is ready to be refined. At this stage, you can sand or carve areas to smooth them, and define nostrils with a sharp crafts

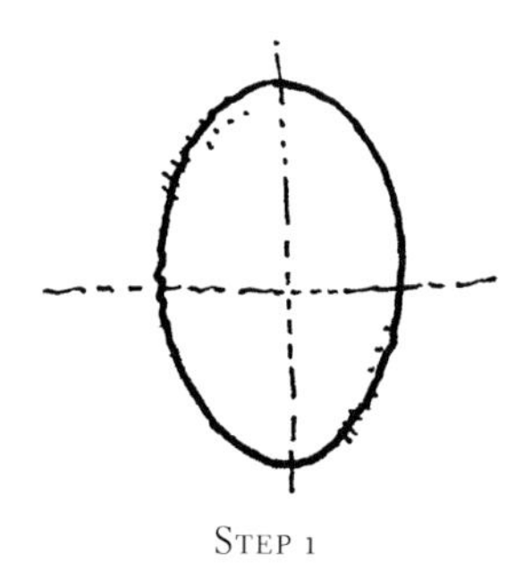

Step 1

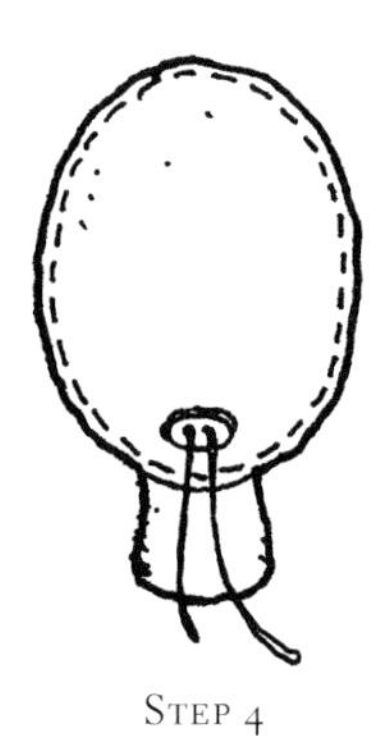

Step 4

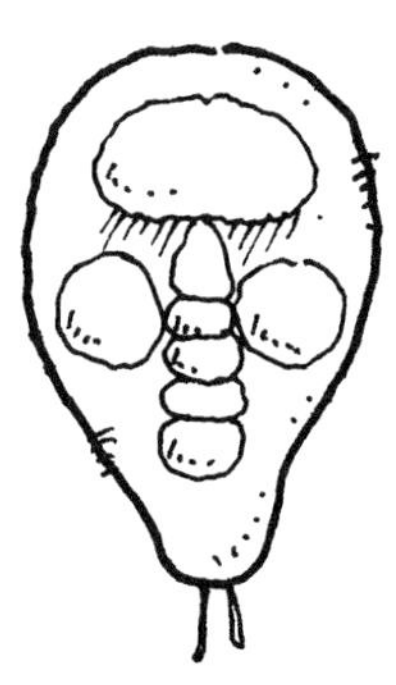

Step 5

knife. More clay can be added to fill in low areas—just wet dry clay with a damp finger before applying more. Let dry thoroughly.

7. With a glue brush, apply a *thin* layer of thick craft glue over throat area. Cut 6½″ × 8½″ (16.5 cm × 22 cm) piece of felt so dominant stretch runs along longer side. Fold in half, then in half again to find center. Position center point over nose. Hold in place with one hand. With your other hand, carefully smooth felt into throat area. Peel back felt and apply glue to mouth area, smoothing and shape felt into mouth area, then nose and eye areas. Glue felt in this way and in sequence shown, allowing it to dry for about 5 minutes after each area is covered.

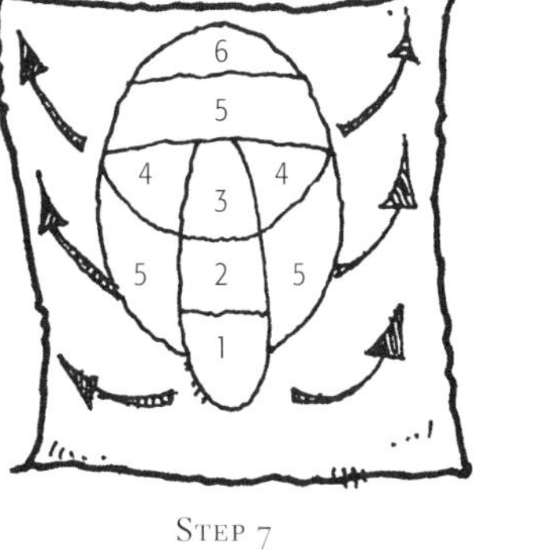
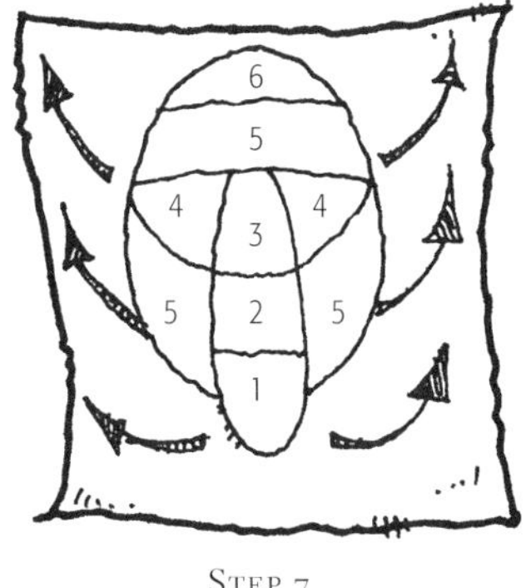

Step 7

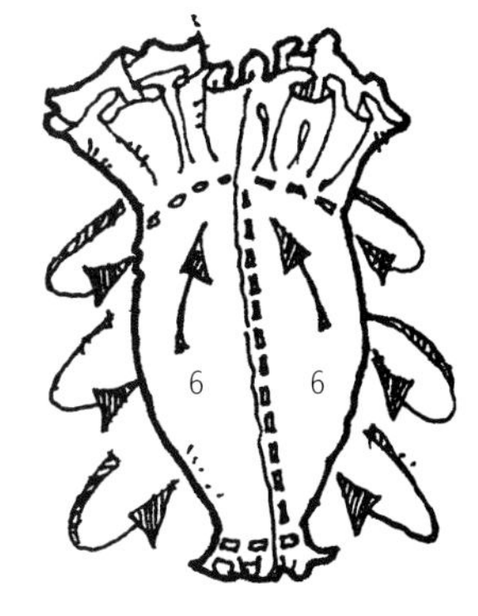

Step 8

8. Continue gluing felt to clay head around to back. Lightly pencil a line down center back of head. Cut off felt on one side even with pencil line. Allow second side to overlap and glue in place. Trim off excess felt around bottom of neck, being careful not to accidentally cut off neck strings.
9. Trace ear piece (template A) on felt with vanishing marker. Stitch very close to edge and cut apart to make two ears. Glue ears in their natural position on side of head by first arranging them backward, gluing only tab. Let dry completely, flip ears back into their natural position, and glue flat to side of head. Pin in position until completely dry, then remove pins.

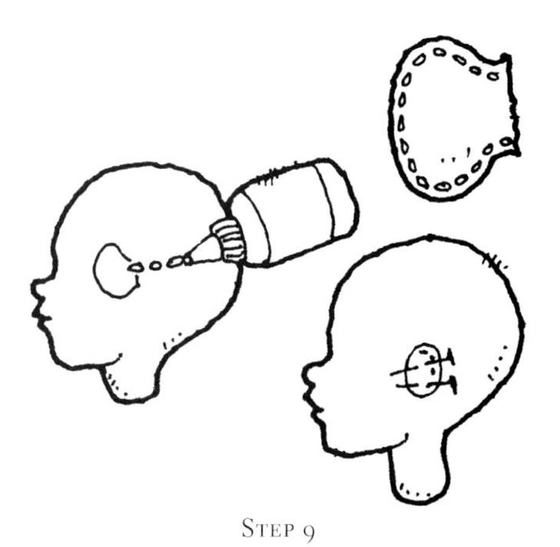

Step 9

Creating the Face

10. Use vanishing marker to outline eyebrows, eyes, and lips according to diagram.
11. Use paintbrush to apply textile medium to eye and lip areas. Push any short fibers back into textile medium to keep surface as smooth as possible. When areas are dry, snip off any stray fibers.
12. Paint lips with desired color. Use small brush to paint circular iris area. Allow to dry, then paint in pupil with black or a very dark gray. Carefully dot in eyelid and lash line. Add white highlights in both eyes.
13. Allow facial features to dry. Brush a layer of varnish over eyes and lips. Use powdered, crushed pastel crayon for cheek color. Apply very lightly with a brush.

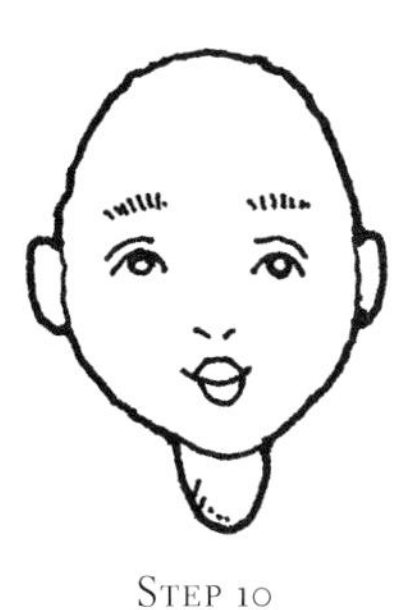

Step 10

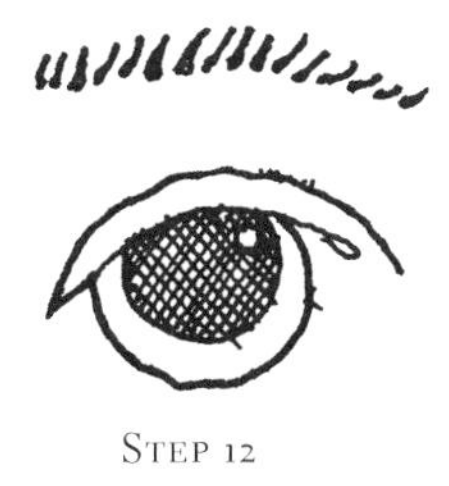

Step 12

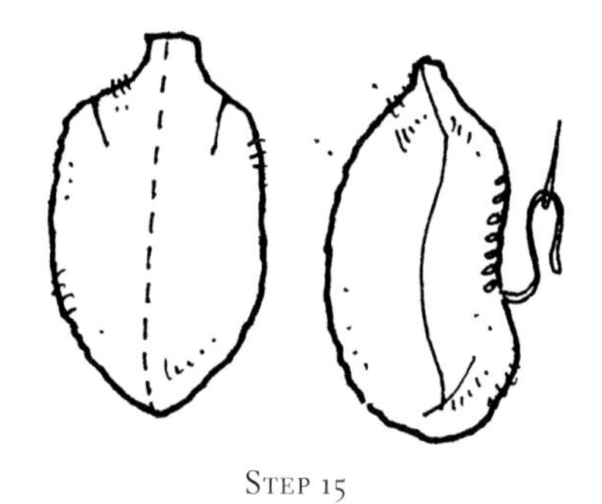

Step 15

Step 16

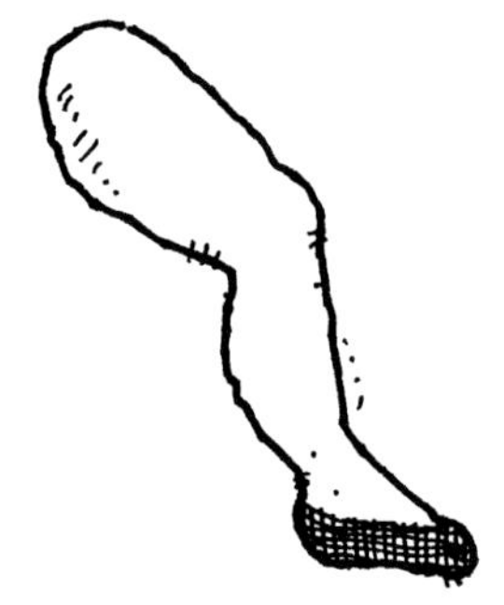

Step 17

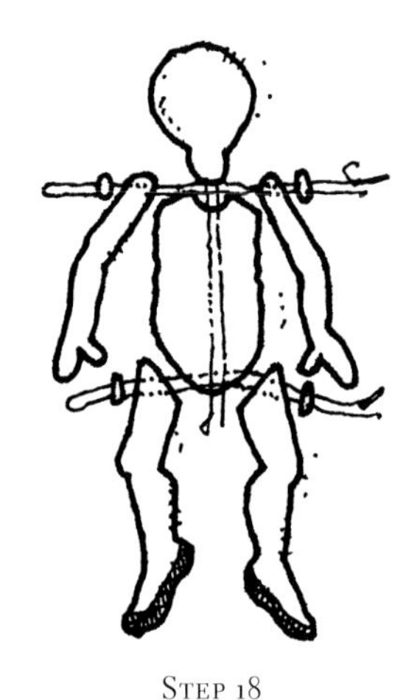

Step 18

Making the Body

14. Cut body pieces (templates B to G) from felt. Stay-stitch each piece to minimize stretch.
15. Sew top and bottom darts on four body pieces (templates B and C). Right sides together, stitch center seams of front body (template B). Repeat for back body pieces (template C), leaving an opening as indicated. With front and back body pieces right sides together, stitch around entire perimeter. Turn completed body right side out through back opening. Stuff firmly and ladder-stitch opening closed.
16. With vanishing marker, outline hands on felt arms (templates D and E). Carefully sew around arms, hands, and fingers with machine set for very small stitches, starting and stopping at opening indicated. Trim seam allowance close to stitching, being careful around fingers. Do not turn right side out. Carefully insert pipe cleaners into fingers and gently stuff hands and arms, making as firm as possible without bursting seams. Insert tiny amounts of stuffing at a time. When stuffing is complete, stitch opening closed.
17. Stitch legs (templates F and G) in same manner as arms. Turn right side out and stuff. Stitch opening closed. Outline shoe on foot with vanishing marker. Brush on textile medium, allow to dry, then clip stray fibers. Use acrylic paint to paint shoes desired color. Allow to dry, then apply a layer of varnish.
18. To assemble body, push neck shape into body piece. Thread head threads on a large needle, and insert needle from tip of inverted neck to crotch of body. Pull thread and head snugly into body. Backstitch and knot neck cord at crotch. Arms and legs are button jointed and hand stitched to body with upholstery thread. Use large dollmaking needle to go back and forth through arms, with buttons on outside. Repeat for legs.

Costuming the Doll

19. Cut out clothing (templates H to N).
20. To prepare blouse sleeves (template H), cut two pieces of felt measuring ¾″ × 4¾″ (2 cm × 12 cm) each, and pink or scallop edges. To embellish, machine appliqué or embroider felt, or decorate with ribbon or lace.
21. Right sides together, stitch center seam in blouse front (template I) from shoulder to crotch. Clip curves, press open, and stitch hem at top front opening. Repeat with blouse back (template J), but do not hem.
22. Right sides together, sew sleeves to front pieces, then to back pieces. Press seams open.
23. Fold back to front with right sides together. Stitch side seams, from sleeve edges to bottom of leg. Stitch inseam and clip center. Turn right side out.
24. Turn under a hem on each sleeve and gather by hand, using embroidery floss or crewel yarn. Leave enough floss so you can gather hems and tie them to fit doll. Repeat for neck and legs. Dress doll in blouse-underwear. Tie floss in bows.
25. Pin trim to center line of front jumper panel (template K) and stitch in place. Place tulle piece on right side, and sew a seam on bottom of panel. Turn and press. Baste side and top seams of tulle to back of panel.
26. With right sides together, sew back seam of two side jumper pieces (template L) together. Start at dot and sew to bottom. Turn and hem edges of top opening. Press seam open.

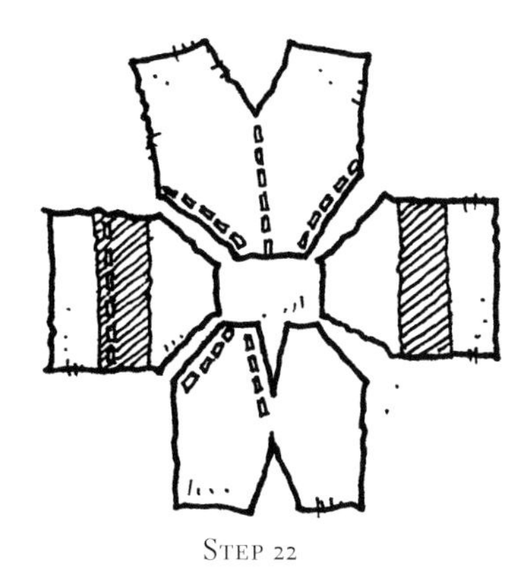

Step 22

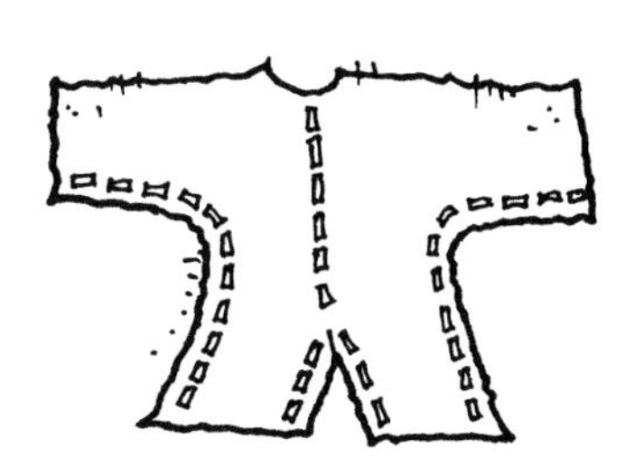

Step 23

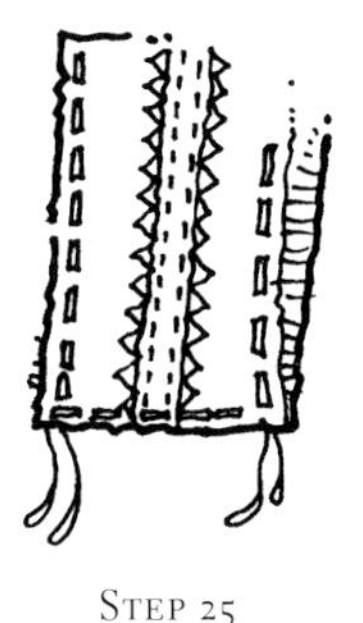

Step 25

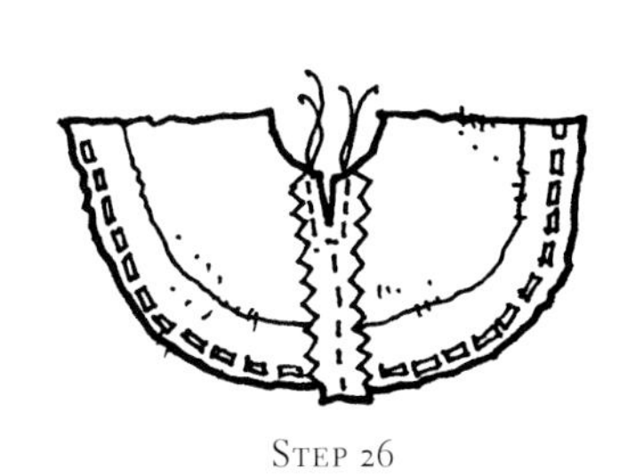

Step 26

27. Stitch back of two felt jumper bottom trim pieces (template M) together. Trim seam allowance and press seam open. Matching back seams, place right side of lower jumper trim on wrong side of lower jumper skirt. Stitch along bottom edge and trim seam allowance. Turn trim to right side of lower skirt and carefully press in place. Machine embroider or hand embroider a decorative edge at top of trim to attach to skirt. Sew front sides of jumper to sides of front jumper panel. Trim and press seams open.

Step 27

28. Cut one felt top band, 1¼″ × 7″ (3.2 cm × 18 cm). Fold band in half, lengthwise. Stitch both ends, then turn, press, and baste open edges. Center and pin to top side of jumper. Sew top seam and turn felt band upward. Gently press. Cut two felt shoulder straps, 1″ × 4″ (2.5 cm × 10 cm). Position straps in half lengthwise. Stitch long edges together, trim and press with seam in center of band on side that will be facing doll.

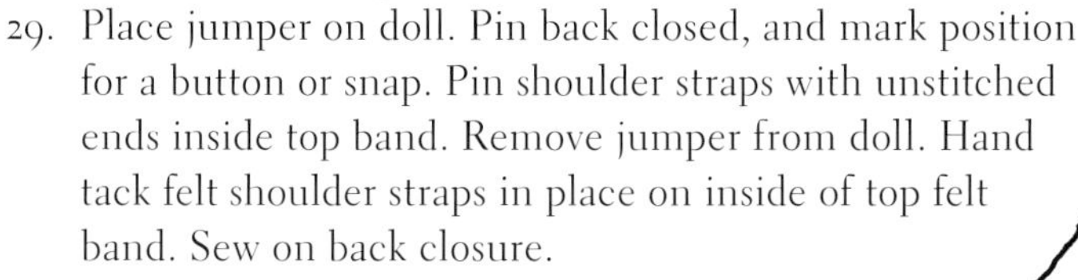

29. Place jumper on doll. Pin back closed, and mark position for a button or snap. Pin shoulder straps with unstitched ends inside top band. Remove jumper from doll. Hand tack felt shoulder straps in place on inside of top felt band. Sew on back closure.
30. Fold scarf piece (template N) in half to form a triangle, right sides facing. Sew side seams and leave an opening (between dots). Turn scarf right side out. Press and stitch opening closed. Center a ⅝″ × 24″ (1.8 cm × 60 cm) ribbon on top side of scarf as indicated on template. Topstitch ribbon to scarf.

Step 28

Making the Wig

31. Note direction of fur, and pin template O to it. Cut out wig pieces, being careful not to snip off long fibers. Fit wig over doll's head, wrong side out, and baste darts to fit doll's head. Remove wig, and machine stitch darts. Wig should fit around ears. Clip out excess fur base in this area, if needed. Apply thin layer of tacky glue around entire inside edge of wig. Carefully place wig in position on doll's head. If there are gaps, secure with a pin until dry. Allow wig to dry thoroughly. Comb hair to desired position. If back of wig is pushing forward, gently comb down and steam press in new direction. Tie scarf on doll's head.

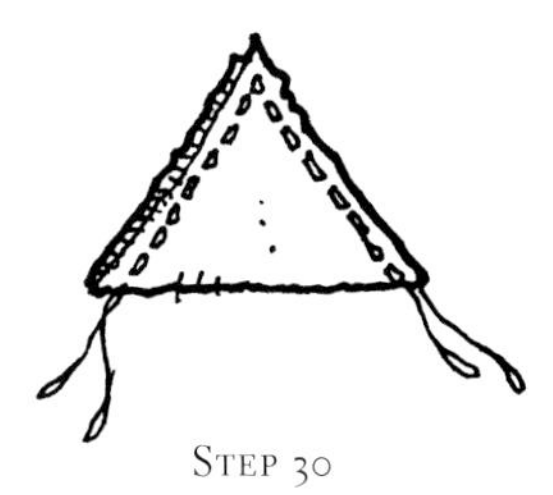

Step 30

Whimsical Personage

Barbara Chapman's dolls always have a bit of the magical and exotic. It is easy to imagine *Whimsical Personage* coming to life in a fairyland deep in the jungles of India. The doll is wearing an antique needlework vest from Uzbekistan and Missoni stockings from Italy. The tassels are from Pakistan, and the lower vest from India.

Whimsical Personage by Barbara Chapman, 1998; 23" (58 cm).

Supplies

- 1 yard (90 cm) quilt batting, 1" (2.5 cm) thick
- 1/4 yard (25 cm) muslin
- Thin yarn such as chenille or ribbon for hands
- Novelty yarn or doll hair for hair
- Florist's wire to make hands (any thin size)
- 6" (15 cm) Styrofoam cone
- 15" (38 cm) strong vinyl-coated wire, such as a coat hanger
- 2 1/2 yards (225 cm) 12-gauge solid-copper electrical wire
- Stuffing
- Acrylic paints (white, plus your choice for the face)
- 1/4 yard (25 cm) fabric for legs
- 1/3 yard (30 cm) fabric for tunic
- 1/4 yard (25 cm) fabric for hat
- 1/2 yard (45 cm) fabric for pants
- Scraps of fabric for vest, boots, and ball
- 1/8 yard (12 cm) of fabric for sleeves
- Assorted trims, buttons, beads, etc.
- Styrofoam ball, about 3" or 4" (8 cm or 10 cm)
- Wire cutters
- Long dollmaking needle
- Small paint brush (size 00)
- Medium-size paint brush

Templates on pages 156–157. Use 1/4" (0.75 cm) seam allowance unless otherwise indicated.

Barbara recommends a stretchy fabric for legs and arms. Stretch velvet is very easy to whip together. For the vest, a textured material, such as upholstery fabric or an old piece of needlepoint or patchwork, works well. Avoid using fabric that frays easily for legs, because it must be pulled tightly over batting. You may wish to exaggerate any feature, finger length, arms, or legs to make your personage more whimsical. The face may be painted in skin tones, if you prefer.

The Dollmaker—Barbara Chapman

elinor peace bailey once described Barbara Chapman's dollmaking as "a link with an ancient mind." Those who have visited her home and seen the exquisite treasures from the Far East, Africa, and other faraway places that decorate it will agree. Barbara's love for art is apparent when you meet her dolls—fairies, magicians, and other fantasy folk who inhabit our daydreams. Barbara imbues her many students with this same sense of magic, as she teaches how to wind yarn around wire to create fingers, arms, and legs, and opens her treasure box to allow her students to choose just the right scrap of silk to add to their own fairy dolls.

Making the Head and Face

1. Trace head (template A) on doubled muslin. Do not cut yet. Machine stitch on lines, leaving back of head and neck bottom open. Trim to ⅛" (0.4 cm) from stitching lines, and turn right side out. Stuff head and neck firmly. To keep stuffing from coming out of neck, gather open end of neck about ⅛" (0.4 cm) from raw edge and pull, leaving just a small opening for coat-hanger wire to be inserted.
2. To sculpt nose, use quilting thread and dollmaking needle, and insert into ear area at side of head. Exit at bottom of nose and make a small stitch in fabric to secure thread. Go back and forth, from one side of nose to the other, following dotted line on template. Start at bottom of nose, and make sure needle goes under some stuffing as you sculpt to make nose as firm as possible.
3. When you get to top of nose, bring thread out one corner of mouth. Take a long stitch to other corner of mouth and pull gently to indent. Exit needle out opposite ear area and knot off.
4. In a small, coated paper plate, mix equal portions of white glue and water. Brush over entire face and neck. Allow head to dry well (3 to 4 hours).
5. Paint head any colors you like. Add flesh tones to opaque white and paint eye shape. Eye pattern may be enlarged or reduced to express your own ideas. Use tiny brush to outline eye and fill in iris. When dry, use opaque white to add tiny "sparkle" dots at ten o'clock and two o'clock on each iris. Set head aside.

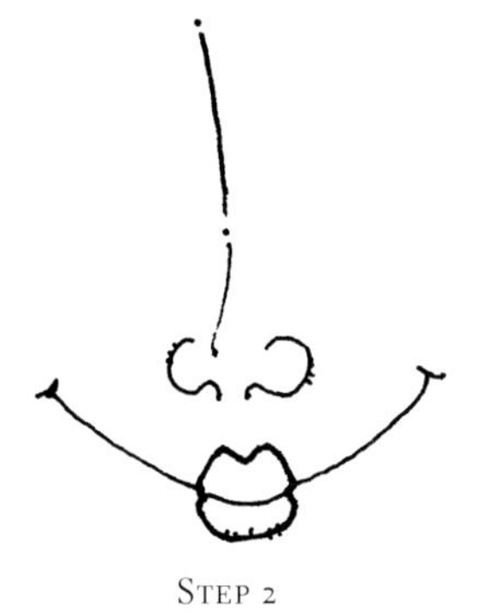

Step 2

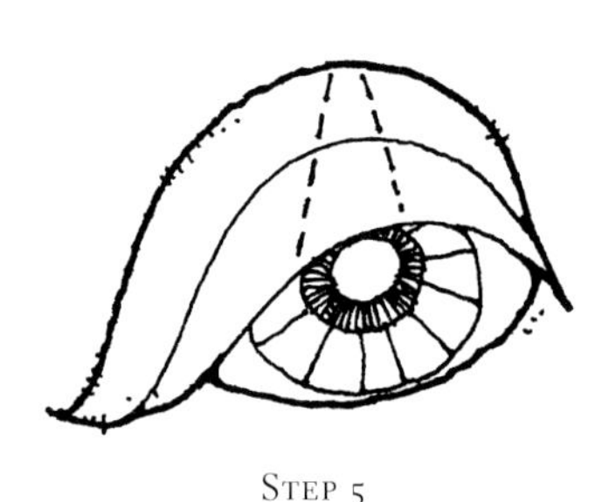

Step 5

Making the Body

6. Cut a 25″ (63.5 cm) length of florist's wire. Leave a long tail of about 12″ (30 cm), and bring wire up to form a bend to make tip of little finger. Continue bending wire to form four fingers. Drop down a little bit to form thumb. Look at your own hand for reference. When you finish forming fingers, wrap wire end around little finger side of hand and twist wires together. Add more wire to wrap between each finger and around palm of hand to stabilize fingers. Try to keep from pulling palm together and making hand too narrow. Do not cut 12″ (30 cm) length of wire that extends from hand. Repeat to make other hand.
7. Wind a piece of yarn through loop near end of little finger several times. Slide wrappings up to tip of finger and pinch wire together. This will help to prevent rest of yarn from slipping off ends of fingers. Wrap over both wires of finger, working from tip to palm. Cut yarn and tie at wrist. Ends will be covered with yarn when you wrap palm and wrist. Repeat same process for all remaining fingers and thumb. Wrap yarn over palm until covered. Work toward wrist, cover, knot yarn off, and set hand aside. Make sure hands are large enough. If not, simply wind more yarn until they are the size you want.
8. To create body, cut a piece of 12-gauge electrical wire about 40″ (100 cm) long. Wrap wire around base of Styrofoam cone. Wire will be twisted in back and ends will stick straight out to side for legs. Remove wire from cone.
9. Cut quilt batting in strips ½″ (1.5 cm) wide. Starting at end of wire (the foot area), bend and pinch ½″ (1.5 cm) of wire to catch batting so it won't slip around as you wrap leg. Wrap wire tightly with batting, working up leg. Add more wrapping to form calf and thigh area. Use a needle and quilting thread to stitch batting to keep it from slipping. A small ball may be sewn on for kneecap. Wrap leg up to area where leg meets loop of wire, but do not cover loop. Continue to stitch more layers of batting to leg until it feels firm.
10. When leg is finished, lay it on a piece of fabric and cut fabric ½″ (1.5 cm) larger than circumference of leg, plus enough to cover upper thigh. Pull

Step 6

Step 7

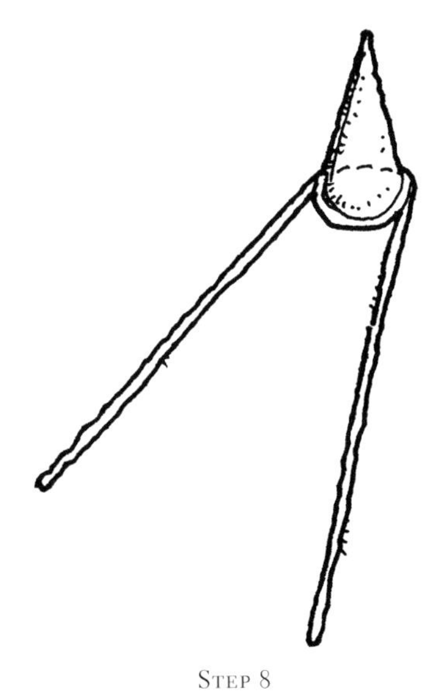

Step 8

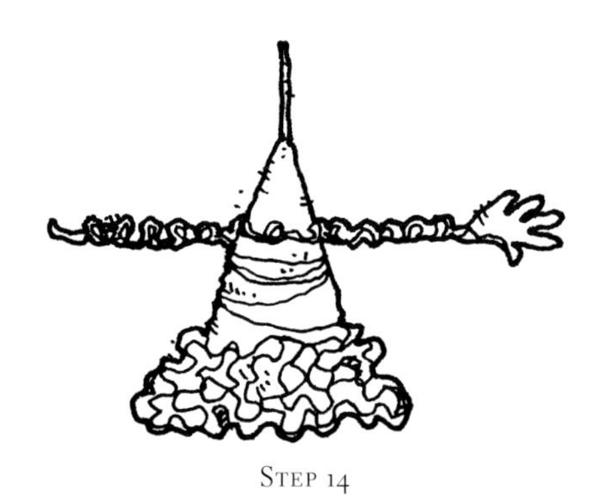

Step 14

Step 17

fabric tightly over leg to cover it, forming a seam down back of leg. Fold under one raw edge of fabric, overlapping it on other edge. Fabric should be form-fitting. Stitch back seam with needle and thread. Turn raw edges of toes inward and stitch together.

11. Slip wire loop back on cone. Cut strips of batting about 6″ × 10″ (15 cm × 25 cm) and insert through leg area and over lower body (base of cone). Tack in place with needle and thread.
12. Cut a piece of fabric about 8″ × 15″ (20 cm × 38m) and cover batting you just attached plus hips. Stitch to legs all around and to batting up to waist.
13. Wrap batting strips tightly from waist up to about 1″ (2.5 cm) from top of cone.
14. Cut about 1 yard (90 cm) 12-gauge wire and wrap around cone, near top, bringing ends out to sides for arms. To gauge length of arms, pull out about 2″ (5 cm) from each side of cone top and bend wire downward (for shoulders). Cut ends of wire about 2″ (5 cm) above center thigh.
15. With thumb side of hand close to body, wrap long wire extending from wrist to shoulder. Wrap florist's wire over hand at wrist, and bring up to shoulder area. Wrap tightly.
16. Insert straight 15″ (38 cm) length of coat-hanger wire straight down through cone with extra length at top.
17. Starting at wrist, wrap batting tightly over arm wires to shoulders. Shape shoulders with extra batting. Wrap around protruding wire for chest. Stitch batting in place with quilting thread.

Costuming and Assembling the Doll

18. Cut tunic fabric 8″ × 16″ (20 cm × 40 cm) or wide enough to fit over upper body. Fold in half lengthwise, and cut a small hole in center. Insert vertical wire through hole. Pull fabric down firmly over torso and trim to desired length. Turn under raw edges; stitch to waist area and up sides.
19. Place arm on fabric of choice and use same process as for covering legs (see Step 10). Stitch fabric to shoulders.
20. Attach head by pushing vertical wire into head. Twist head back and forth to push wire through stuffing. Pull head down firmly, and stitch neck to tunic. If wire is too long, you may either clip so it is at top of head, or allow it to pierce head fabric and use pliers to bend it down at top of head.
21. Hair fiber may be sewn or glued to doll, or tucked under edge of a hat. Make small figure eights of yarn and stitch next to each other. You may cover entire head or just around edge to frame face.
22. To make hat, cut out template B from fabric and fold in half with right sides together. Stitch together with seam at back. Stuff hat with polyester stuffing or excess batting strips, and stitch to doll's head. If you wish tip to bend backward, stuff hat lightly at end and weight with a bell or tassel.
23. To make puff sleeve, cut two pieces of fabric about 5″ × 15″ (13 cm × 38 cm). Place right sides together and stitch two short sides together to form tube. Use a running stitch to gather both edges and slip over arm. Before sewing to arm,

you may wish to stuff sleeve lightly for a more structured look, or you may leave it plain for a softer look.

24. Balloon pants are made the same way, using two pieces of fabric measuring 6″ × 20″ (15 cm × 50 cm). Either sleeves or pants can be made with more slender tubes if that suits your fabric better.
25. A simple vest can be made by cutting two strips of interesting textured fabric. Upholstery remnants work very well. Cut fabric to measure from desired shoulder extension to center back. Sew at center back. Trim front and perhaps lower edge. Crochet an edging or add braid.
26. Add any embellishments—such as buttons, beads, tassels, bells, and so on—to hat, vest, or pants.
27. Boots are made by bending bottom of leg into a foot. Lay on paper and draw around foot. Cut paper to include a ¼″ (0.75 cm) seam allowance. (You may want to stitch one boot together using muslin, rather than experimenting on a piece of expensive fabric.) Stuff boot a little, then trace outline of bottom of foot on a piece of paper. Cut out paper pattern, then cut out two boot soles from fabric. Stitch soles to bottom of boot, then place on doll's foot. Add or remove stuffing to ensure proper fit.
28. To make ball, begin with Styrofoam ball, about 3″ or 4″ (8 cm or 10 cm) in diameter. Glue scraps of fabric to ball and wrap with a variety of threads and thin yarns. Do final wrap with decorative yarn or ribbon and add ornaments such as shells, jewels, or appliqués. Stitch hands to wrappings on ball.

The Maid Was in the Garden

Inspired by the nursery rhyme "Sing a Song of Sixpence," this doll looks as though she has just stepped out of a storybook. Designed to be viewed from the front, you will notice that she has unusually shaped arms, hands, and legs. Skinny little dolls require more care and patience, so read all directions carefully. The extra effort will reward you with a well-made, dainty doll.

The Maid Was in the Garden by Betts Vidal, 1992; 13½″ (34 cm).

Supplies

- ⅛ yard (12 cm) flesh-colored fabric for face and hands
- ½ yard (45 cm) small-scale black print fabric for doll's arms and dress
- ½ yard (45 cm) white batiste for petticoat, apron, pantaloons, legs, and bow
- Narrow lace for edge of petticoat
- ⅔ yard (60 cm) of white 2″ (5 cm) pointed lace for apron
- 2 yards (180 cm) white silk ribbon, ⅛″ (0.4 cm) wide, for torso and pantaloons
- 1 yard (90 cm) black silk ribbon, ⅛″ (0.4 cm), for cap
- 12″ (30 cm) length of wavy wool roving
- 3″ × 3″ (8 cm × 8 cm) piece of Ultra Suede® or suede for shoes
- False eyelashes and white craft glue
- Stuffing
- 2 chenille sticks (or pipe cleaners) for hand armature
- ⅜″ (1 cm) wooden dowels: 5″ (13 cm) for torso and 9″ (23 cm) for anchoring maid to stand
- Scrap of black fabric for blackbird
- 5″ × 7″ (13 cm × 18 cm) wooden oval plaque for stand and fabric to cover
- 1 yard (90 cm) rose trim to cover edge of stand
- Small wicker basket filled with vintage lacy handkerchief or doily to resemble a pile of royal laundry

Templates on pages 158–159. Use ¼″ (0.75 cm) seam allowance unless otherwise indicated.

The Dollmaker–Betts Vidal

The Maid Was in the Garden and other splendid creations by Betts Vidal are created in a room in her home in Hayward, California. It has a large north-facing window alongside dolls and fabric. She arranges various collections, including lavender sticks, butterfly-wing art, apothecary jars full of pearl buttons, miniature chairs, magazine clippings, found objects, crayons, and even doll stands! Betts keeps her studio workable and organized, with fresh flowers and chocolate always at hand. She teaches how to make dolls, twig and velvet miniature chairs, and fabric jewelry.

Making the Body

1. Sew 2″ × 2″ (7 cm × 7 cm) pieces of flesh-colored fabric to 3″ × 4″ (8 cm × 10 cm) pieces of black print fabric as shown for the right arm-hand. Sew 2″ × 2″ (7 cm × 7 cm) pieces of flesh-colored fabric to 2″ × 4½″ (7 cm × 11.5 cm) pieces of black print fabric as shown for the left arm-hand. Place arm-hand templates (templates A and B) over doubled fabrics as shown, with right sides together. Do not cut yet. Sew with black thread around arms, using tiny stitches. Change to flesh-colored thread and sew around hands. Take special care around tiny thumbs. Trim seams to ⅛″ (0.4 cm). A very small cocktail straw inserted in thumb will ease turning. Just coax flat end of a wooden skewer at top of thumb into straw. Be gentle. Now, turn arm, stuff it, and hand stitch opening closed. To give hands a little armature, you may slip in a chenille stick, bent to hand and thumb shape. Remember to bend stick ends under to avoid poking through fabric.
2. Sew 3½″ × 3½″ (9 cm × 9 cm) pieces of flesh-colored fabric to 3½″ × 6″ (9 cm × 15 cm) pieces of black print fabric as shown. Place head-torso template (template C) over doubled fabrics with right sides together. Sew (again, changing threads), clip, and turn right side out. Stuff face area first, and continue adding stuffing behind this until head is firm. Gently poke tiny tufts of stuffing into nose and chin; previously placed stuffing will keep tufts in place. Add clumps of stuffing to cheek area. Draw on closed lids and lashes, or glue on artificial lashes.
3. To sculpt face, use a single flesh-colored thread on a long, thin needle. Enter at back of head, exit at outer corner of mouth. Reenter a few threads over, and

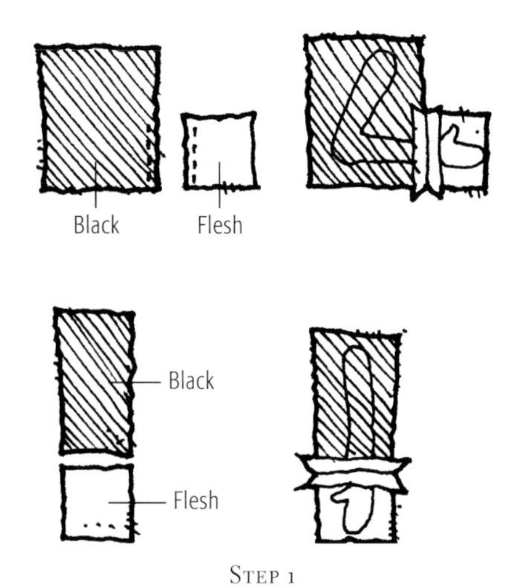

Step 1

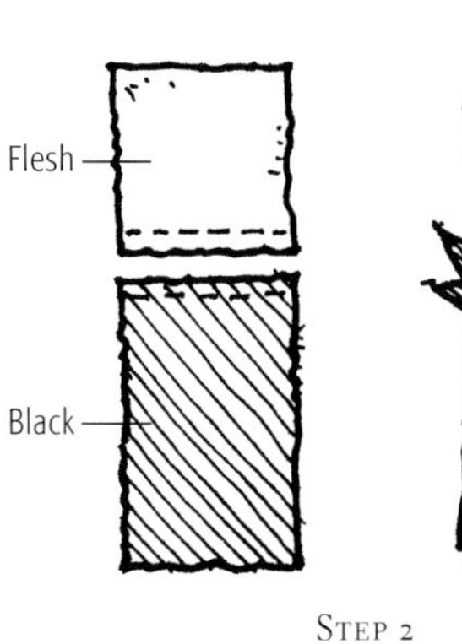

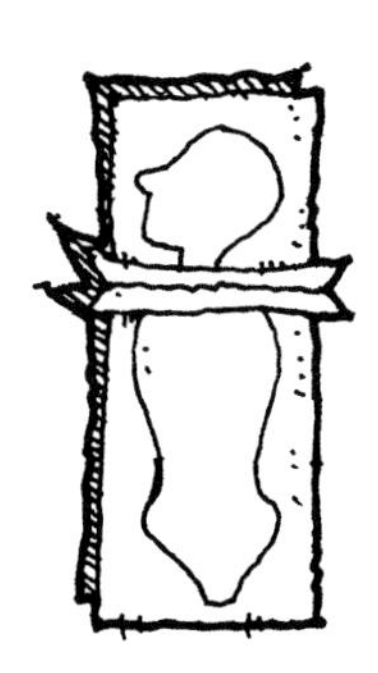
Step 2

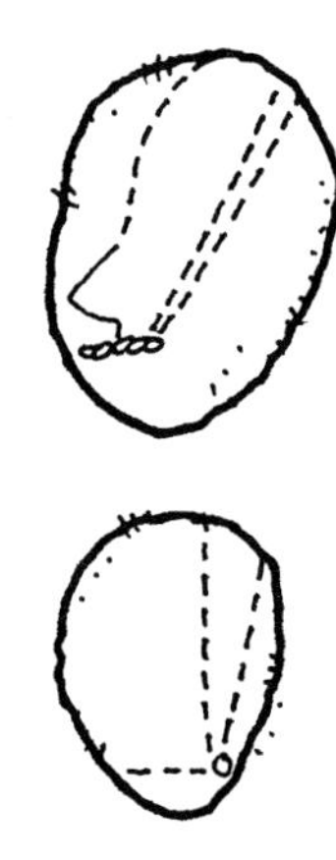
Step 3

exit at other corner of mouth. Tug on thread, and pull over mouth. Enter at first corner, exit to back of head, and anchor stitch in place. This defines lip area. Draw heart-shaped lips; add blush to cheeks, chin, and tip of nose. Tie a short strip of narrow ribbon to nose and clip ends closely.

4. Insert a ⅜" × 5" (1 cm × 13 cm) dowel in neck to keep head from nodding. Stuff around dowel until torso is firm. Hand stitch opening closed. Cut 1 yard (90 cm) of ⅛" (0.4 cm) white silk ribbon into 4½" (11.5 cm) lengths. Arrange across torso, creating a double crisscross on front and back. Hand stitch ends in place. Sleeves and skirt will hide raw ends.

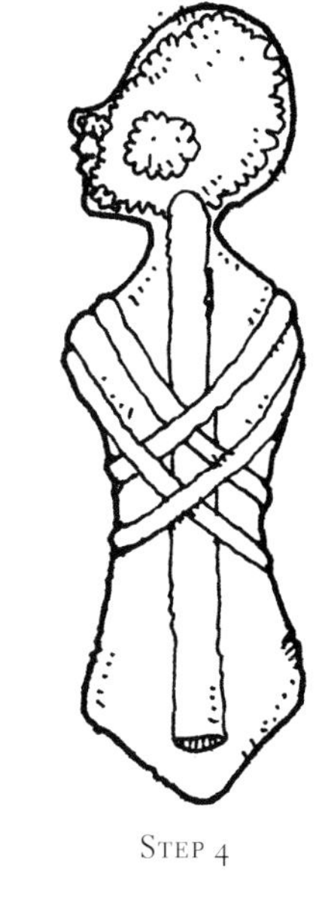

Step 4

Making the Hair

5. A 12" (30 cm) length of wool roving will create a great hairdo. Gently pull roving to make wavy hair. Arrange around head, add a top knot, and hand stitch in place.
6. Gather a 12" (30 cm) length of ⅛" (0.4 cm) black silk ribbon to surround top knot. Add a ribbon trail of about 5" (13 cm).

Step 6

Making the Sleeves

7. Cut two 7" (18 cm) circles of dress fabric. Make an X-shaped slit in center of circles to enable you to slip each one over arm and up to shoulder area. Loosely hand gather ¼" (0.75 cm) from edge. Center circle on shoulder and pin in place. Pull gathers tightly, tucking raw edges inside, and hand stitch gathered edge to arm just above elbow. Repeat for other arm.
8. With dollmaker's needle and double strand of black thread, sew arms to torso. It's best to stitch through arm and sleeve, through torso, then through opposite arm and sleeve. Knot and bury thread. A few extra stitches may be needed to cover crisscross ribbon ends.

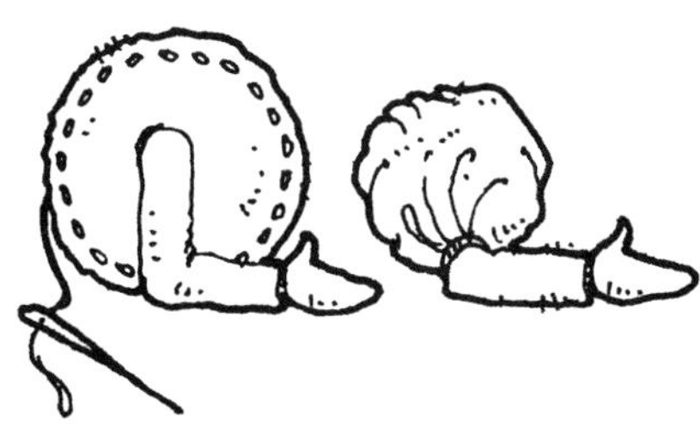

Step 7

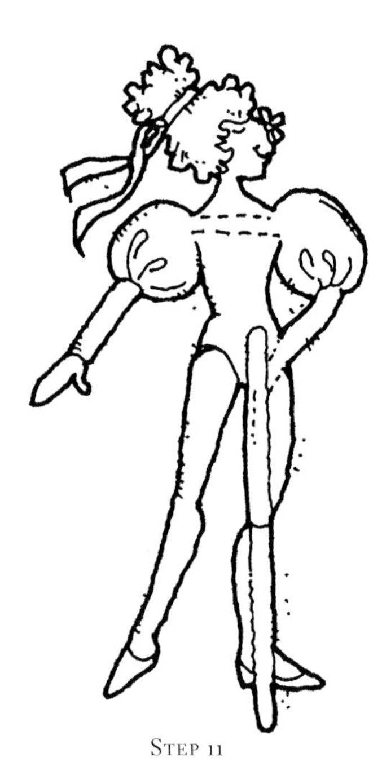
STEP 11

Making the Legs

9. Trace legs (templates D and E) on four layers of white batiste or two layers of white cotton. Sew, trim, clip, stuff firmly, and stitch openings closed. Trace shoes (templates F and G) on black Ultra Suede or felt. Hand stitch to legs, adding a tiny bow at vamp. Only right shoe has a heel; left shoe is tiptoe.
10. Attach legs to torso by whipstitching leg tops to hip indentations.
11. To stabilize doll, sew a 9″ (23 cm) dowel to back of right leg at hip and knee areas. This dowel will be placed into a predrilled hole in plaque on which doll stands. Maid will be positioned to arch her back. Pantaloons are placed over dowel and leg.

Costuming the Doll

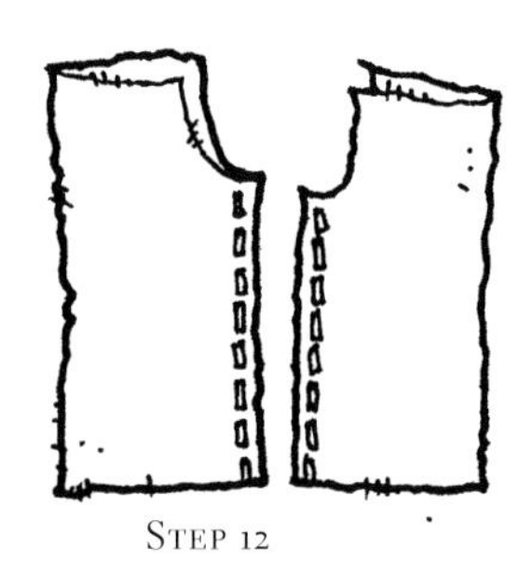
STEP 12

12. Placing template H on fold of fabric, cut two pieces for pantaloons. Stitch legs together at inseam as shown.
13. Turn under deep hem as marked on template. Gather along gather line. Put pantaloons on doll. Pull gathers and anchor stitch to legs just below knees. Tie ⅛″ (0.4 cm) white silk ribbon over gathers. Turn under top hem of pantaloons. Use big pleats to hand stitch to torso just below waist. After sewing pantaloons on maid, you can add tiny bows or ribbon roses at knees.
14. Cut two 15″ (38 cm) circles black fabric for skirt. Place circles with right sides together, and stitch ¼″ (0.75 cm) from outer edge. Trim to ⅛″ (0.4 cm). Fold circle in quarters. Measure 1¼″ (3.2 cm) from point and cut a waist opening. Turn right side out through waist opening, and press skirt. Hand gather ¼″ (0.75 cm) from waist edge. Slip skirt over doll's body and pull gathers tightly. Tuck raw edges inside and hand stitch skirt to waist.
15. Petticoat is made in same way using 14″ (35 cm) batiste circles. Add narrow lace to edge of petticoat. A bit of lace showing under her skirt adds to her dainty look.

Apron

STEP 13

16. Cut a 5″ × 7″ (13 cm × 18 cm) piece of batiste for apron. Sew 5″ (13 cm) pointy lace to side and 7″ (18 cm) to bottom edge. Press and hand gather to fit front of maid's waist. Turn gathered edge under and stitch to waist. Gather 2″ (5 cm) of pointy lace. Hand stitch in place from apron over shoulder, then to back, creating a pinafore look.
17. Add a bow to back made from a 3″ × 36″ (8 cm × 90 cm) strip of batiste. Fold in half lengthwise, stitch along raw edges, leaving a 1″ (2.5 cm) opening in center, then turn right side out. Press and tie into a bow.

Accessories

18. Stitch doll's hands to sides of basket.
19. Trace bird (template I) on black fabric with right sides together. Stitch on drawn lines, leaving tail end open. Trim seams to ⅛″ (0.4 cm), clip, and turn right side out. Stuff to narrow part of tail. Press tail seams together, creating a fan tail. Glue seams together, then trim to fan shape. Stitch bird to basket's edge.

20. Glue a garden print fabric to cover top of 5″ × 7″ (13 cm × 18 cm) wooden plaque. Carefully cut fabric, covering predrilled hole. Paint sides (the routed edges) to match fabric color. Glue rose trim around edge (any extra roses can embellish apron or doll's wrist.). Place dowel (stitched to maid's leg) in drilled hole. Remember to pose her with her beribboned nose in air. So there!

Step 17

Templates

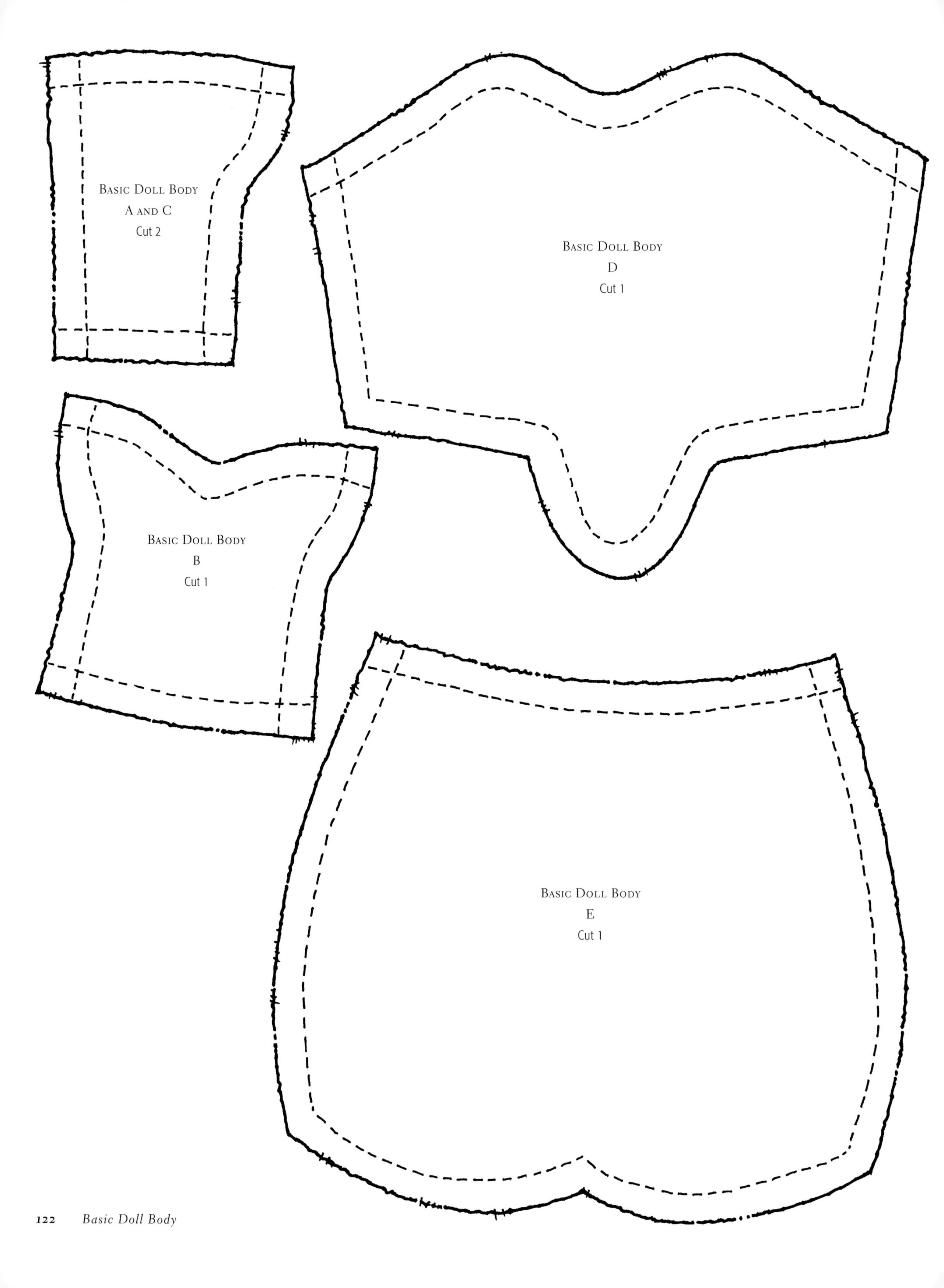
Basic Doll Body
A and C
Cut 2
Basic Doll Body
D
Cut 1
Basic Doll Body
B
Cut 1
Basic Doll Body
E
Cut 1

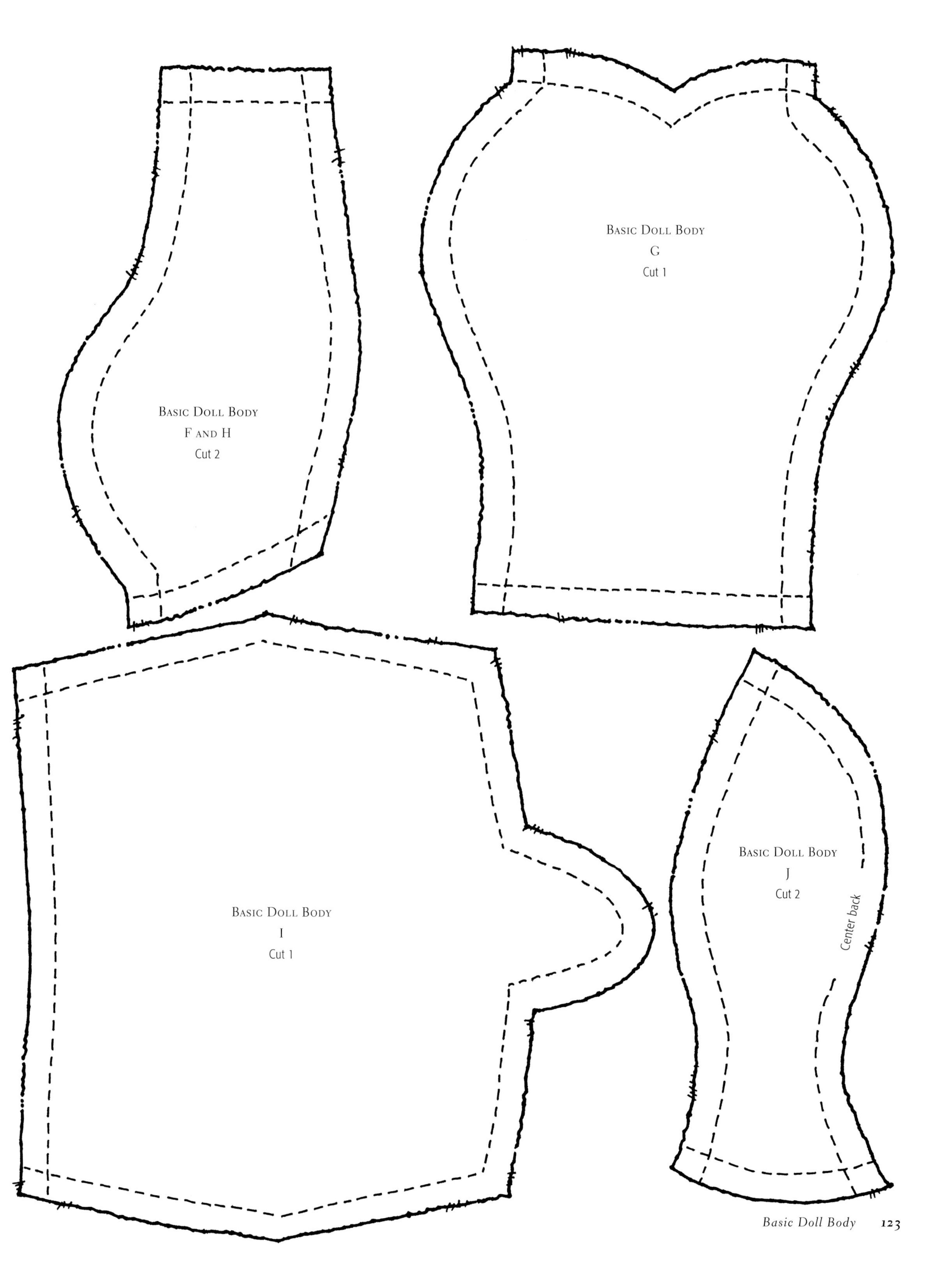
Basic Doll Body
F and H
Cut 2
Basic Doll Body
G
Cut 1
Basic Doll Body
I
Cut 1
Basic Doll Body
J
Cut 2
Center back

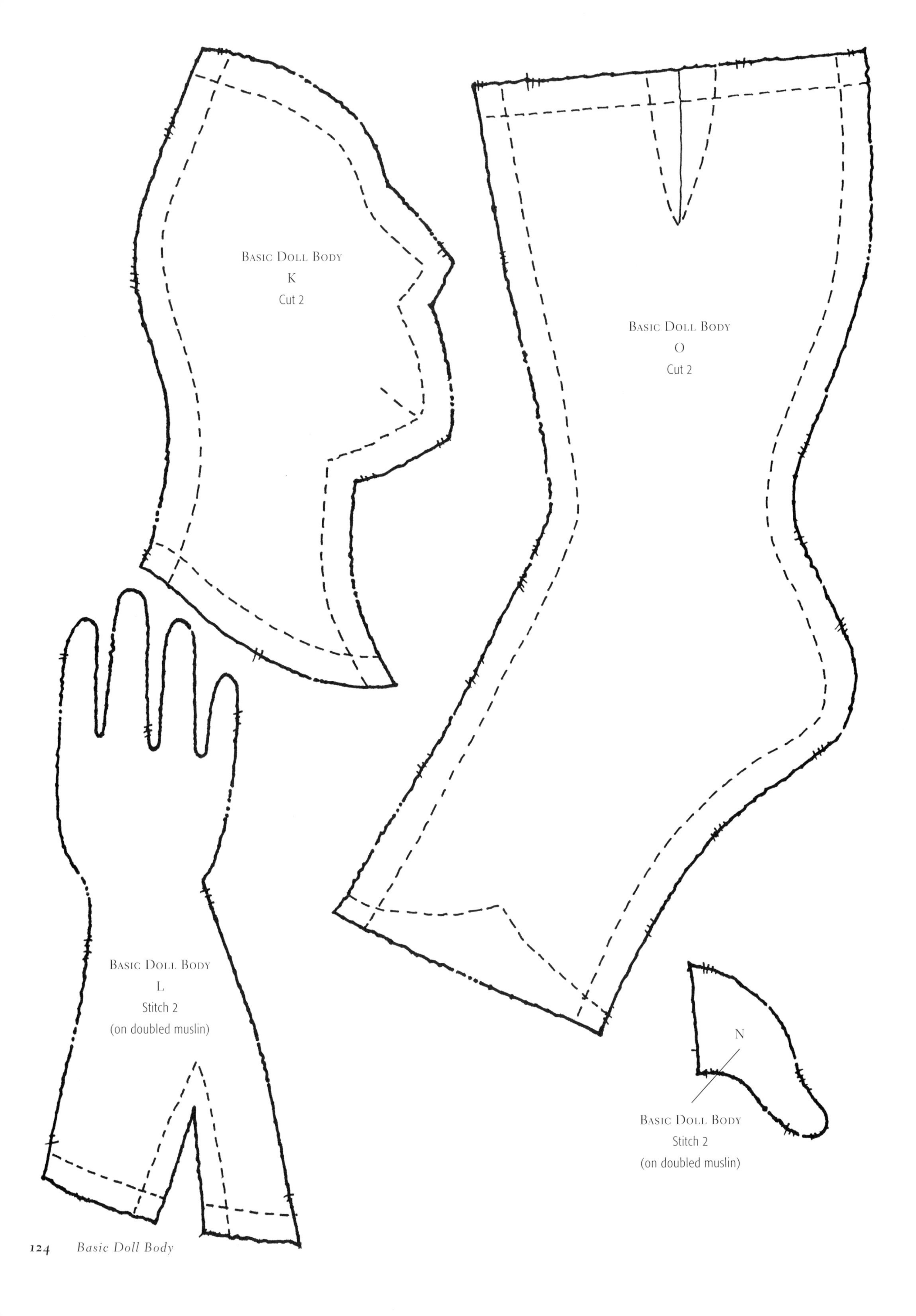
Basic Doll Body
K
Cut 2
Basic Doll Body
O
Cut 2
Basic Doll Body
L
Stitch 2
(on doubled muslin)
N
Basic Doll Body
Stitch 2
(on doubled muslin)

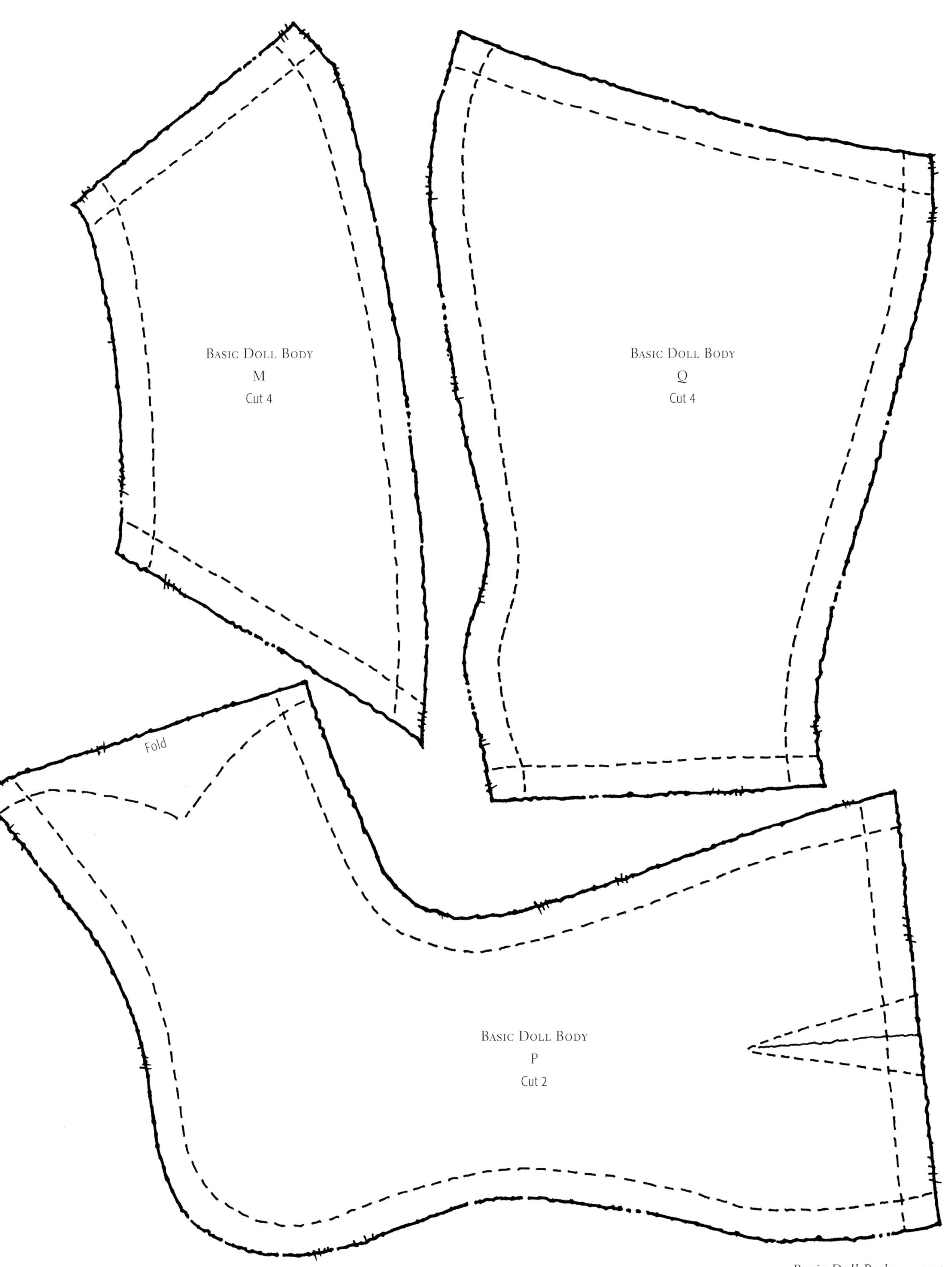
Basic Doll Body
M
Cut 4
Basic Doll Body
Q
Cut 4
Fold
Basic Doll Body
P
Cut 2

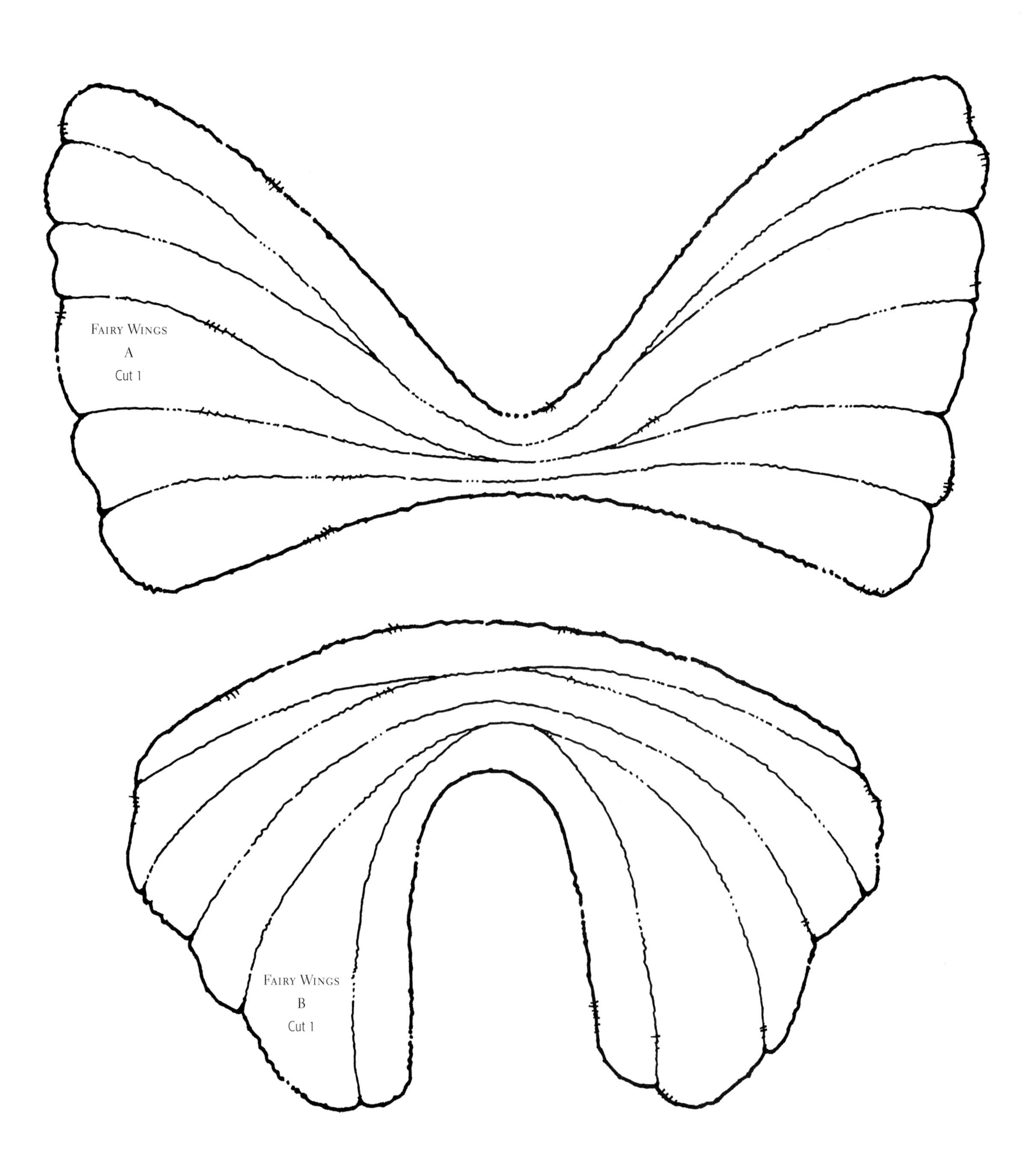
Fairy Wings
A
Cut 1
Fairy Wings
B
Cut 1

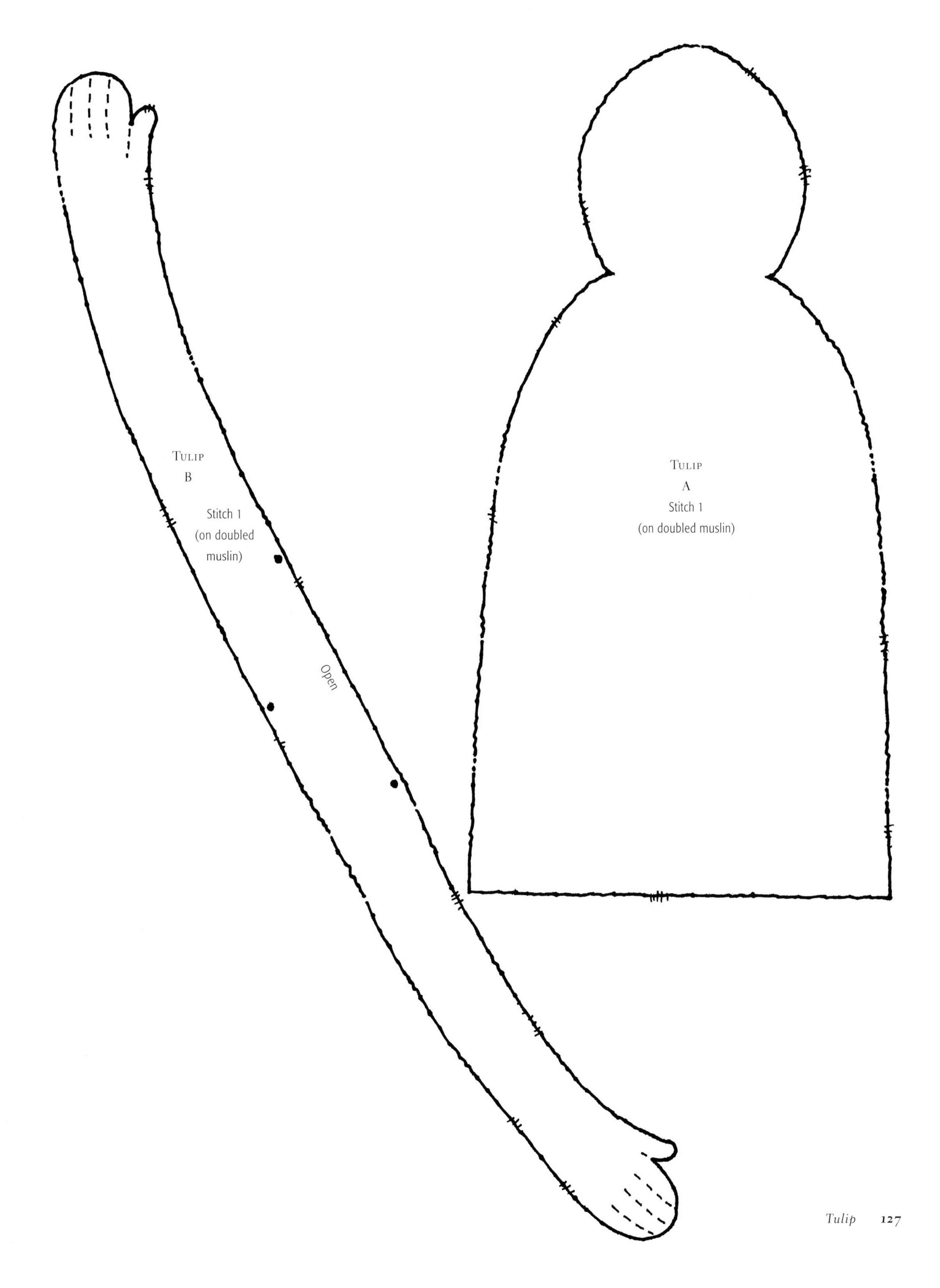
Tulip
B
Stitch 1
(on doubled
muslin)
Open
Tulip
A
Stitch 1
(on doubled muslin)

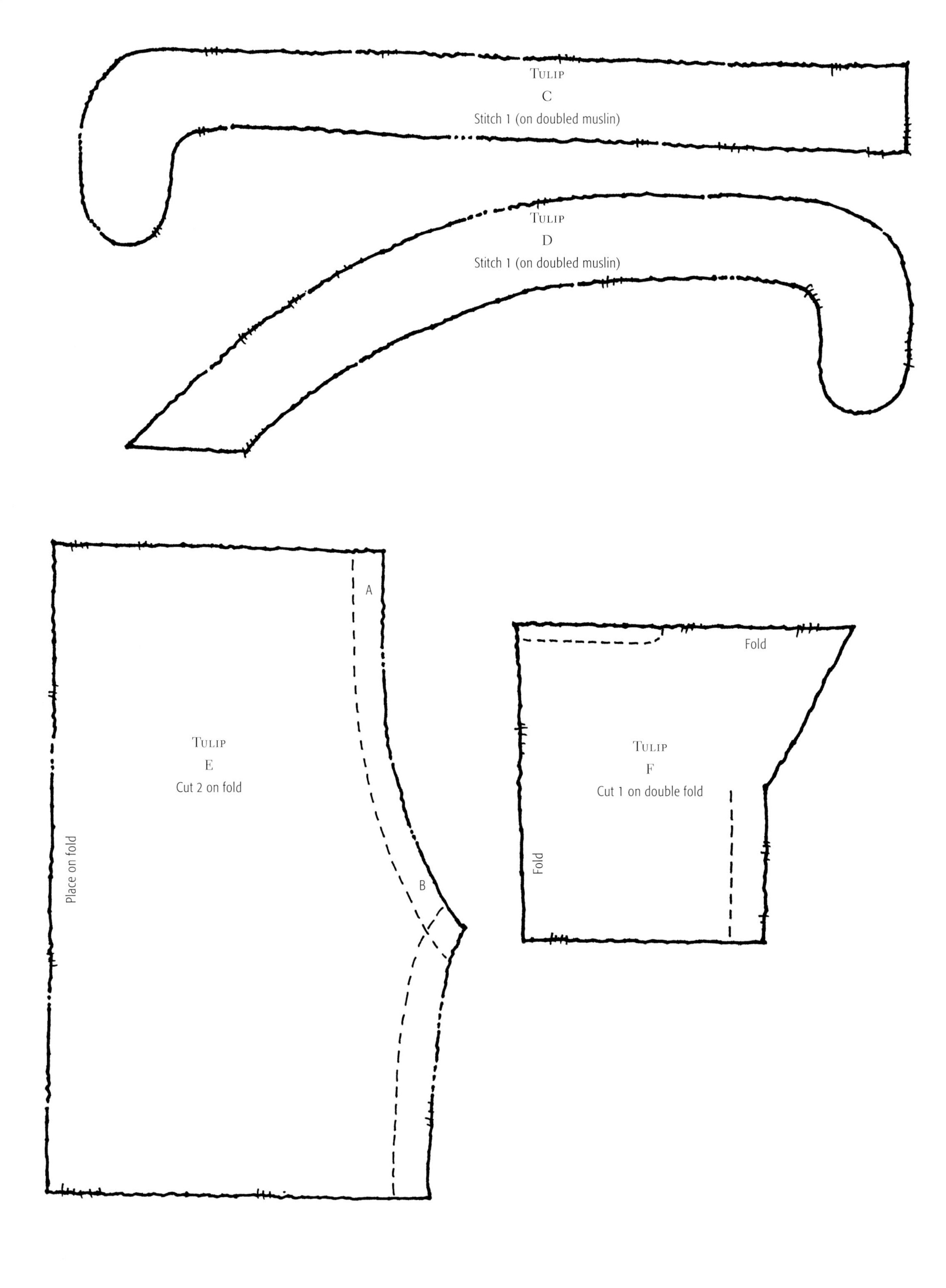
Tulip
C
Stitch 1 (on doubled muslin)
Tulip
D
Stitch 1 (on doubled muslin)
A
Tulip
E
Cut 2 on fold
Place on fold
B
Fold
Tulip
F
Cut 1 on double fold
Fold

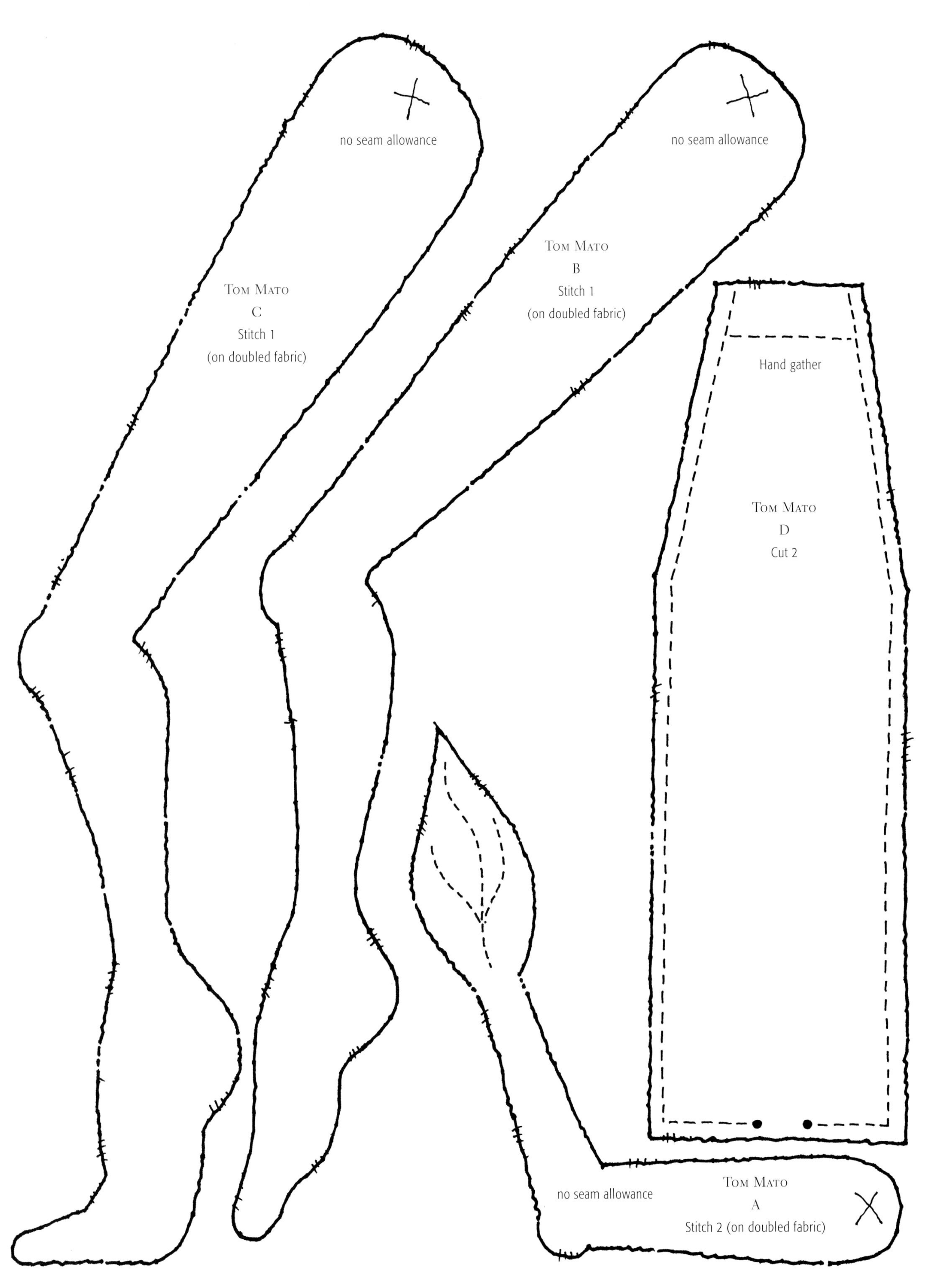
no seam allowance
no seam allowance
Tom Mato
B
Stitch 1
(on doubled fabric)
Tom Mato
C
Stitch 1
(on doubled fabric)
Hand gather
Tom Mato
D
Cut 2
no seam allowance
Tom Mato
A
Stitch 2 (on doubled fabric)

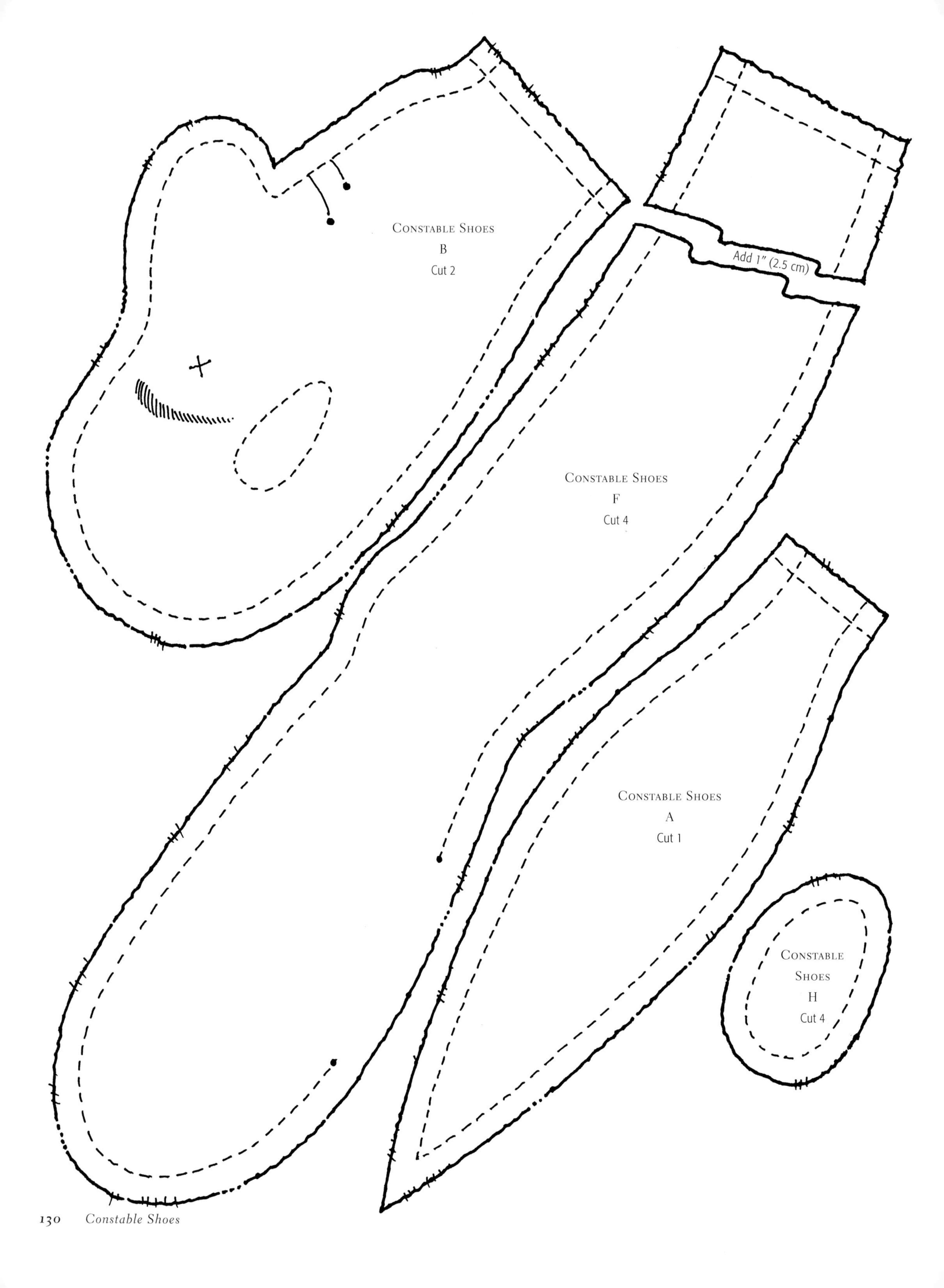
Constable Shoes
B
Cut 2
Add 1" (2.5 cm)
Constable Shoes
F
Cut 4
Constable Shoes
A
Cut 1
Constable
Shoes
H
Cut 4

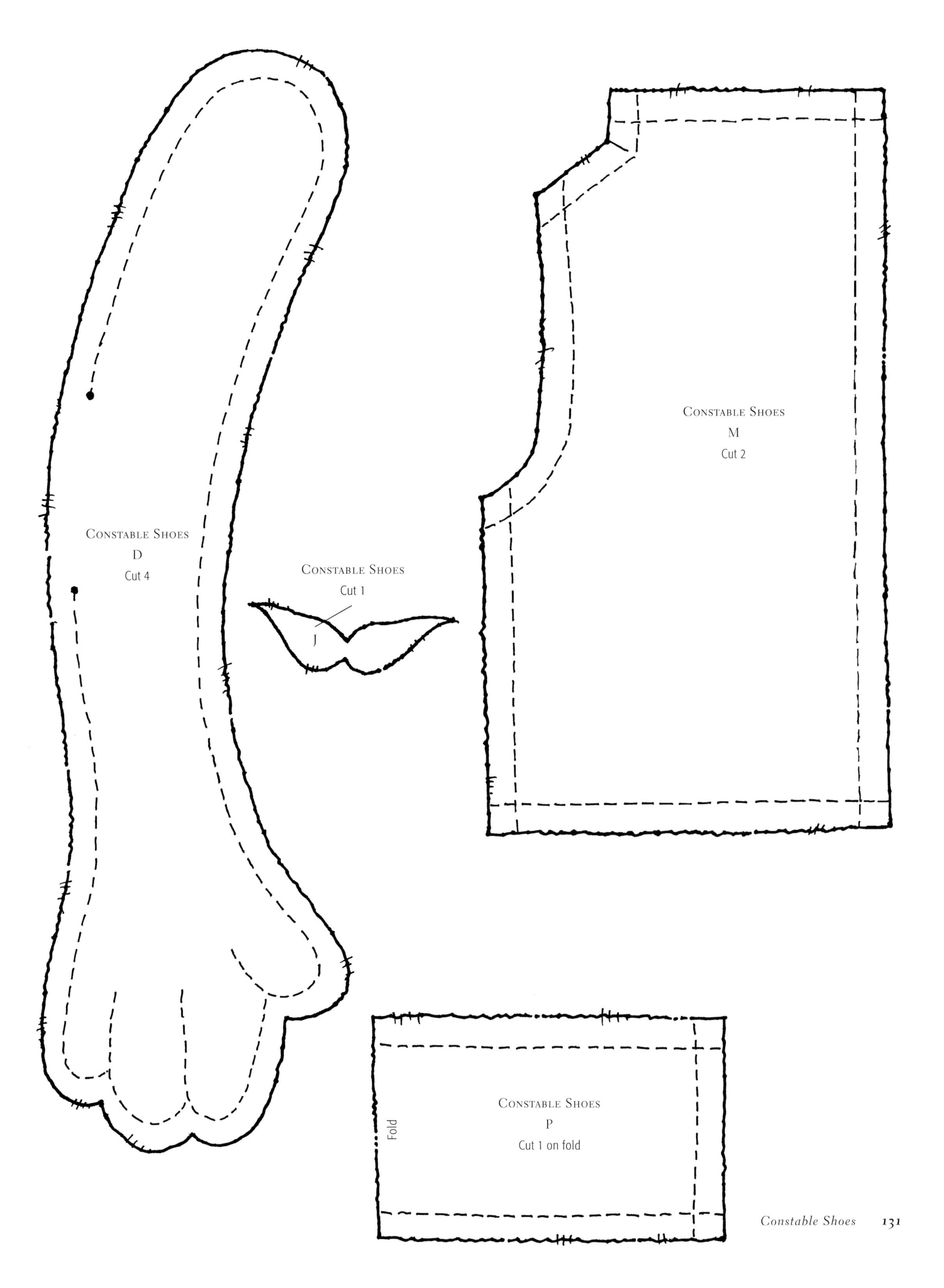
Constable Shoes
D
Cut 4
Constable Shoes
Cut 1
J
Constable Shoes
M
Cut 2
Constable Shoes
P
Cut 1 on fold
Fold

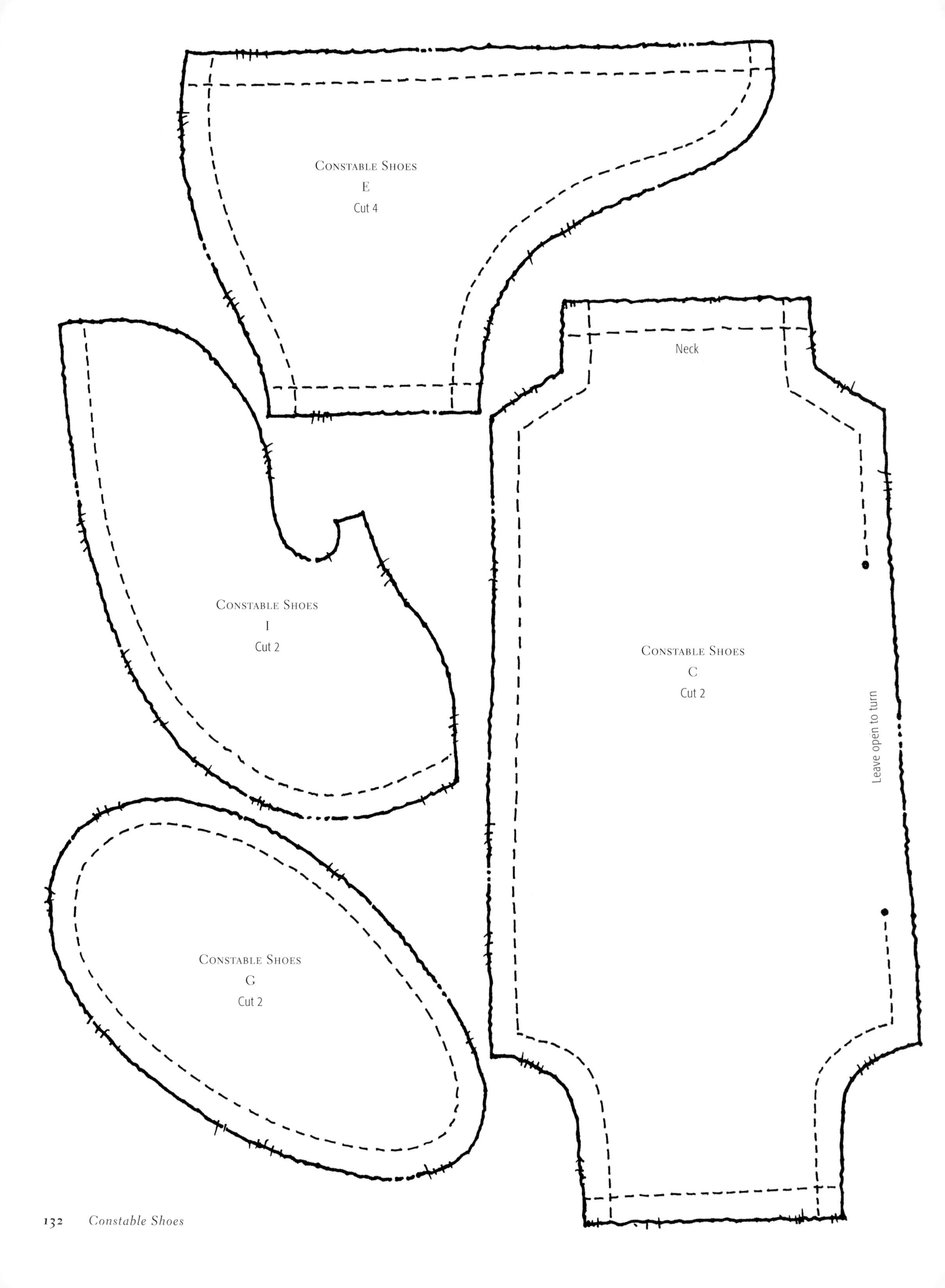
Constable Shoes
E
Cut 4
Constable Shoes
I
Cut 2
Neck
Constable Shoes
C
Cut 2
Leave open to turn
Constable Shoes
G
Cut 2

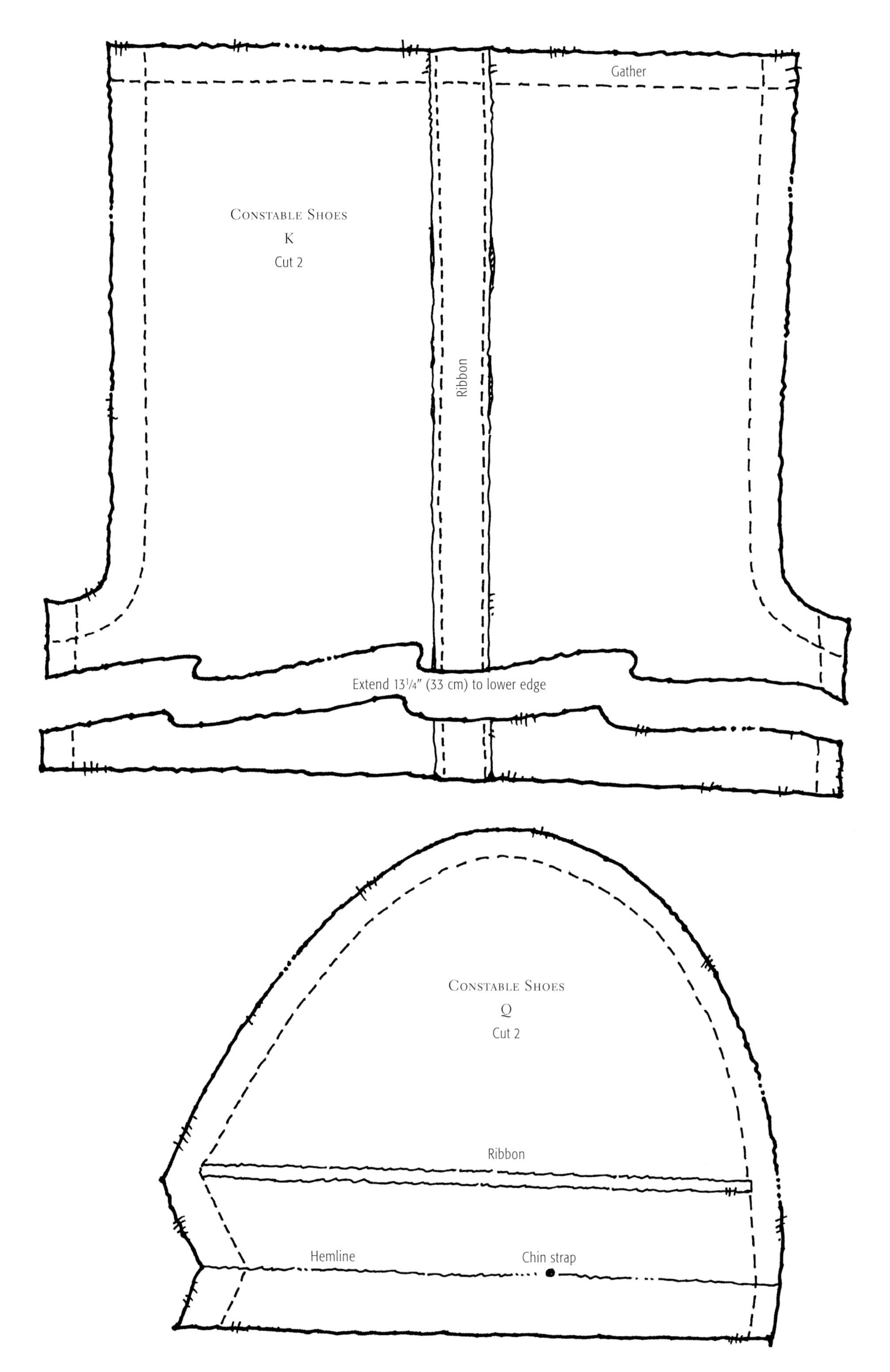
Gather
Constable Shoes
K
Cut 2
Ribbon
Extend 13¼″ (33 cm) to lower edge
Constable Shoes
Q
Cut 2
Ribbon
Hemline
Chin strap

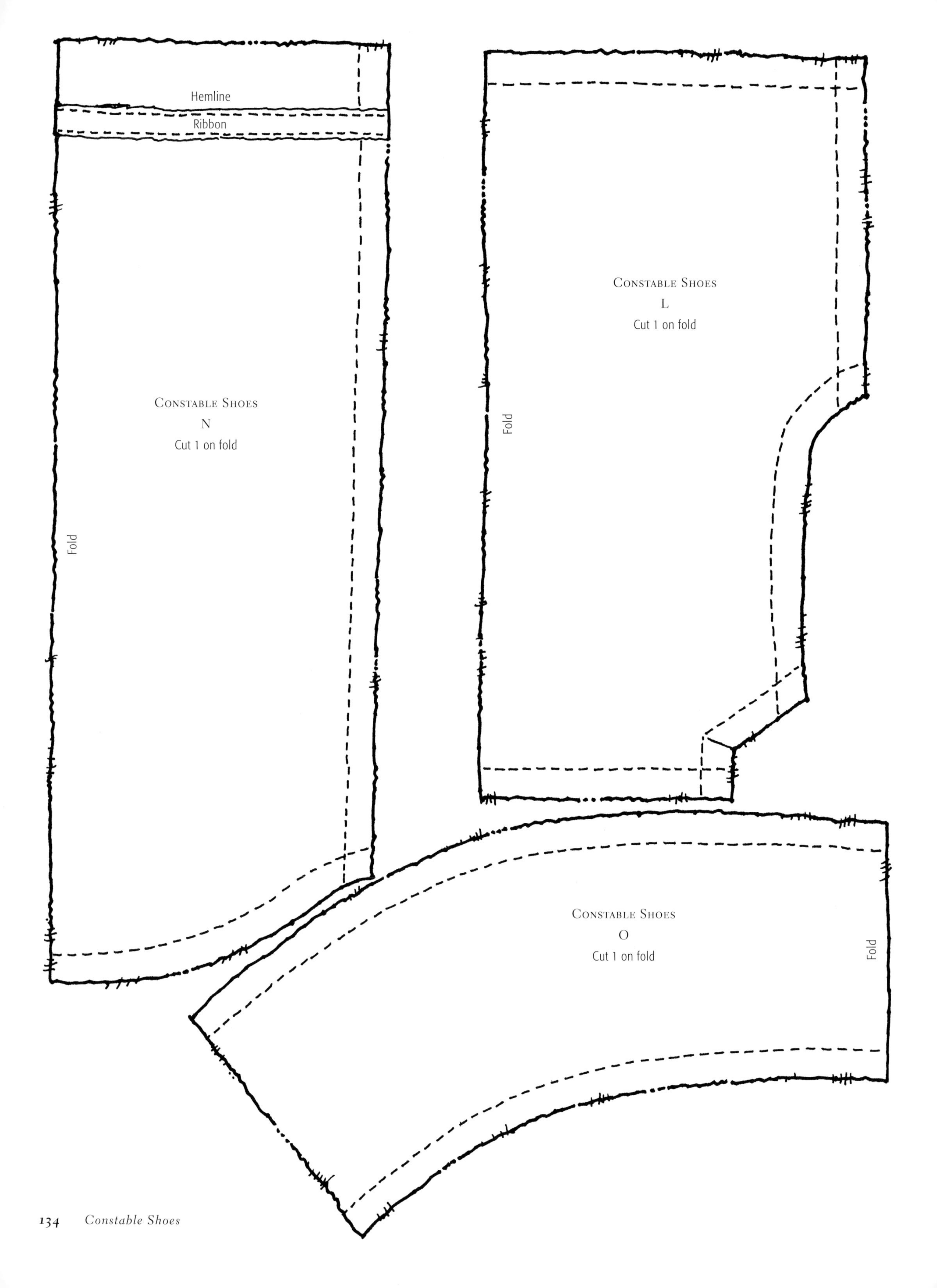
Hemline
Ribbon
Constable Shoes
N
Cut 1 on fold
Fold
Constable Shoes
L
Cut 1 on fold
Fold
Constable Shoes
O
Cut 1 on fold
Fold

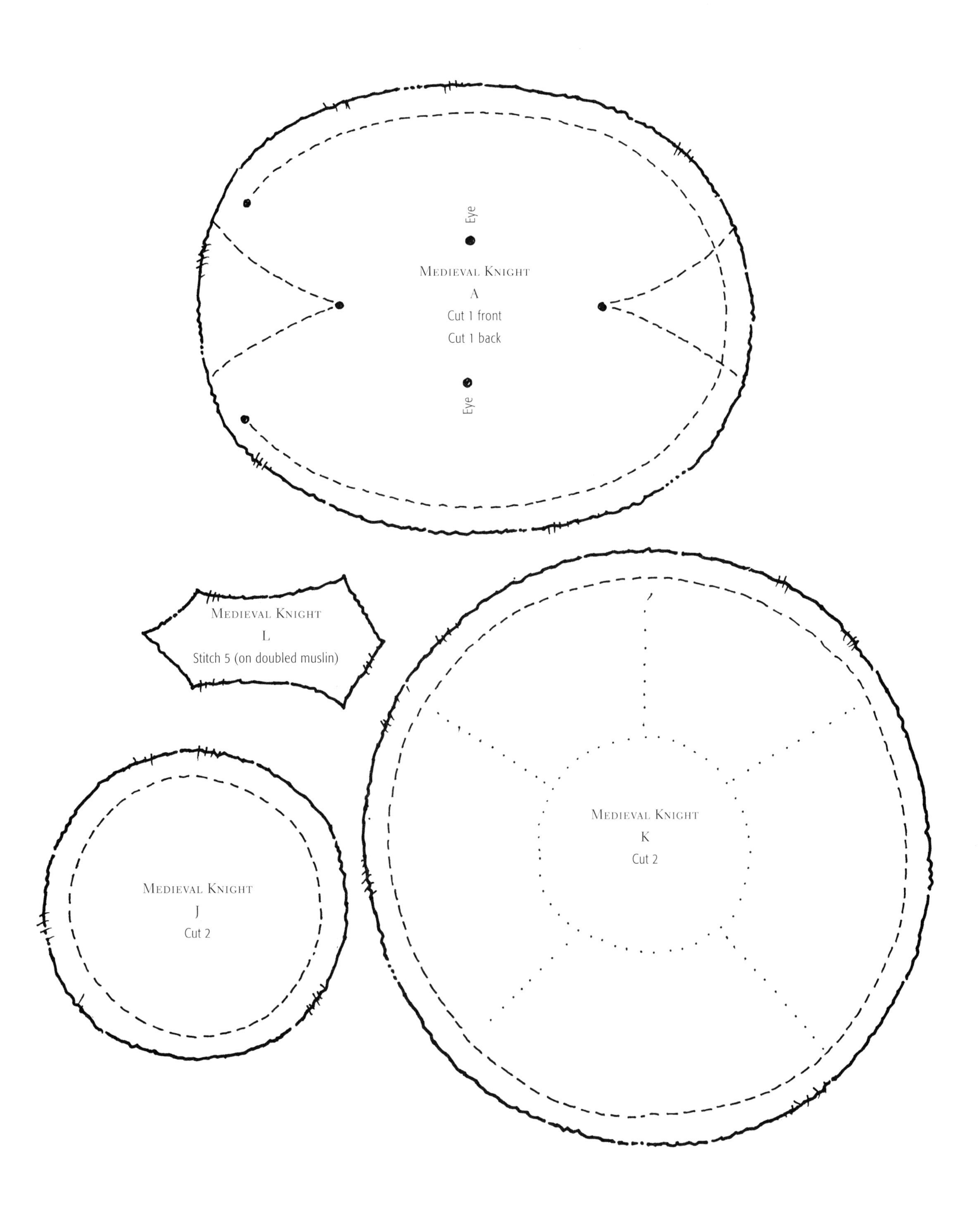
Eye
Medieval Knight
A
Cut 1 front
Cut 1 back
Eye
Medieval Knight
L
Stitch 5 (on doubled muslin)
Medieval Knight
K
Cut 2
Medieval Knight
J
Cut 2

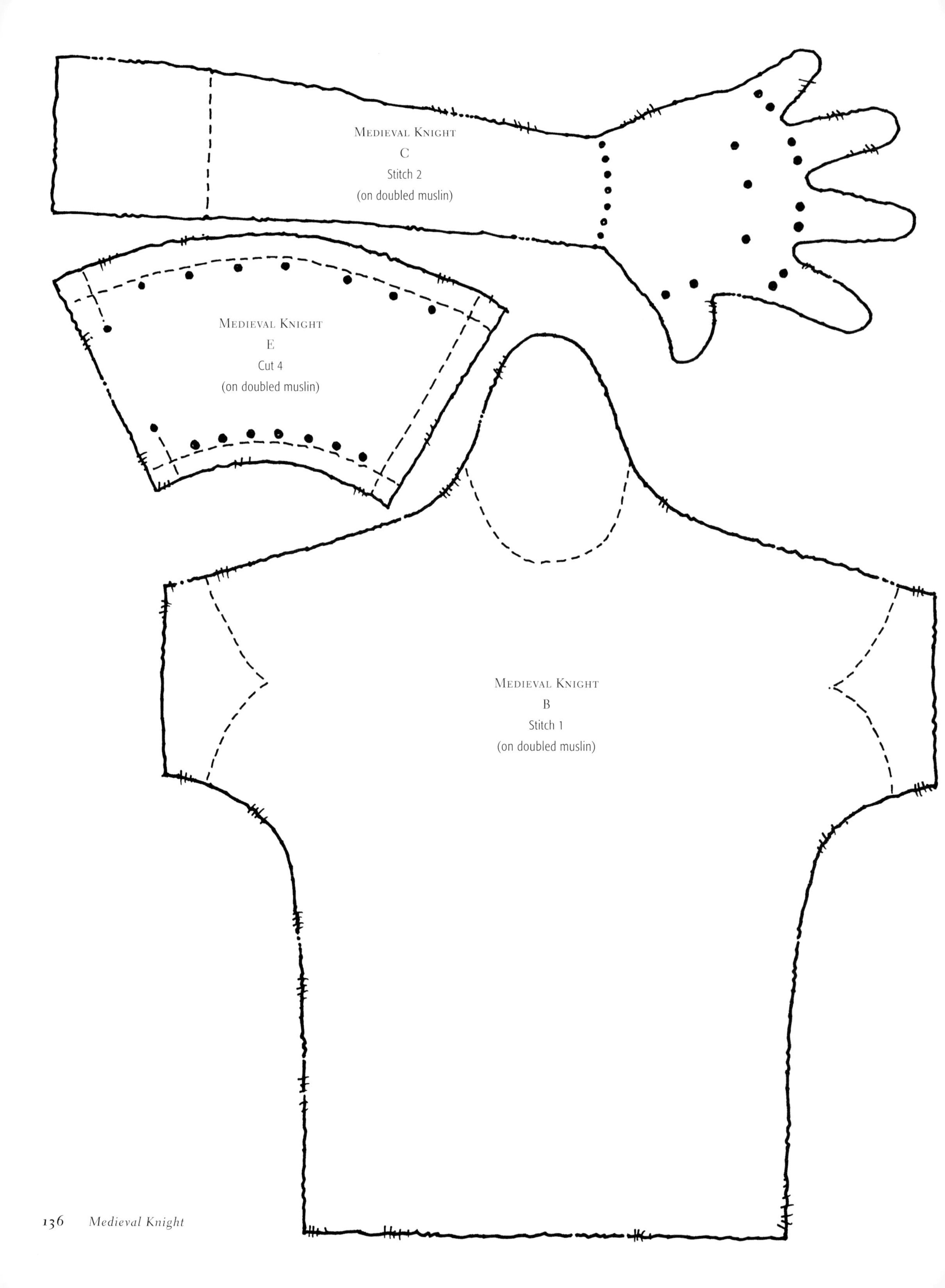
MEDIEVAL KNIGHT
C
Stitch 2
(on doubled muslin)
MEDIEVAL KNIGHT
E
Cut 4
(on doubled muslin)
MEDIEVAL KNIGHT
B
Stitch 1
(on doubled muslin)

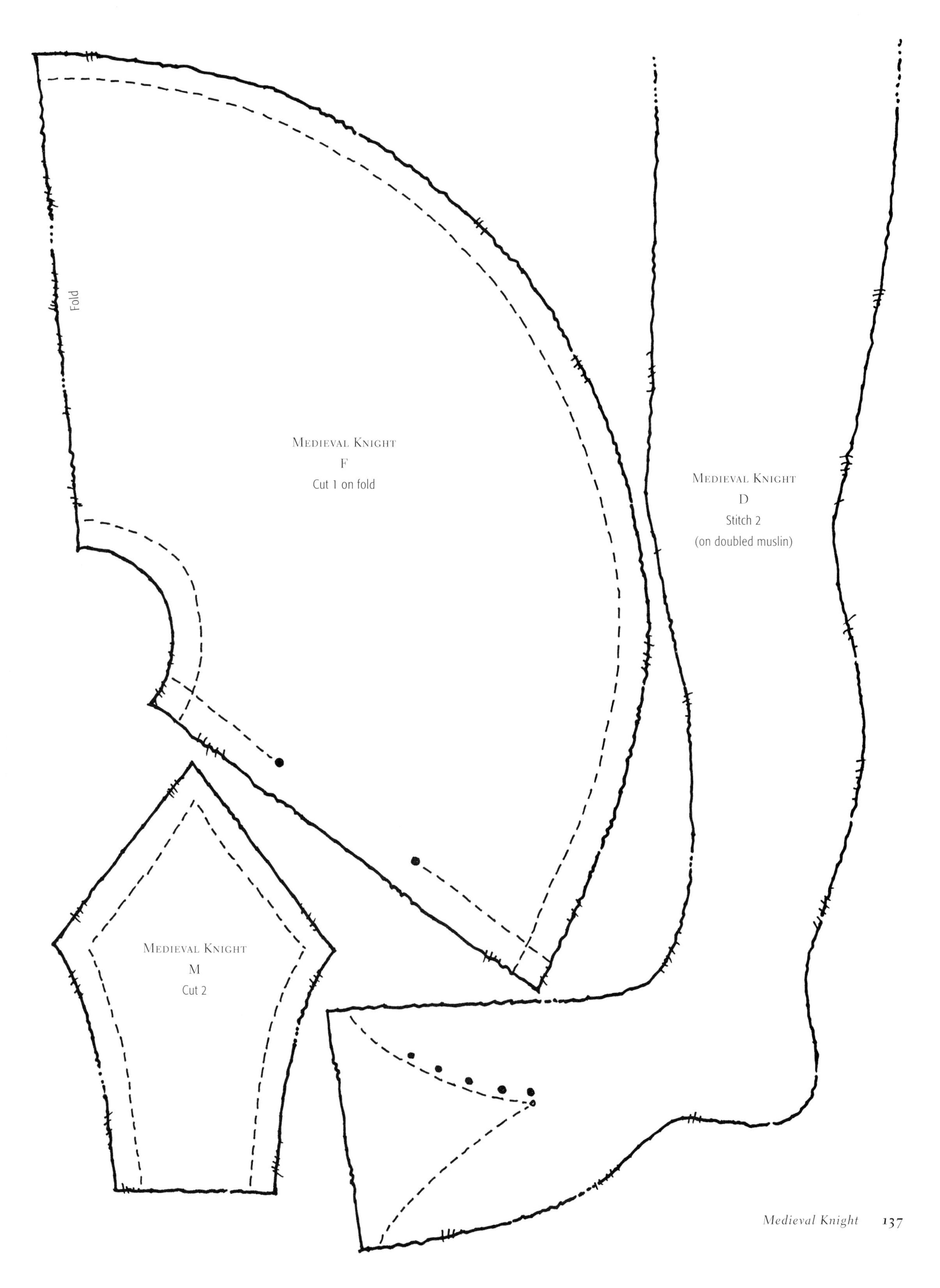
Fold
Medieval Knight
F
Cut 1 on fold
Medieval Knight
D
Stitch 2
(on doubled muslin)
Medieval Knight
M
Cut 2

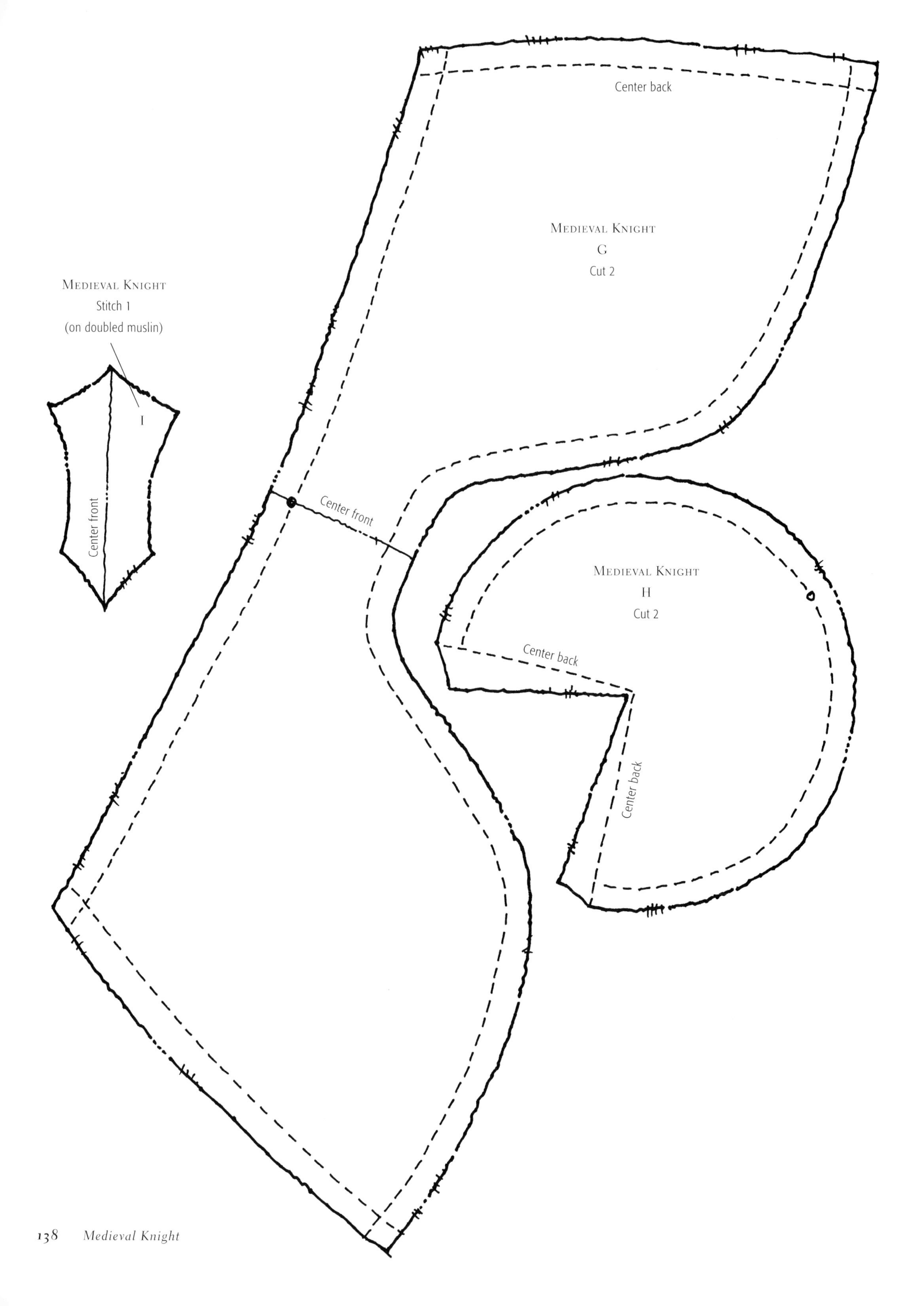
Center back
Medieval Knight
G
Cut 2
Medieval Knight
Stitch 1
(on doubled muslin)
I
Center front
Center front
Medieval Knight
H
Cut 2
Center back
Center back

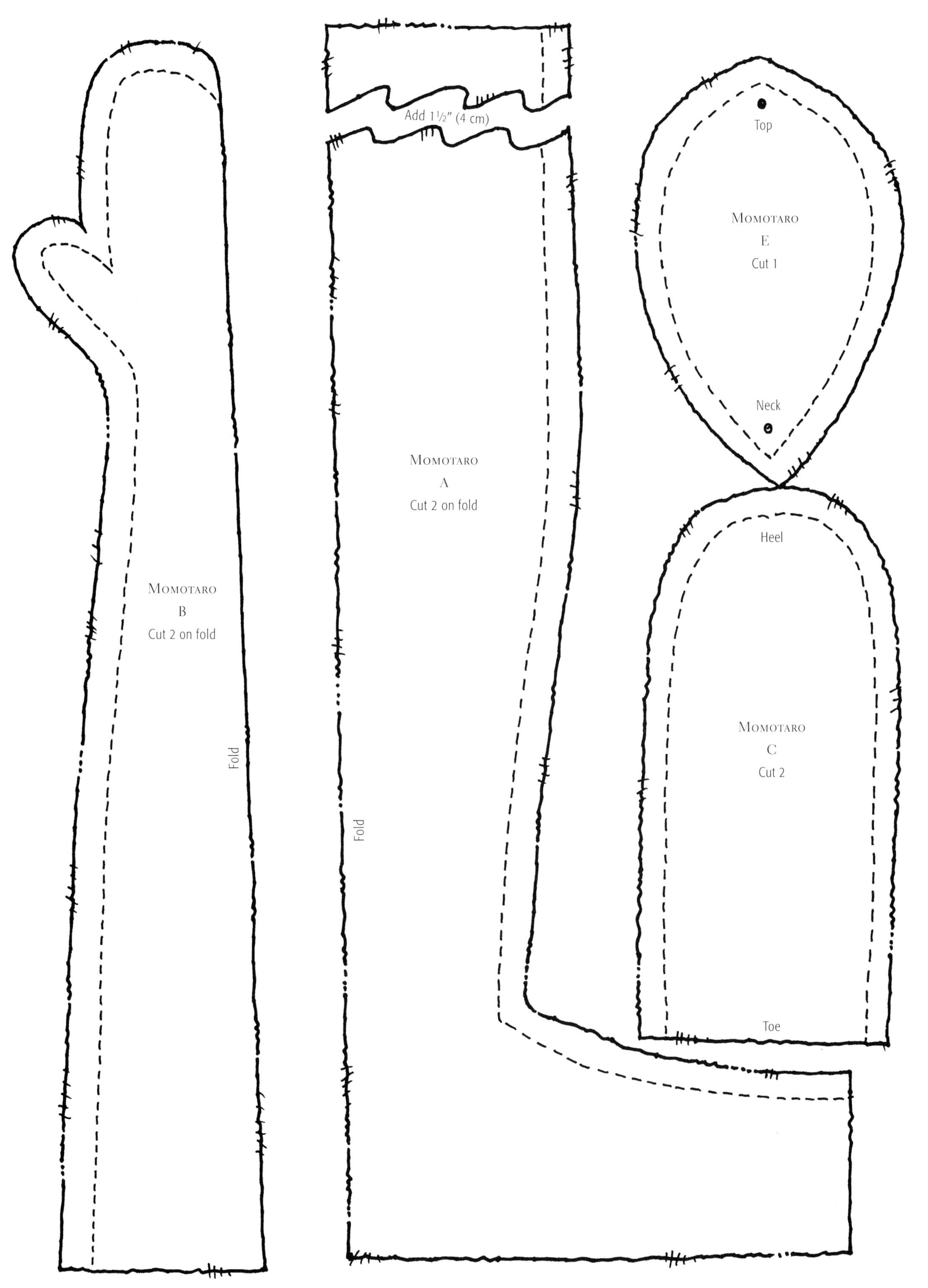
Add 1½" (4 cm)
Momotaro
B
Cut 2 on fold
Fold
Momotaro
A
Cut 2 on fold
Fold
Top
Momotaro
E
Cut 1
Neck
Heel
Momotaro
C
Cut 2
Toe

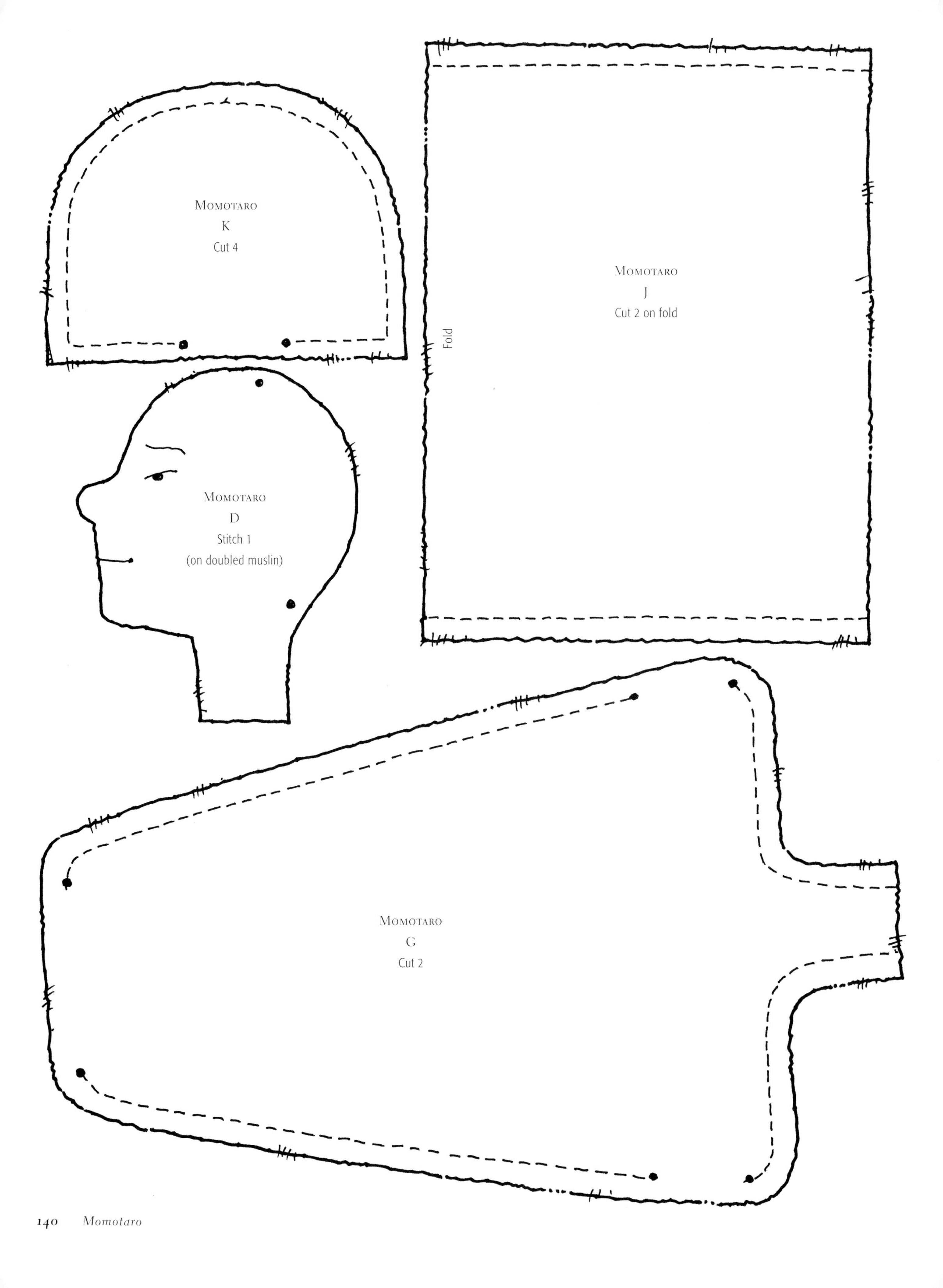
Momotaro
K
Cut 4
Momotaro
J
Cut 2 on fold
Fold
Momotaro
D
Stitch 1
(on doubled muslin)
Momotaro
G
Cut 2

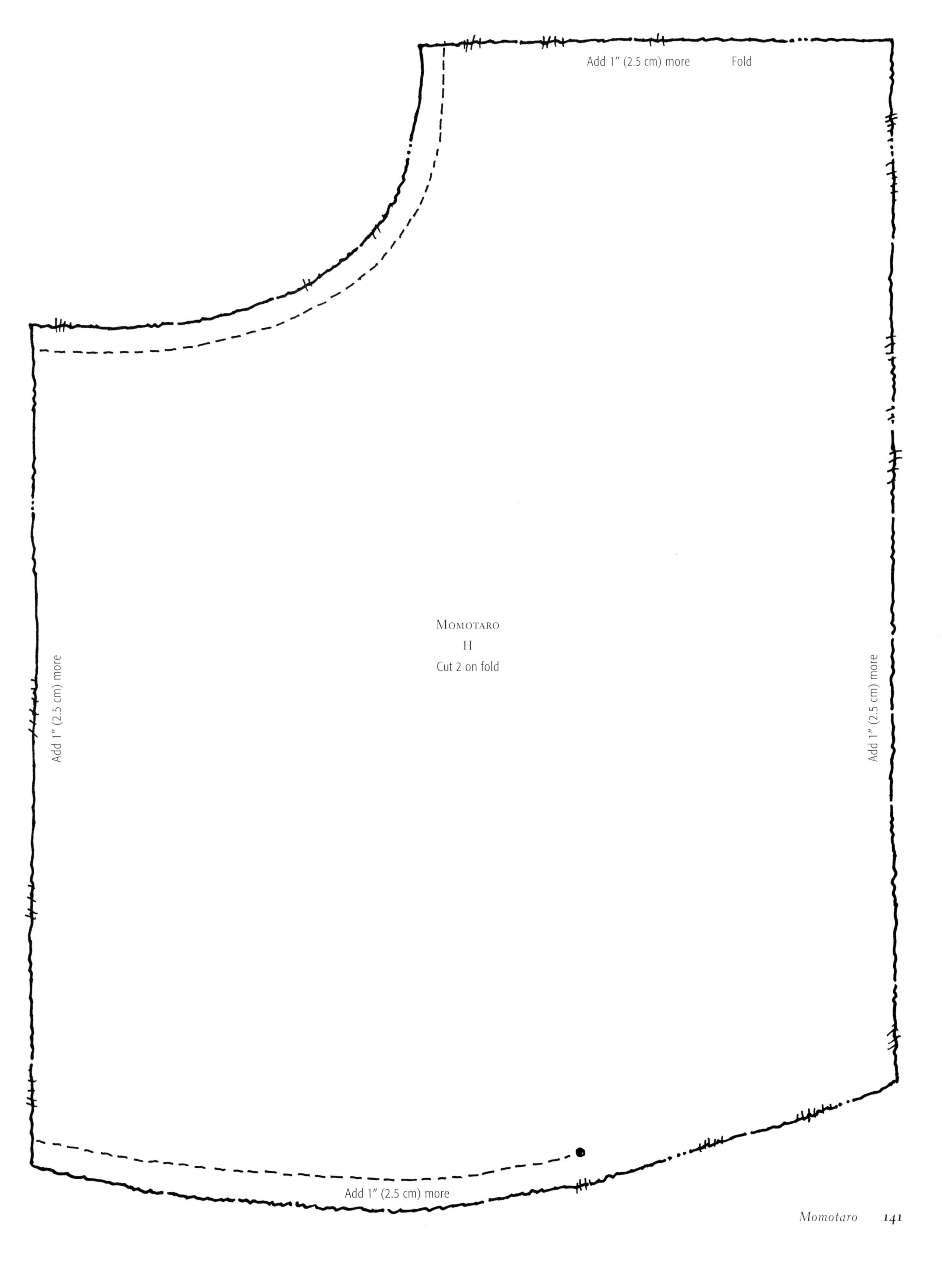

Add 1″ (2.5 cm) more
Fold
Momotaro
H
Cut 2 on fold
Add 1″ (2.5 cm) more
Add 1″ (2.5 cm) more
Add 1″ (2.5 cm) more

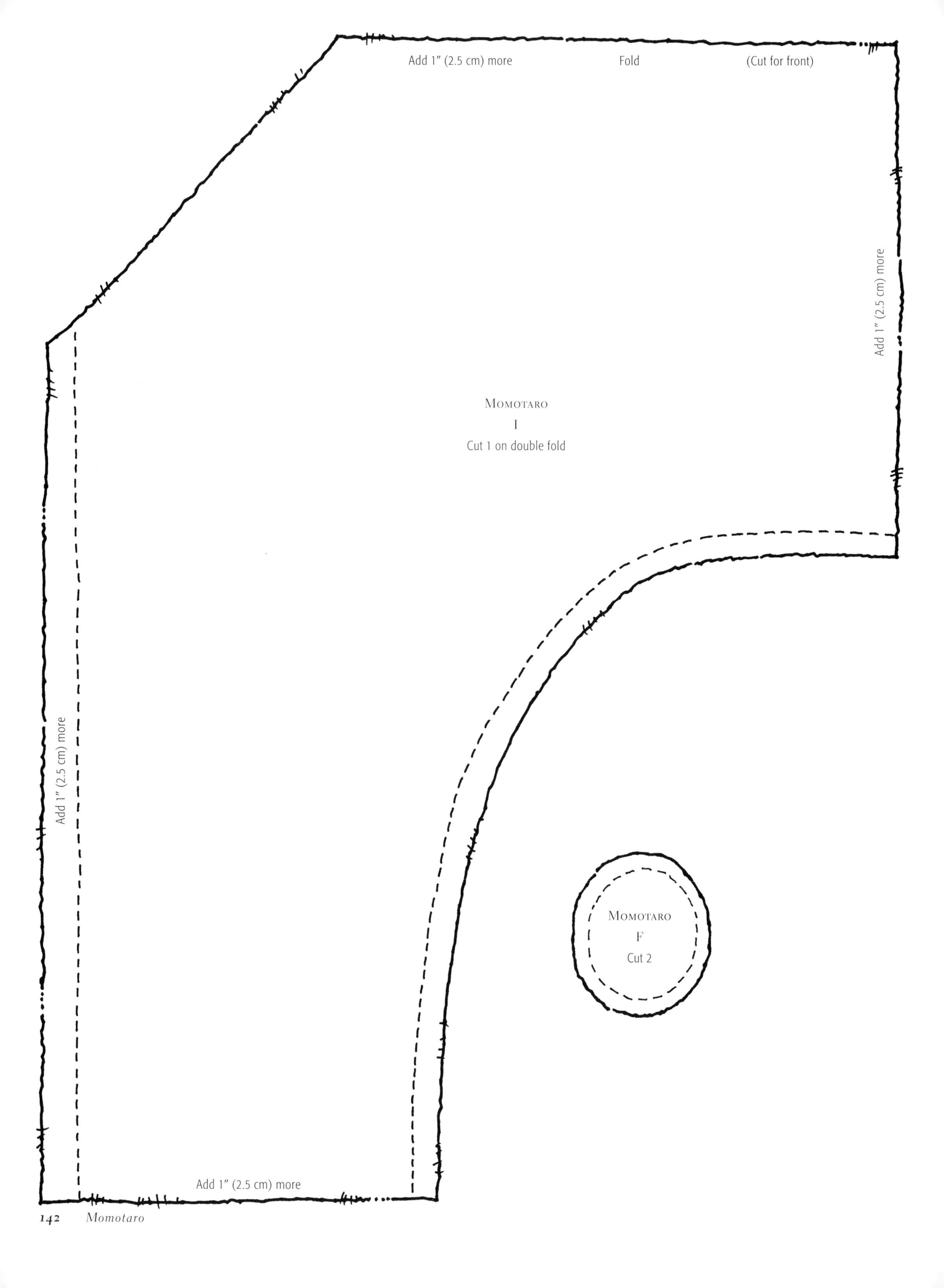
Add 1″ (2.5 cm) more
Fold
(Cut for front)
Add 1″ (2.5 cm) more
Momotaro
I
Cut 1 on double fold
Add 1″ (2.5 cm) more
Momotaro
F
Cut 2
Add 1″ (2.5 cm) more

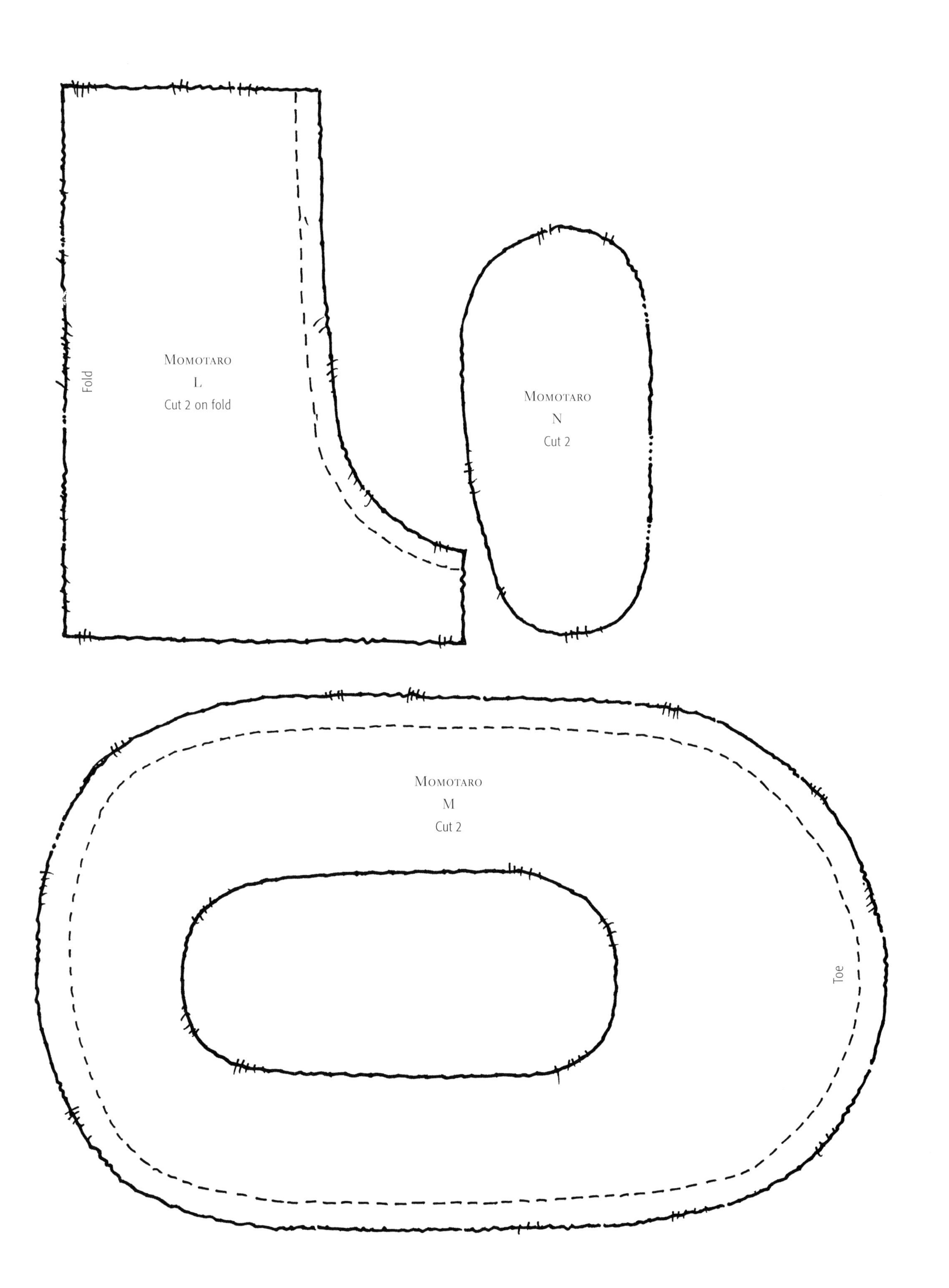
Momotaro
L
Cut 2 on fold
Fold
Momotaro
N
Cut 2
Momotaro
M
Cut 2
Toe

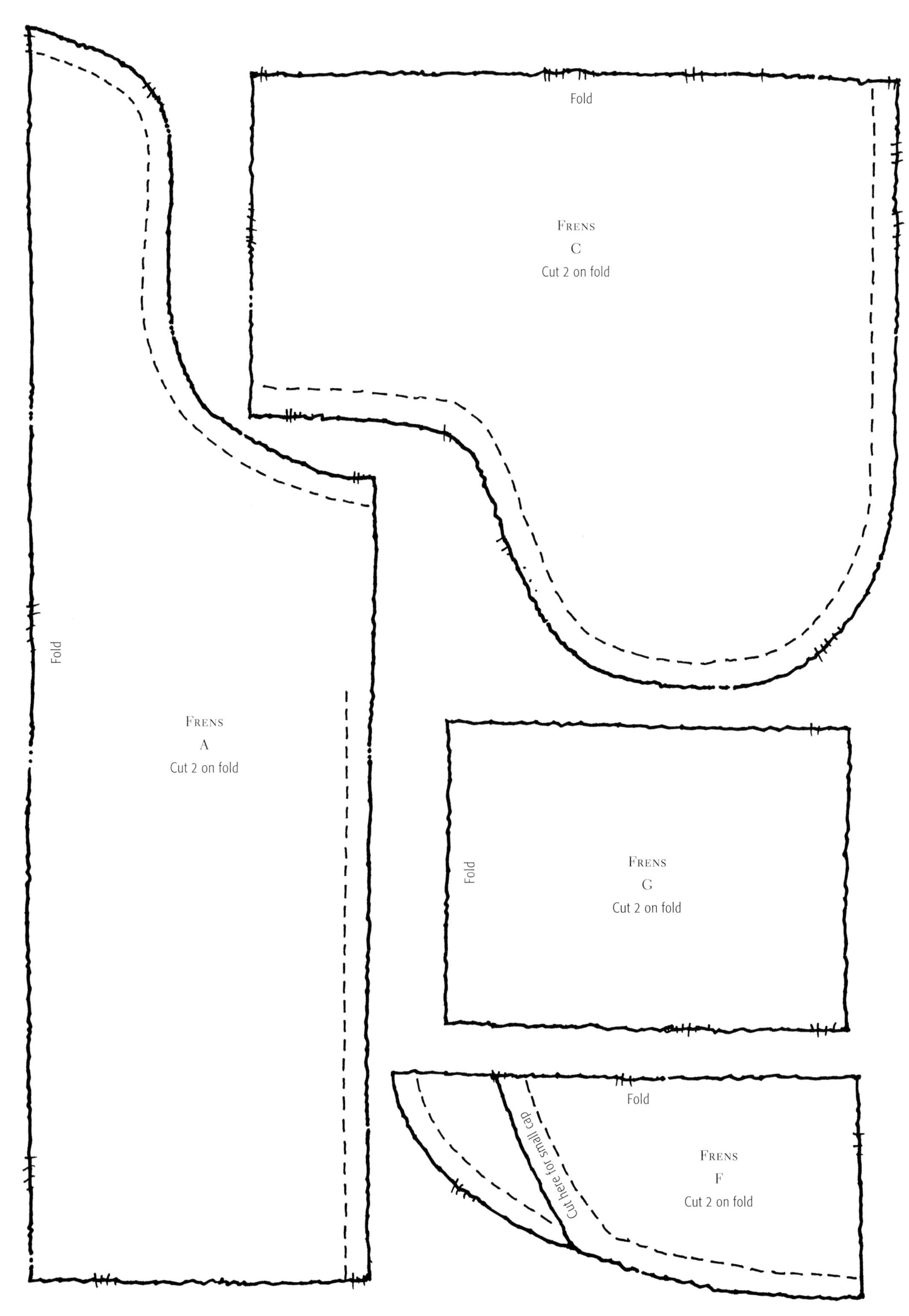
Fold
Frens
C
Cut 2 on fold
Fold
Frens
A
Cut 2 on fold
Fold
Frens
G
Cut 2 on fold
Fold
Cut here for small cap
Frens
F
Cut 2 on fold

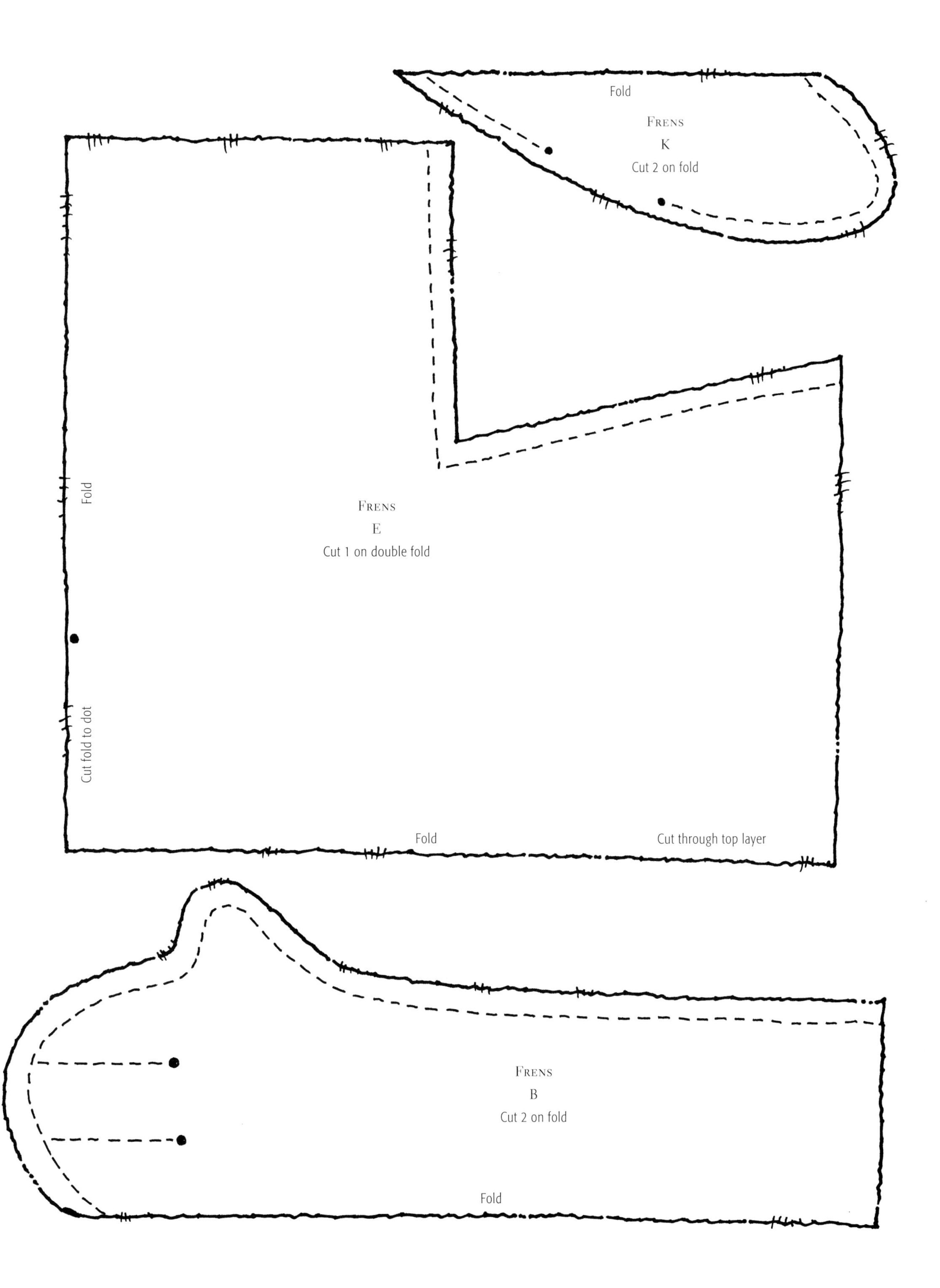
Fold
Frens
K
Cut 2 on fold
Fold
Frens
E
Cut 1 on double fold
Cut fold to dot
Fold
Cut through top layer
Frens
B
Cut 2 on fold
Fold

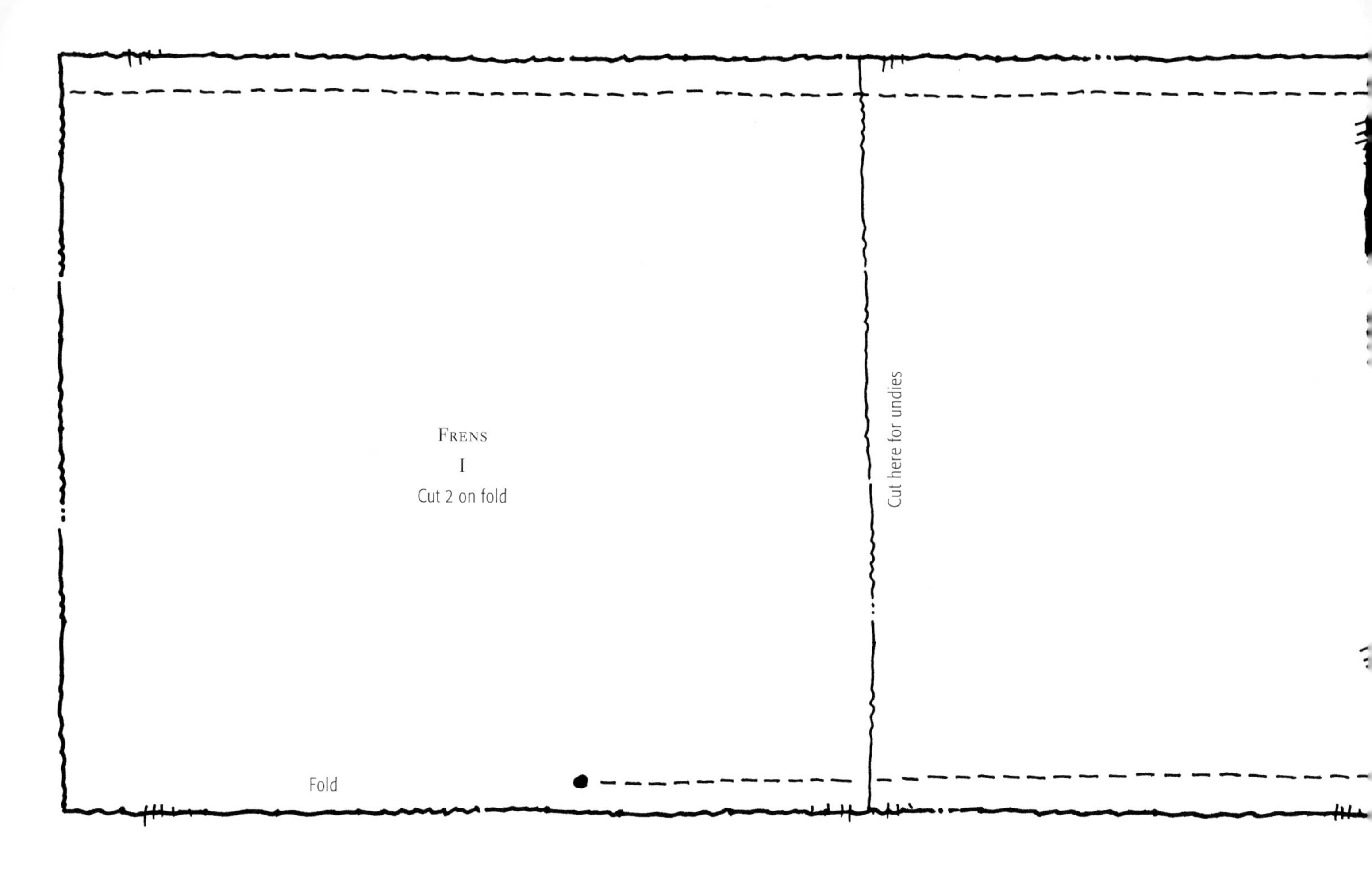
Frens
I
Cut 2 on fold
Cut here for undies
Fold

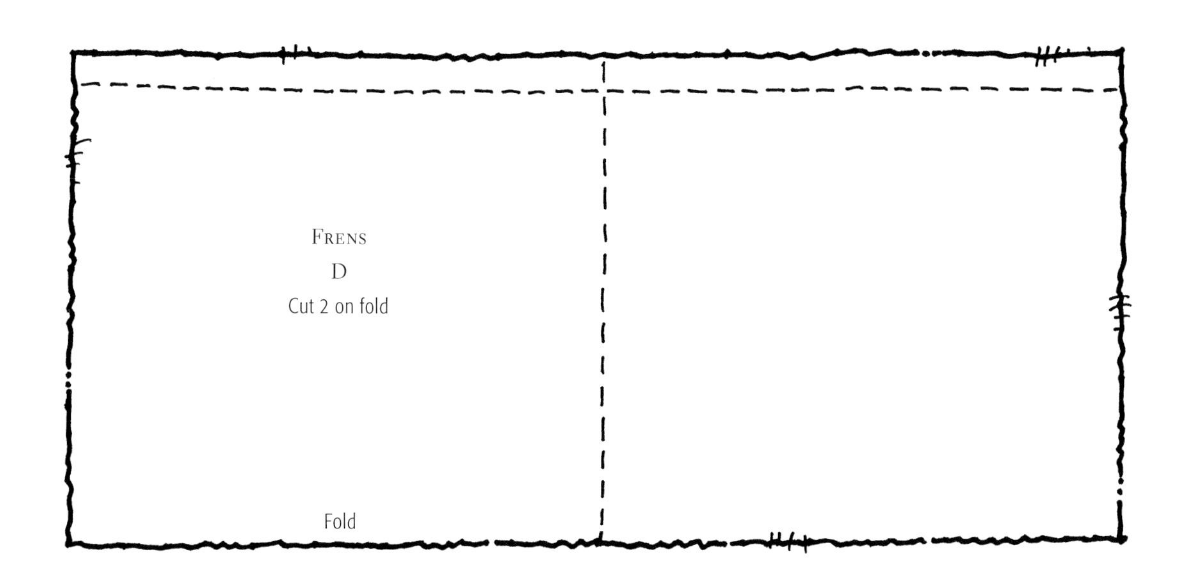
Frens
D
Cut 2 on fold
Fold

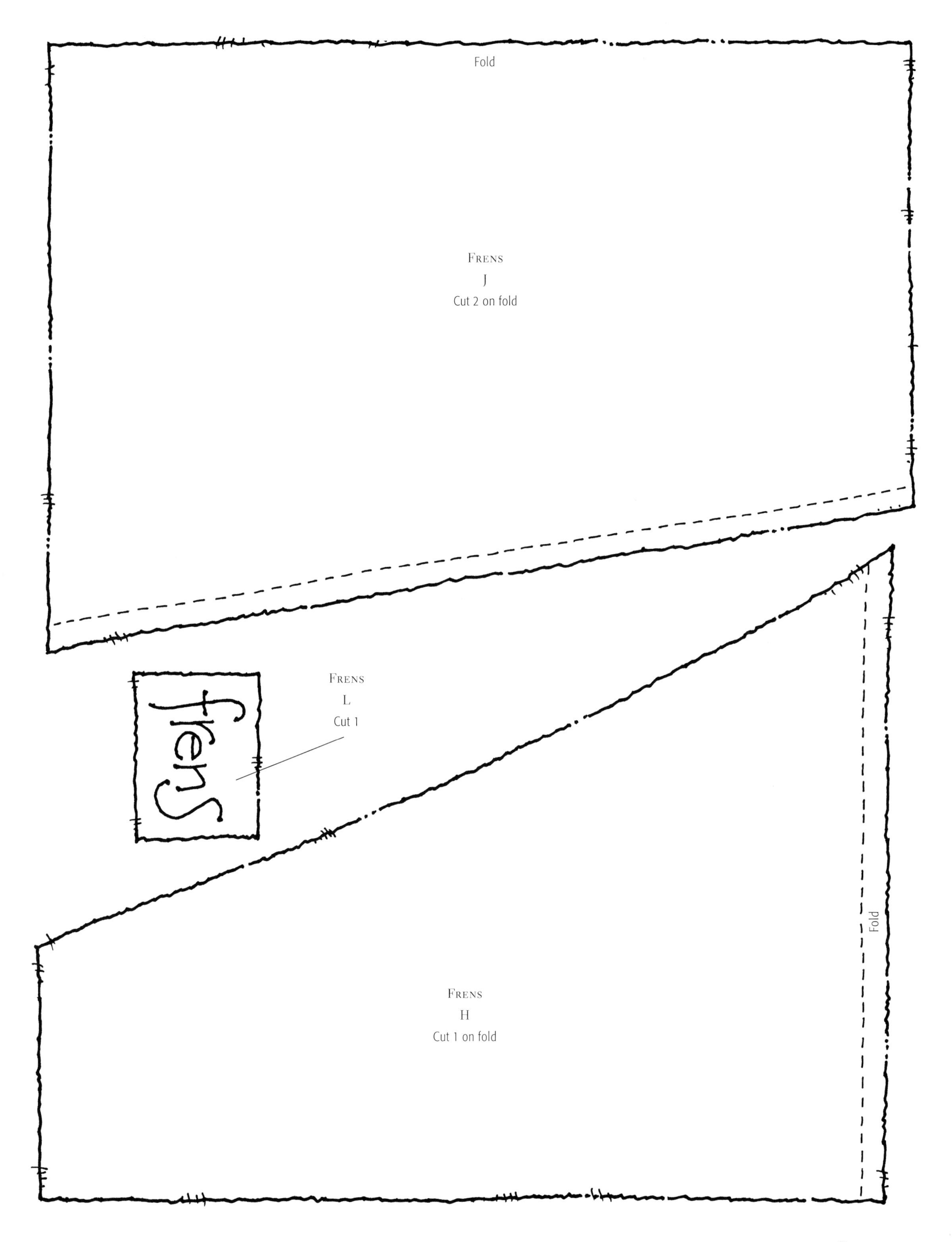
Fold
Frens
J
Cut 2 on fold
frens
Frens
L
Cut 1
Fold
Frens
H
Cut 1 on fold

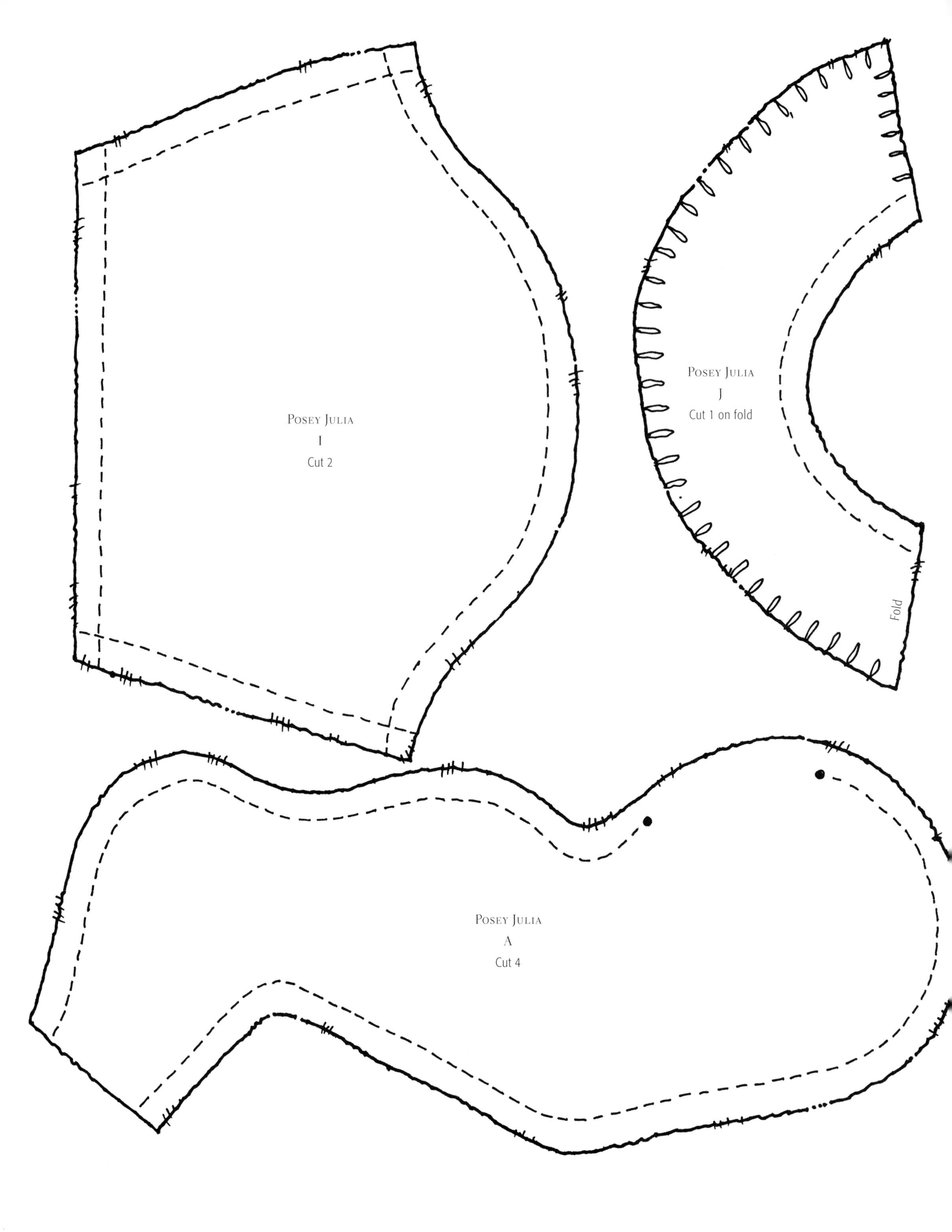
Posey Julia
I
Cut 2
Posey Julia
J
Cut 1 on fold
Fold
Posey Julia
A
Cut 4

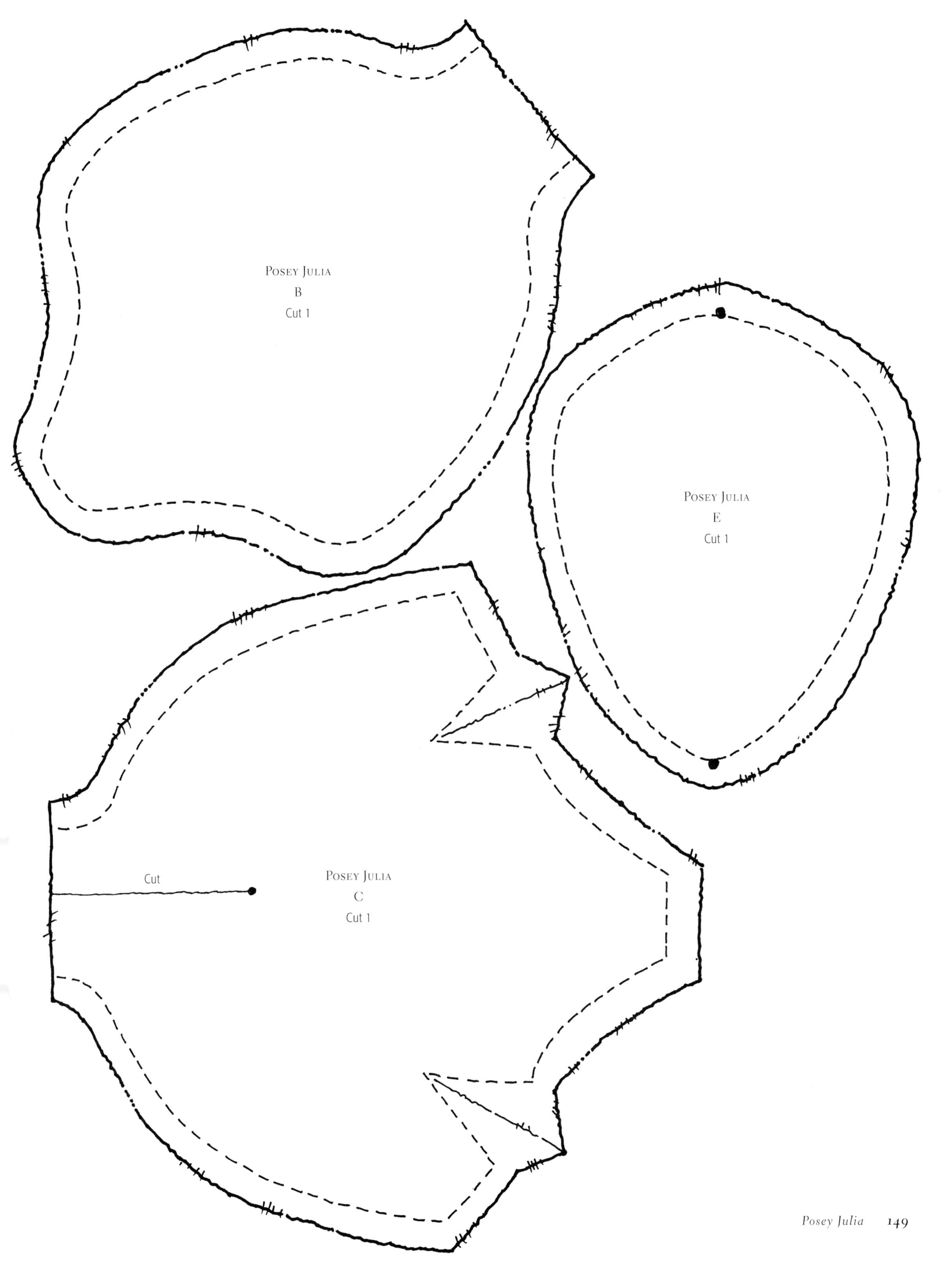
Posey Julia
B
Cut 1
Posey Julia
E
Cut 1
Cut
Posey Julia
C
Cut 1

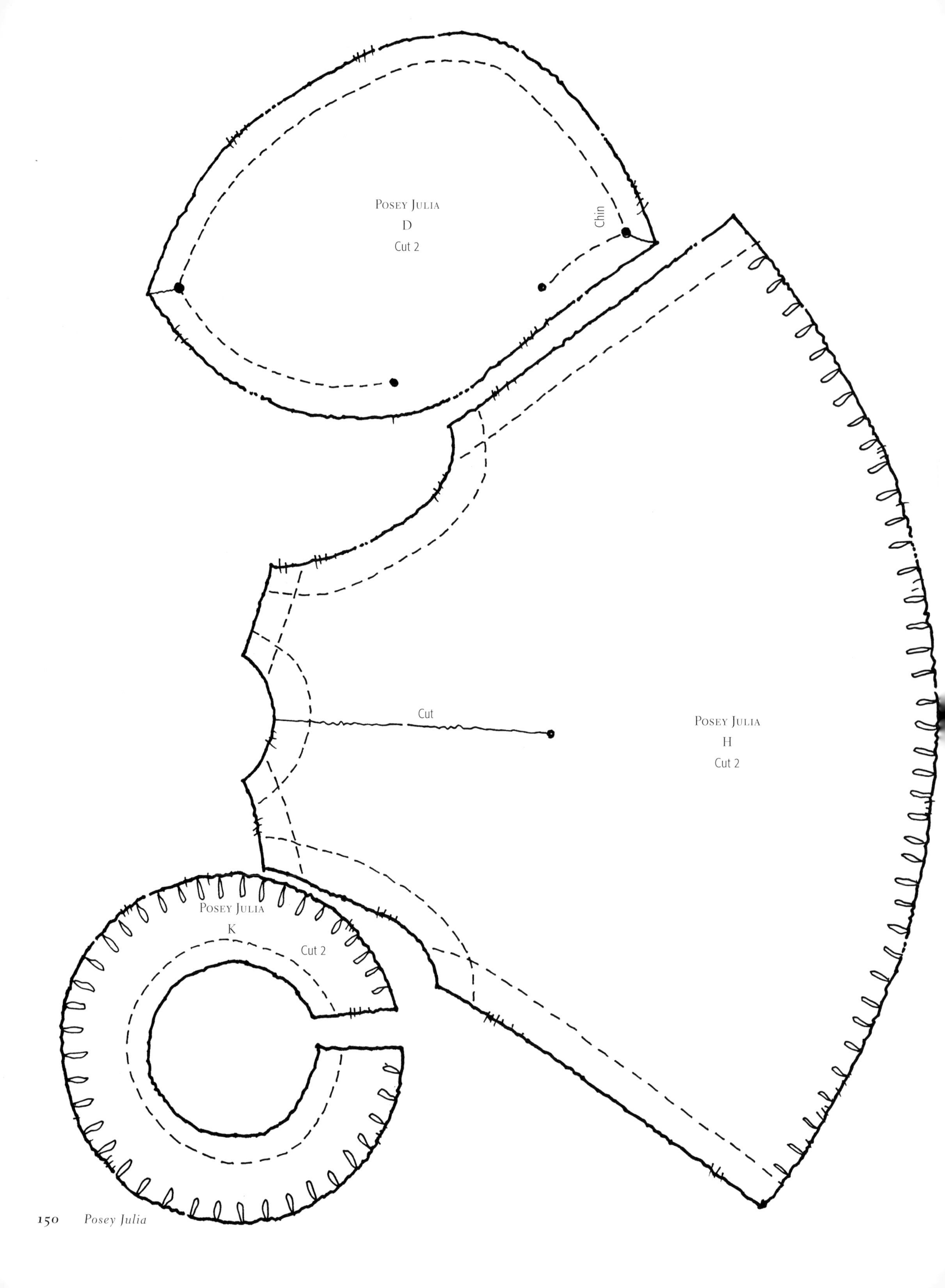
Posey Julia
D
Cut 2
Chin
Cut
Posey Julia
H
Cut 2
Posey Julia
K
Cut 2

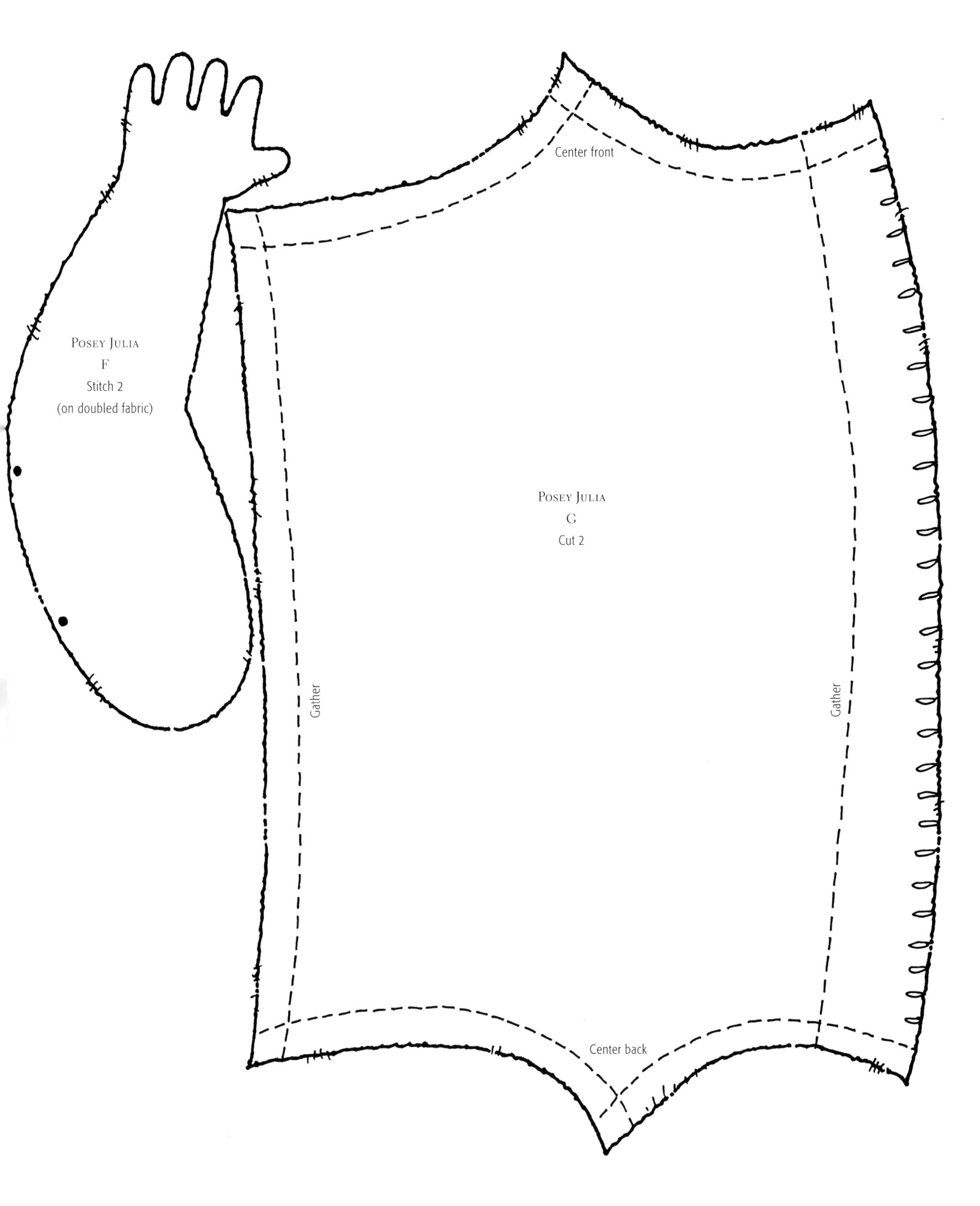
Posey Julia
F
Stitch 2
(on doubled fabric)
Center front
Posey Julia
G
Cut 2
Gather
Gather
Center back

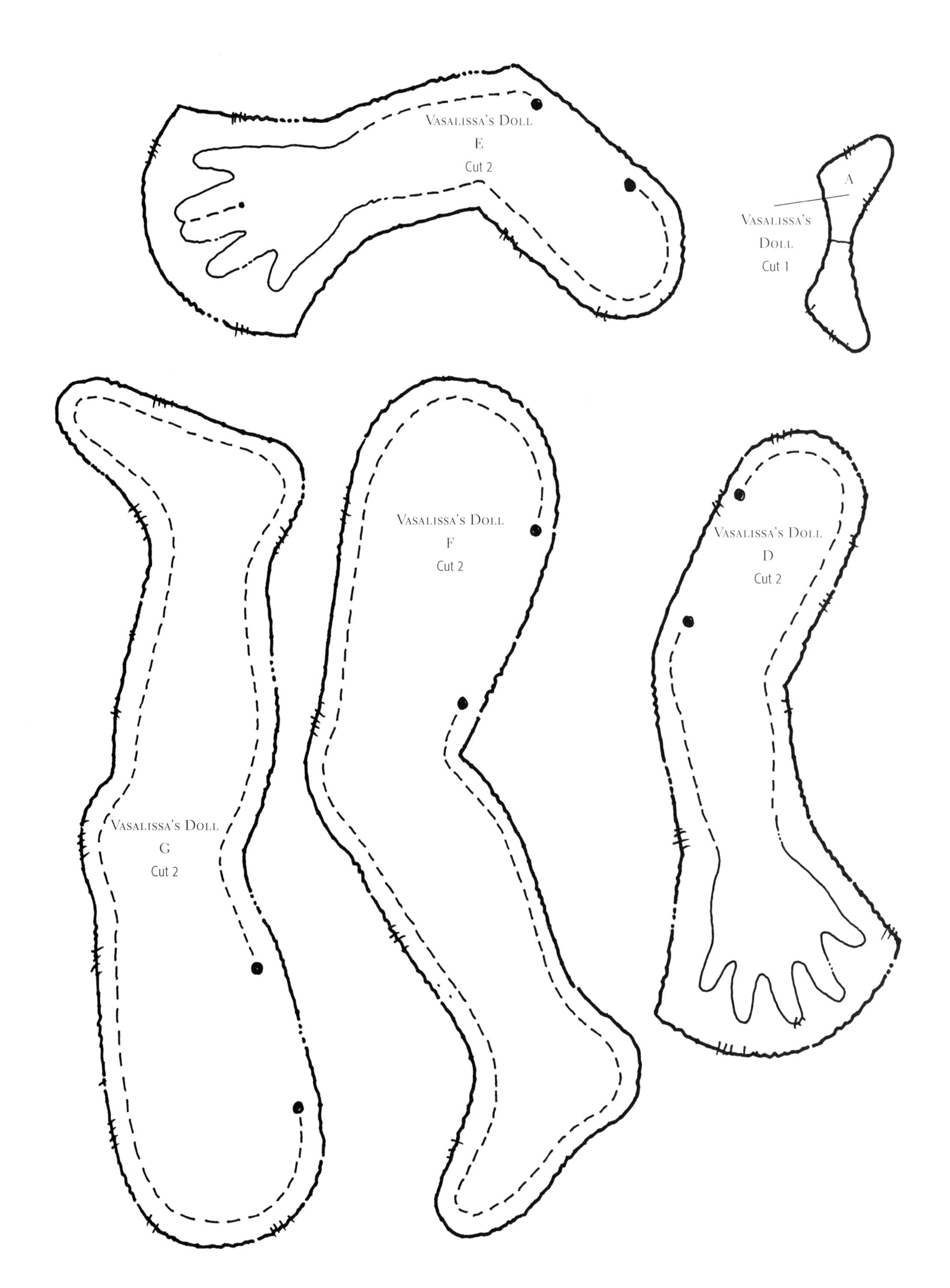
Vasalissa's Doll
E
Cut 2
A
Vasalissa's
Doll
Cut 1
Vasalissa's Doll
F
Cut 2
Vasalissa's Doll
D
Cut 2
Vasalissa's Doll
G
Cut 2

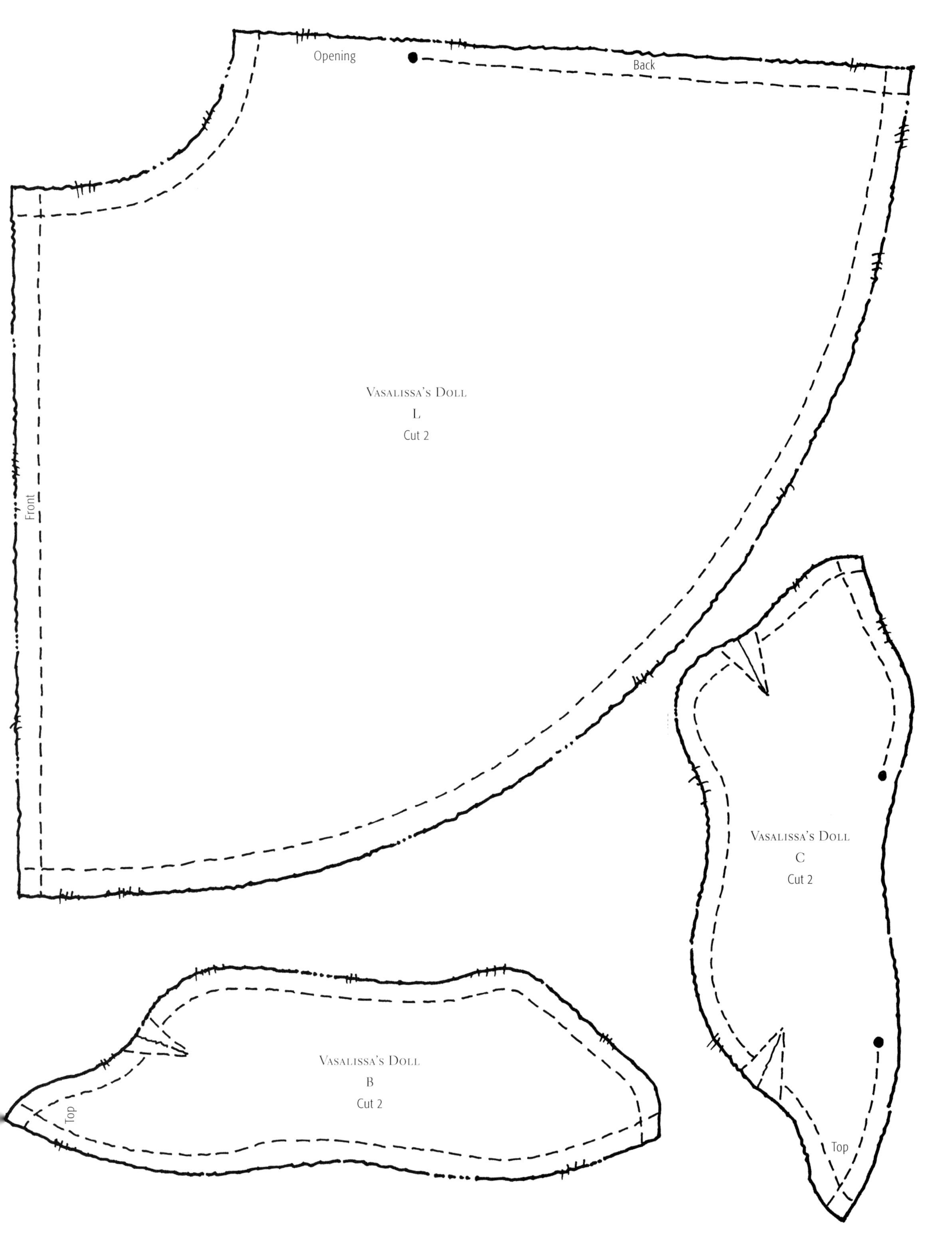
Opening
Back
Vasalissa's Doll
L
Cut 2
Front
Vasalissa's Doll
C
Cut 2
Top
Vasalissa's Doll
B
Cut 2
Top

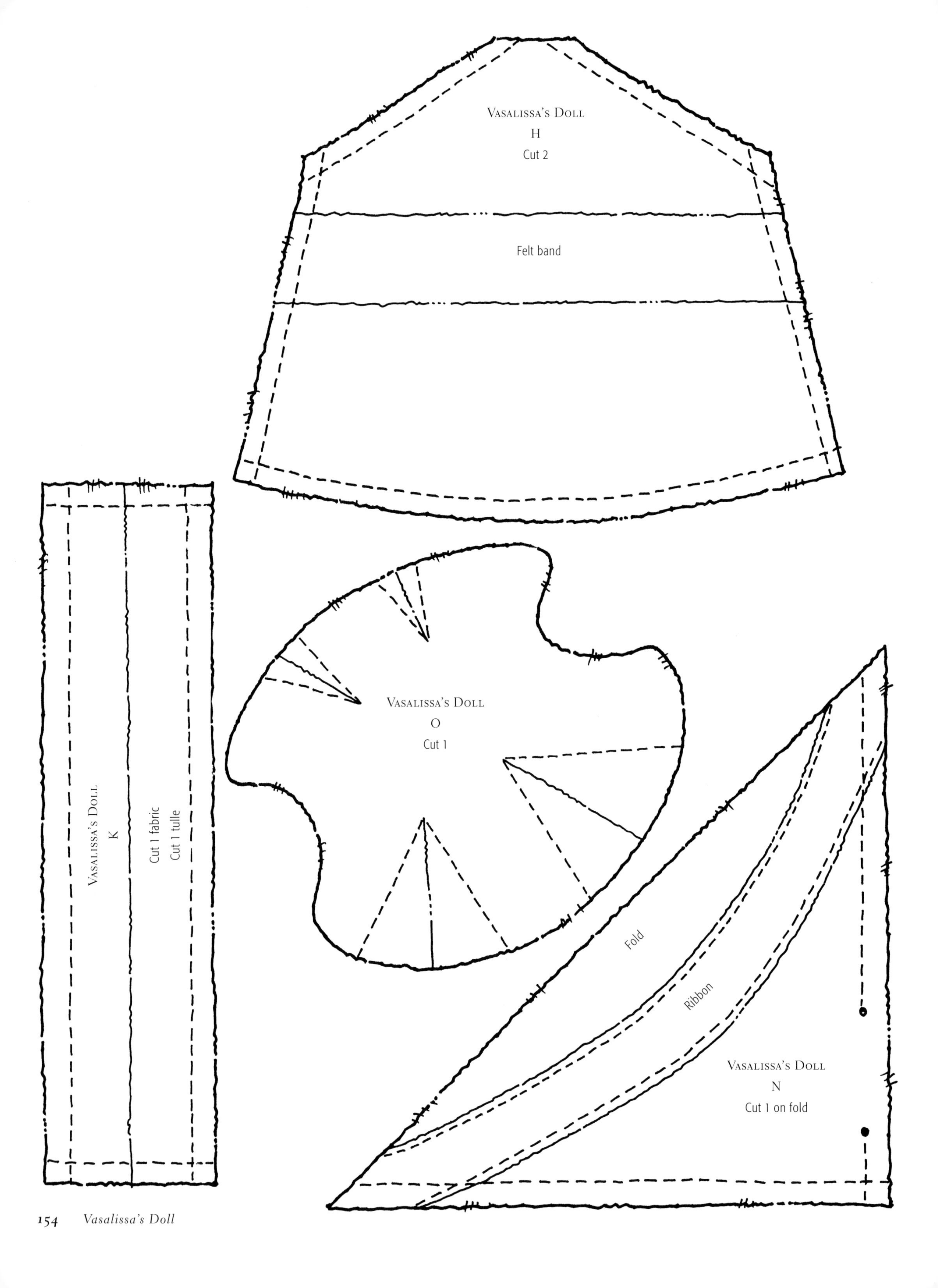
Vasalissa's Doll
H
Cut 2
Felt band
Vasalissa's Doll
K
Cut 1 fabric
Cut 1 tulle
Vasalissa's Doll
O
Cut 1
Fold
Ribbon
Vasalissa's Doll
N
Cut 1 on fold

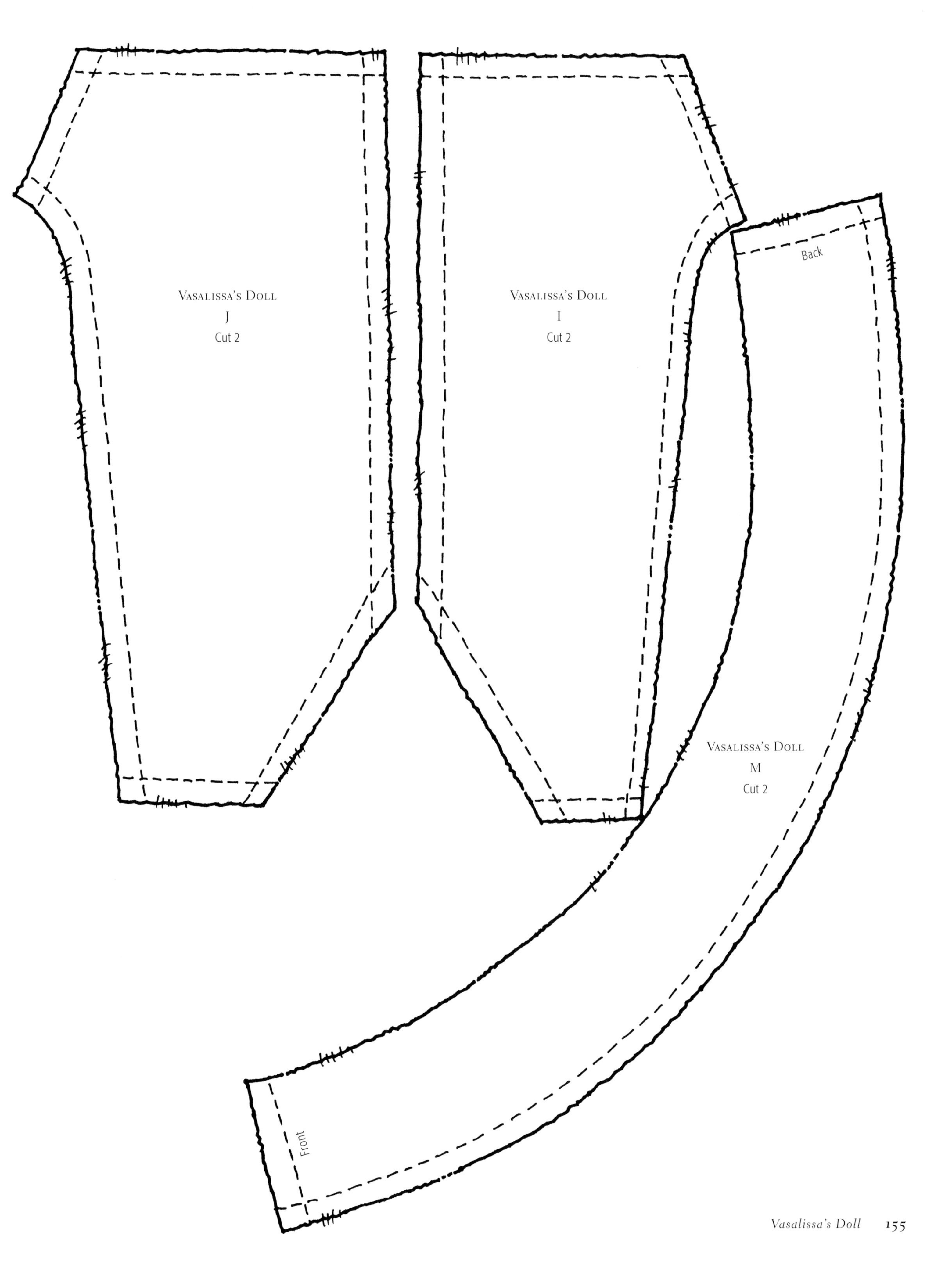
Vasalissa's Doll
J
Cut 2
Vasalissa's Doll
I
Cut 2
Back
Vasalissa's Doll
M
Cut 2
Front

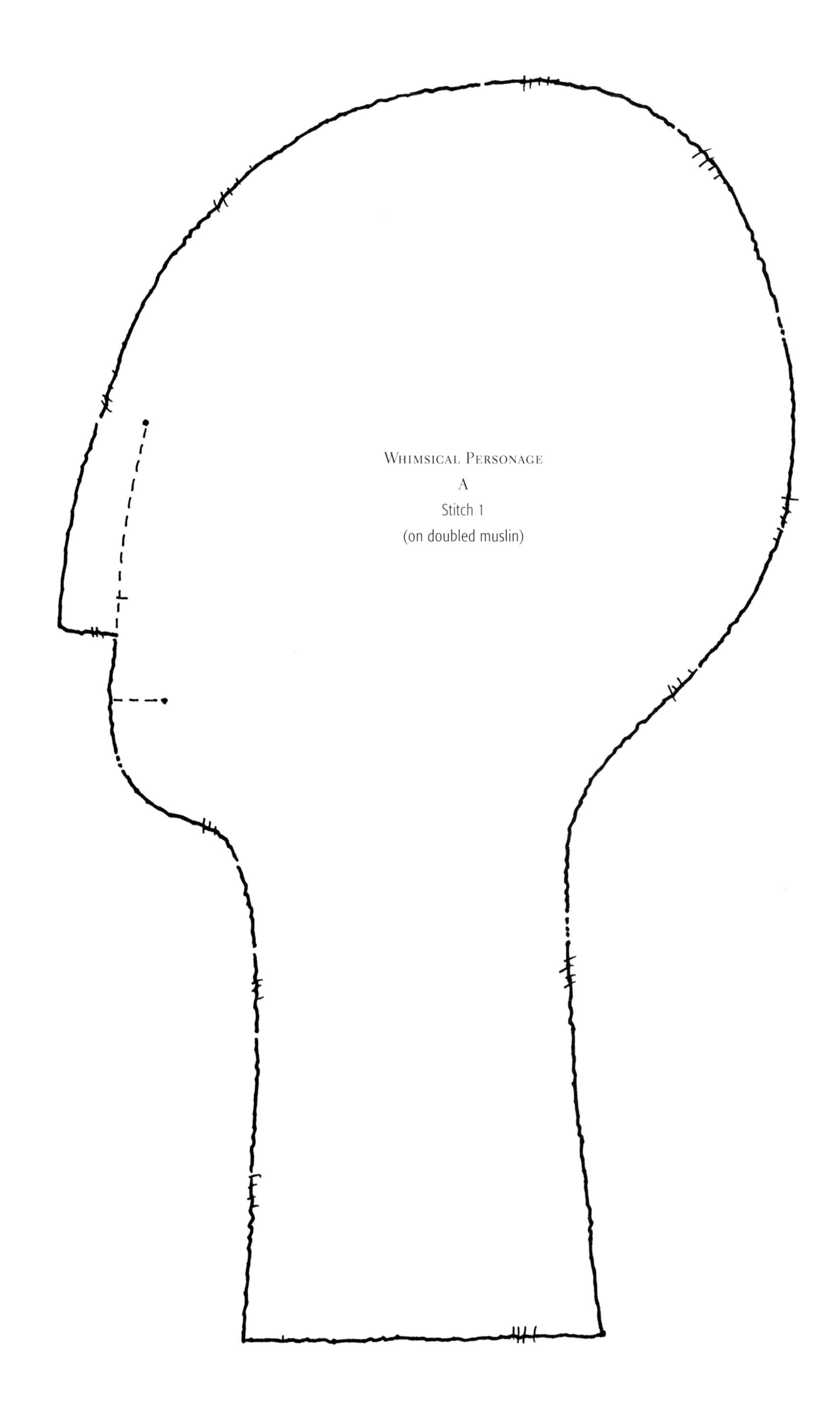
Whimsical Personage
A
Stitch 1
(on doubled muslin)

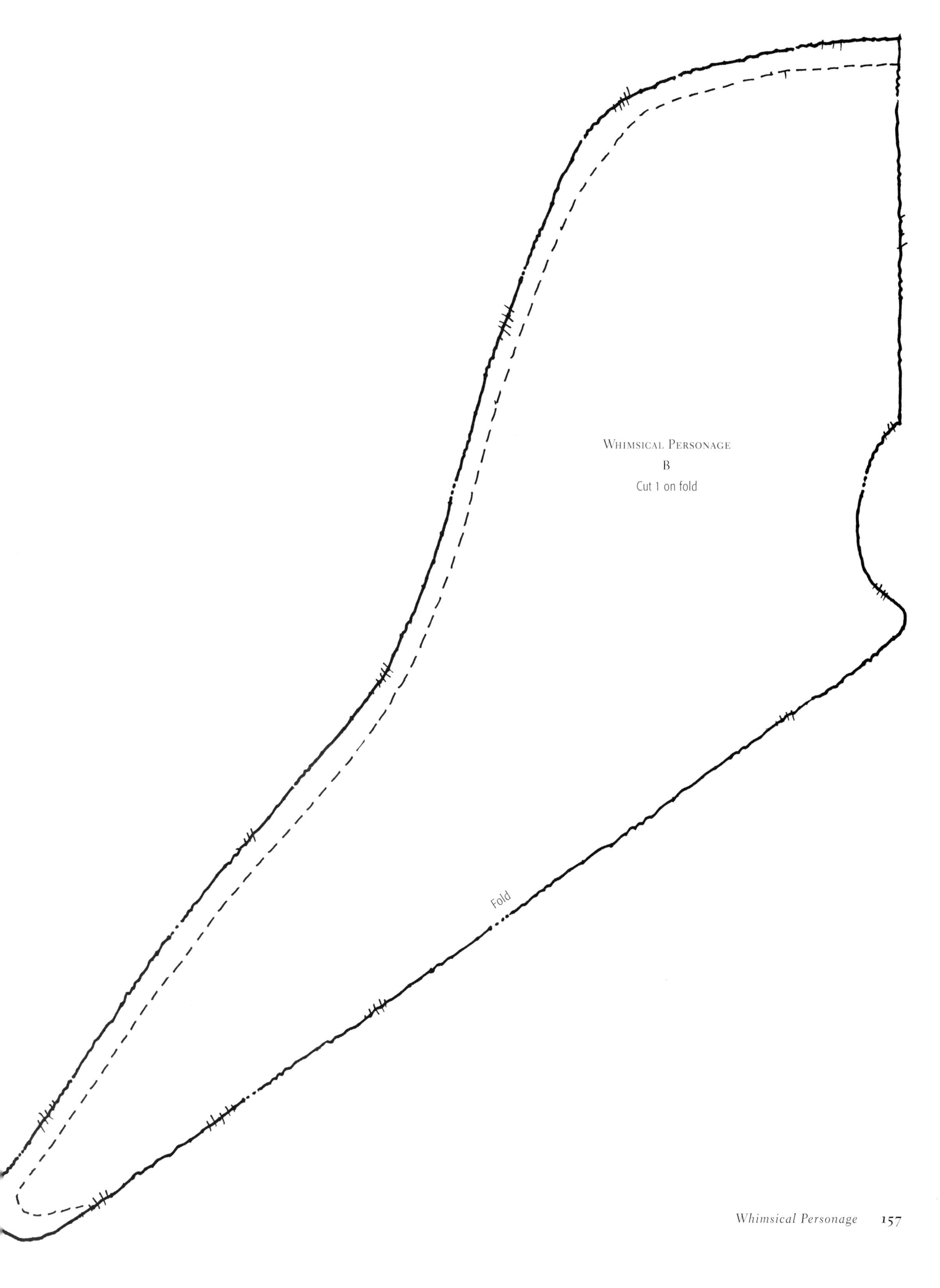
Whimsical Personage
B
Cut 1 on fold
Fold

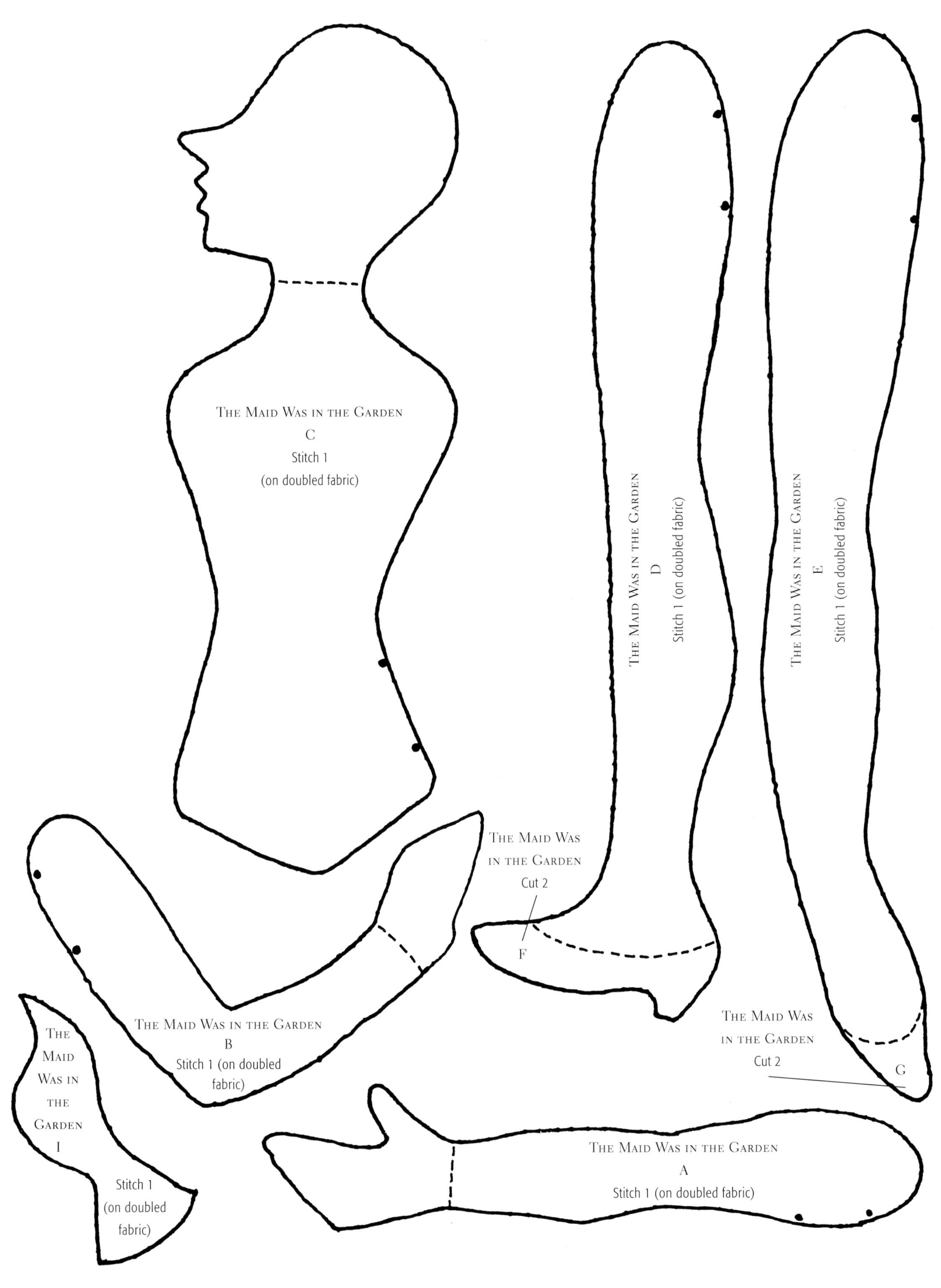
The Maid Was in the Garden
C
Stitch 1
(on doubled fabric)
The Maid Was in the Garden
D
Stitch 1 (on doubled fabric)
The Maid Was in the Garden
E
Stitch 1 (on doubled fabric)
The Maid Was in the Garden
Cut 2
F
The Maid Was in the Garden
B
Stitch 1 (on doubled fabric)
The Maid Was in the Garden
I
Stitch 1
(on doubled fabric)
The Maid Was in the Garden
Cut 2
G
The Maid Was in the Garden
A
Stitch 1 (on doubled fabric)

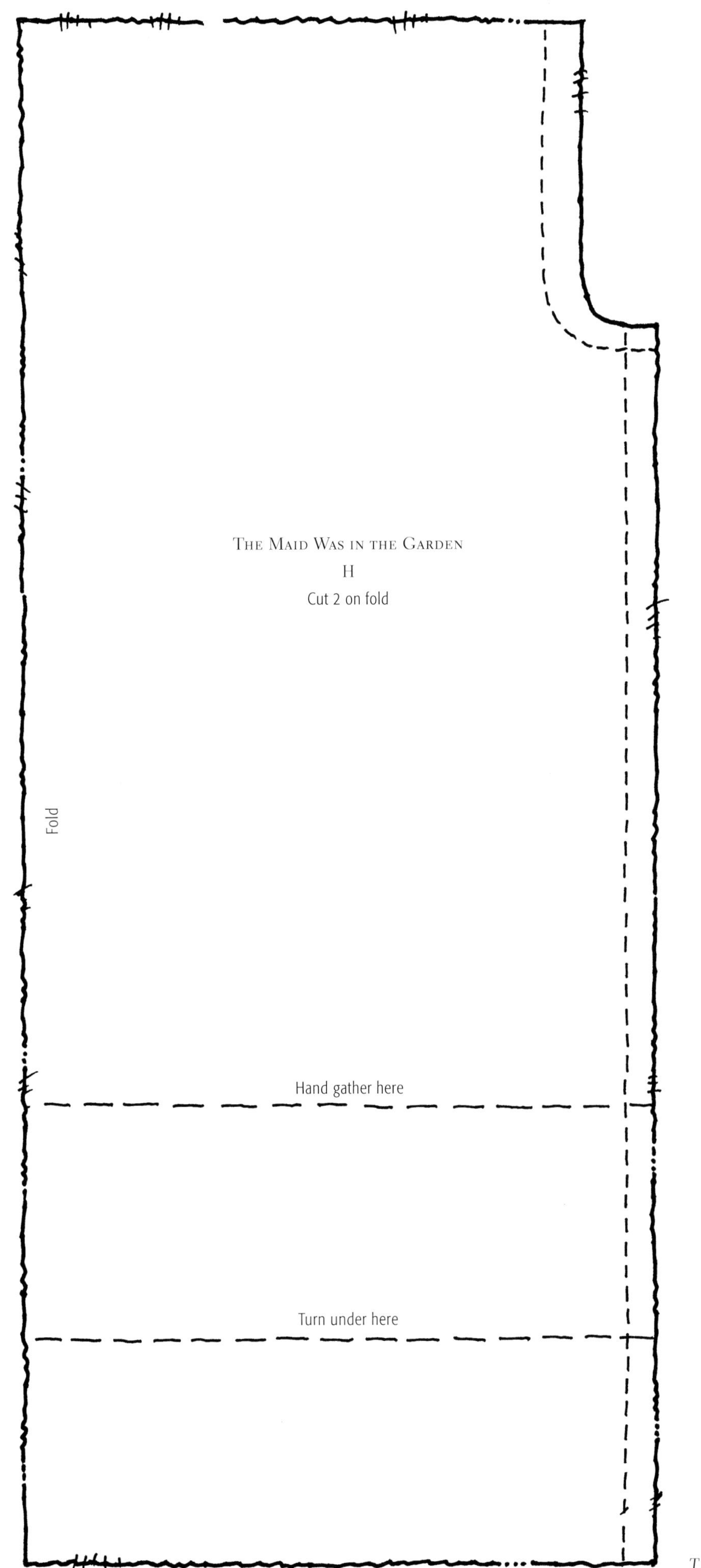
The Maid Was in the Garden
H
Cut 2 on fold
Fold
Hand gather here
Turn under here

Lesson Planning

Most of the projects in *Crafting Cloth Dolls* require paints in the dollmaking process. If you have a crafts store, you have many paints and brushes to choose from. If you run a quilt shop or other fabric shop, you may not stock paints. In that case, when you are featuring dollmaking classes, purchase large bottles of the paints required for the class, as well as a good supply of brushes. Have other supplies on hand, such as paper cups with water, paper towels, and plastic-coated paper plates for mixing paints. You can include the cost of these supplies in the class fee.

Most classes will not accommodate huge numbers, and I recommend fifteen or fewer students, in order to give each of them individual attention. It helps to have supplies organized in advance, individually bagged or boxed. Make sure that when you sign up students, they pay their class fees in advance. That will help to ensure their commitment to the class and will enable you to have enough supplies on hand. Always plan for one or two extra people, as there are often last-minute attendees, as well as students who may want to make another doll at home.

Some of the dolls are too complicated to make in a class, but many projects in this book are ideal to build a class around.

1. *The Basic Body*

Using my pattern for the basic doll body in Chapter 2 (see page 7), go step-by-step to create a doll's body. Encourage your students to experiment. This doll is a little more complicated and would be an intermediate-level project. It provides a good opportunity to have a follow-up class in creating patterns for doll clothing, using the dressmaking steps outlined on pages 51 through 54.

2. *Rita Carl's Tulip*

This doll (see page 65) is easy and fun to make. She can be dressed seasonally or suspended over a flowerpot (from a bent wire hanger), and makes an ideal beginner-level project.

3. Annie's Frens

These wonderful, simple country dolls (page 93) will have great appeal in a classroom setting. Encourage people to experiment with them. Have your flannel and country prints on hand for your students to purchase. These dolls are sure to be a hit! You might offer a boxed lunch as an optional part of the class.

4. Let's Make Hair!

The class will focus on some of Bonnie Hoover's wonderful wig-making ideas (see page 45). Each student should bring ten finished heads. This might even be a fun class for students to exchange heads before they start. Have interesting buttons, fibers, and embellishments on hand for the students to purchase, and let them have fun. You will want to have some finished samples to show them. They can mount the heads on hoops, or stitch clasps on the back to make them into doll brooches.

5. Wings and Shoes

This easy class will teach students to make fairy wings and shoes—Annie's wings (page 56) and Christine's shoes (page 55) will be the foundation. Students should bring a completed doll body for the shoes, but can make wings for any doll. This can be an all-day class, or two half-day classes.

6. Experimenting with Paint

Have your students bring a doll body they wish to paint and antique. Follow the general instructions for *Constable Shoes* (see page 75) for the necessary steps. Not all crackle products give the same result, so be sure to understand your products and experiment with them in advance. Jo Sonja's® is my favorite, with the most predictable results. Remember not to overbrush these products, and the thicker you put it on, the larger and more noticeable the cracks. Some crackle products, such as Americana's Weathered Wood, require a layer of paint over the top to produce the crackled effect. This might be a nice look for a doll stand.

7. Felt-Making and Other Great Clothing Tricks (Lecture)

Unless your shop has a washer and dryer (which most don't), you will need to make this a lecture. You should make some felt to pass around (see Elise Peeple's directions on page 97). This might be an opportunity to include some of the other embellishment techniques, such as Brenda Gehl's wonderful stitching (and paint overlay) to give dimension to her knight's armor (page 81). You might also try "aging" the doll's face or hands. First soak the doll pieces, then use a large, soft brush to apply a wash (such as a mix of water and Burnt Umber acrylic paint). The same effect can be achieved by tea-dyeing the fabric (see page 7) or by painting the doll with strong coffee. As a grand finale, you might want to find slides of dolls from clubs in the area, and have a slide show to show dollmaking at its best.

Resources

elinor peace bailey
Association of People Who Play with Dolls, 1779 East Ave., Hayward, CA 94541. Send a self-addressed stamped envelope (SASE) for information on newsletter.

Rita Carl
For a catalog of patterns, send an SASE to Reet's Rags to Stitches, P.O. Box 578, Miranda, CA 95553.

Antonette Cely
Patterns, book, and seminar information available from Cely Communications, Inc., 3592 Cherokee Rd., Atlanta, GA 30340-2749; phone, (770) 936-9851; fax, (770) 451-3257; website, www.cely.com.

Patti Medaris Culea
Send an SASE to PMC Designs, P.O. Box 720463, San Diego, CA 92172-0463; E-mail, pmcdesigns@aol.com; website, www.PMCDesigns.com.

Brenda Gehl
For patterns, select materials, dolls, fiber art, and a class schedule, contact Gehlery Creations, N88 W16475 Main St., Menomonee Falls, WI 53051.

Miriam Christensen Gourley
For information on the Fabric Folke line of dollmaking patterns, check the website, www.fabricfolke.com.

Bonnie Hoover
For patterns, information, and an order form, send $1.00 plus SASE to Bonnie Hoover, 26889 Lakewood Way, Hayward, CA 94544.

Sue Little
Contact ilittle@flash.net.

Sue McFadden

Supplies for felt dollmaking, including several patterns, and beautiful imported felt (30% wool/70% viscose) in flesh shades and white. For a brochure, fax (814) 466-3099 or E-mail mcfadden@lazerlink.com.

Elise Peeples

For a catalog of patterns, send $1.00 plus SASE to Elise Peeples Dolls, 23403 NE 92nd Ave., Battleground, WA 98604. Doll classes offered to clubs, guilds, and shops. One-of-a-kind dolls available for sale.

Virginia Robertson

Patterns and dollmaking books. For a catalog and teaching schedule, send $3.00 to Virginia Robertson's Quilting and Cloth Doll Supplies, 202 Railroad Rd. Dolores, CO 81323.

Christine Shively

Patterns. 8717 Hilltop Rd. Ozawkie, KS 06670.

Betts Vidal

Teaches dollmaking, twig and velvet miniature chair making, and fabric jewelry making. For information, send an SASE to Betts Vidal Designs, 26163 Underwood Ave., Hayward, CA 94544.